AVID

READER

PRESS

DISPOSABLE

AMERICA'S CONTEMPT FOR
THE UNDERCLASS

SARAH JONES

AVID READER PRESS

NEW YORK AMSTERDAM/ANTWERP LONDON
TORONTO SYDNEY NEW DELHI

AVID READER PRESS
An Imprint of Simon & Schuster, LLC
1230 Avenue of the Americas
New York, NY 10020

First Avid Reader Press hardcover edition February 2025

AVID READER PRESS and colophon are trademarks of Simon & Schuster, LLC

An earlier version of chapter two was first published on the Intelligencer
website, https://nymag.com/intelligencer/article/covid-deaths-injustice.html, on
November 10, 2020, and is licensed from Vox Media, LLC with permission.

For information about special discounts for bulk purchases,
please contact Simon & Schuster Special Sales
at 1-866-506-1949 or business@simonandschuster.com.

The Simon & Schuster Speakers Bureau can bring authors to your live event. For
more information or to book an event contact the Simon & Schuster Speakers
Bureau at 1-866-248-3049 or visit our website at www.simonspeakers.com.

Interior design by Ruth Lee-Mui

Manufactured in the United States of America

1 3 5 7 9 10 8 6 4 2

Library of Congress Cataloging-in-Publication Data

ISBN 978-1-9821-9742-1
ISBN 978-1-9821-9744-5 (ebook)

For the dead, and everyone they left behind

CONTENTS

DISPOSABLE

ONE

AN ACT OF SOCIAL MURDER

For too many people, misery is the formal policy of the United States. The lucky few at the top tell a different story about this country. America is fair, they say, and the meritorious rise to the top. The reality is less flattering. It's still rare to find a self-made man, despite hard-won progress for the American underclass. Instead, an old story still holds true. For centuries, the American ruling class has inflicted economic insecurity on the less-fortunate millions. They've had many champions in many eras, and in 2016, they helped elect another. In Trump, the slumlord president who presided over the first wave of mass death during COVID, they had not just a president but a peer. His victory was a triumph for the ruling class. With Trump in power, and a sophisticated conservative apparatus at his back, they were secure. Our moguls and titans of industry could thus adopt a selective blindness. The world of the poor is not invisible except through a trick of the mind: a person must work hard not to see it. Shutdowns and mandates generated pain for everyone, including workers who lost pay and health insurance; the ruling class, as usual, suffered the least. Public health measures did not look like lifesaving measures to them but rather infringements, which erected borders around their customary liberties. The same liberties were not available to the underclass, to the disposable. Some were trapped in frontline jobs, where they could not avoid coworkers or the public. Still more lived in congregate settings, often in crumbling conditions, which inevitably exposed them to the virus. When COVID struck, people like Richard Proia had few choices and no chance.

Angelina Proia remembers her father, Richard, as God-fearing, "fun-loving and gentle," a kind man in an unkind world. After losing his job as an accountant in the crash of 2008, the Rochester, New York–based Proia struggled to find steady work. He pieced together gigs in an endless search for stability. He was a baseball umpire, though it netted him only $40 to $50 a game, and he performed occasional accounting work for local governments. The work was never enough. The recession and its consequences followed him for years. "The benefits, the pay, he never got that back," Proia said. "He was only able to get half of his pension because they fired him right before he would have received his full pension." So Proia aged into poverty. This is a relatively common happenstance in the United States. Over 17 million older Americans live on incomes at or below 200 percent of the federal poverty line, and many more can barely meet monthly expenses, even on marginally higher incomes.[1] The outbreak of COVID-19 coincided with an uptick in senior poverty, too: while pandemic aid reduced[2] poverty for most in 2021, rates increased in adults aged sixty-five or older, the *New York Times* reported[3] in 2022.

Tracey Gronniger of Justice in Aging's Economic Security team explained that the federal poverty line doesn't adequately capture the number of senior adults living with economic insecurity, as Proia did before his death. According to the Elder Index, a tool created by researchers at the University of Massachusetts Boston's Gerontology Institute, a senior in poor health who rents rather than owns a home in the Rochester metropolitan area must make $30,000 minimum to meet basic expenses in 2023.[4] Housing tops health-care costs to siphon up most of a person's monthly income—and Gronniger says there's often little support for seniors who need affordable housing. "You have a lot of people who are struggling to afford their house, afford medications, afford all of the things that you need as you get older. And they're doing it on these incomes that are pretty fixed and that are very limited in terms of how they can expand what they can do," she explains. Proia lived in Plymouth Gardens, an apartment complex for low-income seniors, where Angelina believes he may have caught the virus. There were other cases, she tells me, and "there wasn't a lot of sanitation and precautions and people were just kind of crammed in the building." When Proia needed to go out, he had to rely on public transportation, which created another opportunity to come into contact with COVID. "He didn't have a lot of money," Angelina says. "He went from being middle class to poor. And so he was taking the bus to places. He may have caught it on the bus, too." She'll never know for certain, but she does believe her father's poverty placed him in danger.

Proia first went to the hospital on April 3, 2020, after feeling unusually lethargic. The hospital swiftly sent him home. "Because of the lack of testing supplies that were available, especially to people who don't have a lot of money, he was sent back home because he had no fever and because he could breathe," Angelina explains. At the time she didn't take her father's potential illness seriously, she adds; the two had a rocky relationship toward the end of his life, and at the time she found it difficult to believe that COVID might directly affect her own family. "I kind of brushed it off," she adds. "I'll regret that for the rest of my life." Proia began to quarantine as a precaution, and his health began to worsen. His sister called paramedics to his home on April 5, but they wouldn't take him to the hospital: Proia still didn't seem sick enough to rate much professional concern. The following day, Angelina's stepmother, who did not live with Proia, sent a caretaker to check on him. By then, he was in trouble. He had a temperature of 103 and seemed delirious. This time when he returned to the hospital he received a COVID test, which showed him to be positive for the virus. Proia had already been ill for days; his hospitalization occurred too late to save him. Doctors ventilated him, but to no avail. Proia died on April 16, alone.

The inequality that claimed her father's life frustrates Angelina. "You hear stories of people even being able to get the vaccine that have a lot of money and they don't meet the criteria. And I suspect it was the same way with tests," she says. "My father wasn't one of those people, he didn't have access to those kinds of resources." Now Angelina is left with her memories and regrets. When COVID shortens a life, it often forecloses the possibility of reconciliation. Proia's illness moved so swiftly that Angelina had no time to tell him how much she loved him. "Had I known for certain that he had COVID, I would have said more things to him," she insists. "I would have probably apologized for the horrific things that I did to him and have said to him in the past. I would have tried to make peace with our relationship if I knew that there was a possibility he could die, which,

4

you know, is obviously a possibility with COVID," she adds. "I just feel like it would have given our relationship some personal closure." Instead there's only silence.

A gulf separated Richard Proia from John, a difficult man who'd benefited from significant material privileges throughout his life. He had never lived on his own with any success, his niece Ellen told me. (Their names have been changed at Ellen's request to protect the family's privacy.) He lived in the basement of his parental home well into his sixties, and dwelled at the same time in the shadow of his father, who appeared to be all that John was not. John had failed to launch himself into the wilderness of the world, but his father had conquered it. A decorated military officer, he passed his drive for success on to Ellen's father, an Ivy-educated attorney, but not to his other son, John. John lingered. John festered. Eventually, John snapped.

There was no reason for his outrage, Ellen thought. Nothing about John's easy existence contradicted the messages he heard on conservative talk radio and later read on the internet, the ones saying that anyone in America could succeed with minimal effort. He did not have to reconcile the messages of Rush Limbaugh with personal poverty or institutional prejudice. John had every advantage. He was healthy. He was white. He was well-off and would inherit more upon the deaths of his parents. Yet he struggled to connect with others, to form any but the most fragile ties with other people. He spent his working life as a civil servant for the military before he departed it, aged, with a pension and a faltering social life. Then came the pandemic, and John's ensuing radicalization would spawn a crisis that engulfed him and his entire family.

The pandemic, Ellen said, is when the trouble started. John's father died just as the lockdowns descended. John had never been liberal. Yet Trump woke something in him, as the president did in so many men like him. So John marched to the right with the election of Trump, and as his personal and national anxieties increased, his march broke into a sprint. John listened to Trump. Not the CDC, certainly not Anthony Fauci. He refused to wear a mask. He objected to lockdowns. Even though he still lived with his ninety-seven-year-old mother, he became reckless, risking illness and death, both hers and his own.

John started going to protests. Anti-lockdown protests, anti-mask protests, and, after the election, a Stop the Steal protest. "I was really upset about that," Ellen says. In late 2020, she'd traveled from her home in New England to the family base in northern Virginia for the holidays, quarantining and testing so she could be sure she wouldn't endanger her mother, who is John's ex-sister-in-law, or her grandmother. Ellen wore masks in her grandmother's house. John would not. Then January 2021 arrived, and with it the biggest Stop the Steal rally of all. "We knew he was going to go to that, just based on his patterns of behavior. He had all the psychological reasons somebody might be seeking a tribe and inclusion. He had Rush Limbaugh ornaments on his Christmas tree. He had Trump ornaments on his Christmas tree," Ellen, a professor, tells me.

On January 6, Ellen, her mother, and her grandmother's home health aide played cards and watched rioters storm the Capitol on television, and they all knew that John might be nearby. "I have no idea whether he actually joined the rioters. I suspect he didn't just because I think he probably might have bragged about it if he had," Ellen theorizes. The home health aide, a woman from Sierra Leone, worried for herself and for Ellen's grandmother, her charge. Her family back home depended on her paycheck. Perhaps she could keep

John away, restrict him to the basement he lived in to protect Ellen's grandmother from harm.

What happened next, Ellen learned from the home health aide: John arrived home and came up to sit with his mother—a rare occurrence for him—so he could tell her all about his day. Five days later, Ellen's grandmother tested positive for COVID. So did the home health aide, and so, inevitably, did John. Nobody knows quite how the virus entered her grandmother's home, but John's activities raised concerns.

"He refused to be tested for quite a while," Ellen says. "My father was hounding him about how he needed to get tested. And he kept refusing, saying, 'I don't want to get a false positive and then have to quarantine.' And he was saying this even while his mother was in the hospital on a ventilator and dying of COVID concurrently." Like many families with a loved one sick in the ICU, Ellen's family relied on video calls to keep her grandmother's spirits high. "I tried always to talk to my grandmother during these calls in case she could hear," Ellen adds, quietly. "I think she quite likely could at some point." It was, she remembers "wrenching."

Ill and vulnerable, Ellen's grandmother didn't possess all the advantages of her son. Neither did her home health aide, whose safety depended on the habits of her employers. But it was the senior woman who would pay for her son's radicalization with her life. At the age of ninety-seven her failing health couldn't withstand the onslaught of COVID. On January 26, Ellen's grandmother died, a casualty not just of COVID or her own failing health, but perhaps of her son's right-wing ideology. John's political heroes promised him a glimmer of power and belonging after a lifetime of thwarted entitlement and anger; they also encouraged him to reject any remaining empathy he had, along with science and public health. In doing so he also placed himself at risk, though he was more likely to survive than his mother. Others he sacrificed, all for his newfound sense of purpose.

John has showed "no remorse," Ellen tells me, for possibly sickening his mother. She spoke to me a week after the funeral, a short outdoor affair in Arlington National Cemetery. "But my uncle had really wanted to have an indoor two-hour memorial service, which he would sing at, the next day. And he was very upset that other people did not think it was a good idea to hold a long indoor memorial service," she says. Some delusions are difficult to break.

Like all major disasters, the pandemic is a moment of revelation. Through it, we see America as it is, and not as it we would like it to be. Wealth does exist here. John had it, though he was no titan of industry. When he fell ill, his means entitled him to the best care the country could offer. American prosperity is real enough for people like John, but it exists so far in the distance for so many that, for millions, it might as well be a mirage. For the masses, prosperity will never be tangible without serious political intervention.

Those dynamics didn't originate with the pandemic. COVID is a biological entity; it can only manipulate the world it inherited on waking. What the pandemic did, and continues to do, is strip the world back until its workings are visible to all. By December 2020, COVID had killed one in every eight hundred Black Americans. Through July 2020, Latinos were more than four times as likely to be hospitalized for COVID compared to whites and were nearly five times as likely to die. More than 500,000 Americans died by March that first blighted year, and the dead accumulated in the country's most marginalized communities.

Behind the numbers, there are lives. Injustices. Institutions that failed or never existed at all. To consider them is to learn a story about America.

Using education in combination with race as a measure of socioeconomic status, Justin Feldman, a social epidemiologist and a visiting scientist at Harvard's François-Xavier Bagnoud Center for Health & Human Rights, found "very large differences" in terms of COVID mortality. The data showed "that within every racial group, people with a high school degree or less were doing quite a bit worse than people with a college degree or more." The results, he adds, weren't "fully explained by racial inequality, and racial inequality wasn't fully explained by socioeconomic inequality, so they're both operating at the same time."

Feldman found that effect within every racial and ethnic group he studied. "What I found, for instance, was that Black men with a college degree or more died at lower rates than Black men with high school or less. So they were better off," he explains. "But they were dying at about the same rate as white men with a high school degree or less."

Trends in COVID mortality were built on long-standing social inequalities. "You can think about some of the main ways people get exposed to COVID, like the workplace and housing, closely tied to people's ability to get particular jobs or afford housing that's not crowded or not multigenerational," Feldman says. For many people, inadequate access to health care meant they developed comorbidities that predisposed them to serious cases of COVID. People who live in a place with a relatively high rate of poverty "tend to have higher rates of COVID mortality," he adds, which is an artifact of segregation. The past lives on, even in the middle of death.

Numbers stand for wealth as well as for the dead. A fateful arithmetic subtracted lives from the lower classes and added, almost inexorably, to the fortunes of the wealthy. During the pandemic a few flourished—and even congratulated themselves for their acts of charity. In the prologue to *Davos Man*, his account of billionaire plunder and its consequences, journalist Peter S. Goodman quotes Marc Benioff, the founder of Salesforce: "In the pandemic, it was CEOs in many, many cases all over the world who were the heroes," he said. "They're the ones who stepped forward with their financial resources and their corporate resources, their employees, their factories, and pivoted rapidly—not for profit, but to save the world."[5] Benioff's bold words disguise a more cynical reality. The pandemic was often good for CEOs. While thousands of people lined up at food banks and filed for unemployment, the rarefied class to which men like Benioff belong made bank.

Trump is easy to mock. At times he almost seemed to beg for it. Racist, ignorant, and gaffe-prone, he reveled in liberal ire, first as a candidate and then as president. Yet Trump is capable of a certain cunning. He knew who put him in office, and understood, on a deep level, whom he served. It wasn't the working class. Though in 2015 and '16 the political habits of poor whites fascinated journalists and dismayed liberals, in truth Trump won wealthier voters, while Hillary Clinton succeeded among the poorest. As the *Washington Post*'s Philip Bump theorized in one column, Trump may have won higher-income voters in lower-income areas.[6] At the same time, his presidential campaign benefited from a few wealthy backers, like the right-wing billionaire Mercer family.[7]

Once in office, Trump fashioned himself a champion of the white working class while he worked on behalf of the wealthy. By the time the pandemic arrived, he'd signed tax cuts that transferred over a billion dollars in savings to less than a hundred wealthy households, all while waging war on welfare for the poor.[8] Trump's priorities didn't change with the pandemic. When Trump signed the CARES Act into law, he did more than distribute checks to the American people. He also authorized tax breaks that once again benefited the wealthy.[9] In June 2020, ProPublica, a nonprofit investigative news outlet, reported that the CARES Act had handed out billions in tax breaks for the nation's wealthiest households. Five provisions total cost the U.S. Treasury about $258 billion in 2020 alone.

The pandemic would deliver further windfalls to people far wealthier than John. As Americans began to stay home, they turned to e-commerce for basic goods. Jeff Bezos grew his personal fortune by 67 percent, or $89.6 billion, from the beginning of the pandemic to the end of 2021, the year he stepped down as CEO of Amazon.[10] His workers weren't so blessed. Desperate for protective gear, appropriate safety measures, and sufficient paid leave, Amazon warehouse workers walked off the job in Staten Island, Shakopee in Minnesota, and Chicago.

The walkouts represented a fraction of Amazon's national workforce. Yet the company perceived them as a public embarrassment and reacted with aggression. When Chris Smalls organized a walkout at his Staten Island warehouse, the e-commerce giant fired him the same day, and then concocted a plan to smear him.[11] At a meeting of executives, Amazon's general counsel, David Zapolsky, said that Smalls, who is Black, is "not smart, or articulate, and to the extent the press wants to focus on us versus him, we will be in a much stronger PR position than simply explaining for the umpteenth time how we're trying to protect workers."[12] On May 1, 2020, Amazon discontinued the unlimited unpaid time off policy it had implemented to encourage workers to stay home sick. A month later, in June, the company stopped paying workers a $2-per-hour pandemic bonus.

.   .   .

But the pandemic wasn't over, and in New Jersey, Courtenay Brown was afraid. The navy veteran worked for an Amazon Fresh fulfillment center, where she packed groceries for a country sheltering in place. "The moment New York City shut down and no one was really going anywhere, they were just like, 'You know what? We're going to open up the zip codes. We want to see if people are going to order online,'" she remembers. "They hopped on the bandwagon so fast." This, she tells me, "was really horrible." The work increased, but the labor pool did not. Her center had "a huge decrease in workers" because people feared for their loved ones. "They didn't want to get them sick and take their chances to die," she says.

In the beginning of the pandemic, Amazon did provide hand sanitizer and protective gear to workers. Brown, then an activist with United for Respect, a coalition of retail workers organizing for better conditions on the job, explains that at her fulfillment center managers kept the materials locked up away from workers. She feels that Amazon didn't do enough. "They ain't done a damn thing," she complains. She works in close quarters with dozens of other people, and the cleaning is lackluster. "You know a typical Walmart aisle?" she queries. "Cut that in half, and then imagine having five or six other people in the aisle. You have people restocking shelves, people picking, people cleaning . . . not like *cleaning* cleaning. Usually, there's somebody that dropped something on the floor, so they got to come mop and stuff. We're not that lucky to have them actually clean the shelves."

The day we spoke, the U.S. reached a milestone: 900,000 dead from the virus. Brown could have been one of them. She contracted COVID around late 2021, and she's convinced she got it at work, one victim of a larger outbreak at her warehouse. Amazon didn't close the facility. "No, they let that shit go full wildfire, literally, to the point where most of us got sick and we were in here struggling," she says. When she was at home with the virus—"I felt like I was dying"—Amazon was messaging her. Not to check up on her health, but to see when she would return to work. "They kind of had no choice, because they were that desperate; there was very few people here," she theorizes.

When she first began working for Amazon, she lived in a motel room with her sister, another Amazon worker. "Basically, we had only a few options, either pay for the room that we're staying at, feed ourselves, and get ourselves to work, or try and go look for a place. We couldn't do all four," she explains. "Usually, we would starve." The company has since instituted a $15 starting wage for warehouse workers, and Brown moved into an apartment with her sister, but when we spoke she said they still struggle to pay the bills. "We're barely making it through," she tells me.

Of Bezos, she adds, "What he made, yes, it's amazing, it's cool. I love the concept, it's definitely dope, but at what cost?" Bezos knew what was going on in his warehouses, she insists. The day he took his Blue Origin rocket to the edge of space, he thanked his workers for sending him there. Brown was not impressed. Months later, his words still rankled. "For him to be able to know all of this stuff is going on and not do anything about it, to keep just getting richer and then turn around, 'Oh yeah, thanks for letting me do all of this while you guys are suffering,' it takes a special kind of piece of shit to be able to do that," she says.

Though Brown survived her encounter with COVID, many like her have not and will not. The poorer a person is, the shorter her life is likely to be. She's more likely to age into poverty, to skip medical care that she needs, to live near environmental pollution. Her work is necessary, but she is replaceable. She belongs to a sacrificial category of person.

So did my grandfather. Once a man, now he's a number, too. Charles Tibbetts died of COVID in September 2020, an early casualty of a regional surge in southwest Virginia. The virus discovered my grandfather in a vulnerable state. His age and poor health placed him at high risk for serious illness and death. We who loved him knew he was under threat. From February to August we watched him with fear. He would go into an emergency room, and then to a short-term rehabilitation facility, and then, when his insurance refused to cover more care, he'd have to leave and the cycle would begin again. In 2020 there were no vaccines. Only masks and hand-washing and hours spent indoors, piecemeal mitigations swallowed up by systemic failure. When he fell ill on the last night of the Republican National Convention, the news felt predetermined and preventable all at once. Even now the questions haunt us. What if we could have afforded care that kept him in his home? Or a higher-quality nursing home?

But we didn't have the money, and neither did my grandfather. Though he shared race and gender with John, my grandfather was not the son of privilege. In some respects he had more in common with Courtenay Brown. Born in Maine to a family on the sharp edge of a working-class life and deep poverty, he served a stint in the army and spent his prime years in odd jobs. Together he and my grandmother managed to send my mother to college, where she became the first in her family to graduate. Decades later, I made my way to college, too, and then to a postgraduate program, and then a succession of white-collar jobs.

Our mobility wasn't enough to save him or even ourselves from the horrors to come. Viewed from a great distance my family can seem as though it is proof of the American dream. Though my grand-parents didn't graduate from college, my mother did, and later, she found steady work as a music teacher. Both grandchildren also gradu-ated from college and hold professional jobs. Yet our progress has been slow. I rent. So did my parents for most of my childhood. Then, when I turned eighteen, the state interceded in an act of eminent do-main. Our old rental is now a wide spot in a rural highway over the mountains. Eminent domain meant the destruction of my childhood home, but the payout allowed my parents to buy a house, well into middle age. My brother and I have no assets, and I owe the equivalent of my first starting salary in student loan debt. With my husband, I live in one of the most expensive cities on earth, and our jobs keep us there.

So how could I save my grandfather? Or anyone else in my fam-ily, if they needed it? The American dream is fickle and fragile. I could not keep my grandfather alive. But perhaps I can understand what killed him.

There are differences between my grandfather and Courtenay Brown, and between Courtenay Brown and Ellen's grandmother. Despite the tragedy that befell them, Ellen's family could afford quality in-home care for her ailing grandmother, a bubble, which only the force of John's radicalization could puncture. I couldn't provide the same protection for my grandfather, and Brown, a working-class Black woman, couldn't hide from the pandemic at all. Yet in their own way, each is a victim of capital.

Trump's attitude toward lockdowns was widespread within his own party. The reason wasn't difficult to discern. Lockdowns threat-ened the economy. Trump knew who had elected him, and they expected him to make good on their investment. When Trump spoke of reopening America, he knew he wasn't risking himself, or his political allies. They were in power, and if they fell ill, they'd have access to the best health care available. Trump risked Ellen's grandmother, who was far sicker than he became, and thus more vulnerable. He risked my grandfather. He risked the disposable. Victims of social Darwinism, the disposable indict figures and forces that are far older than Trump, in life and in death.

Popularized, in part, by Richard Hofstadter in his intellectual history, *Social Darwinism in American Thought*, the term has come to represent a prevalent set of beliefs about the poor. To the social Darwinist, the poor are lowly by nature—which means their suffering is natural, too. The elite, then, bear no responsibility for the condition of the underclass. The early social Darwinists, who certainly did not apply the term to themselves, drew from laissez-faire economics as much they did from biology. So did their predecessors. Eight years before Darwin published *On the Origin of Species*, the influential English polymath Herbert Spencer wrote *Social Statics*, which was "an attempt to strengthen laissez faire with the imperatives of biology," as Hofstadter put it.[13] It was Spencer, not Darwin, who coined the phrase "survival of the fittest," and he had nothing but contempt for the poor. "The whole effort of nature is to get rid of such, to clear the world of them, and make room for better," he wrote in *Statics*.[14] Spencer's ideas received a warm reception in America, especially among its elites; Hofstadter wrote that Spencer's success arrived in part because "he was telling the guardians of American society what they wanted to hear."

Spencer himself defended an older logic, which took on a particularly brutal form during the great famine in Ireland. By the time the famine began in 1845, "a consensus" had emerged in England, argued

author John Kelly. Irish poverty "had become so terrible, it was drain-
ing the Irish people morally as well as physically," he wrote in *The
The Graves Are Walking: The Great Famine and the Saga of the Irish
People.*[15] Influenced by thinkers like Thomas Malthus, who warned
that poor relief would lead to overpopulation, the English elite provided little aid and absolved themselves of additional responsibility,
while they inveighed, often, against the Irish themselves. "Providence,
who sent the potato disease, meant that many should die," said one
Lord Brougham, a former lord chancellor of England.[16] In 1846, the
Economist wrote that the famine in Ireland was "brought on by their
own wickedness and folly." England's role in creating the famine went
unremarked and unexamined.[17]

The English elite treated their own underclass little better.
Though a system of poor relief existed, the workhouse was designed
to work the poor, and to reeducate them in the virtues of personal
responsibility, rather than to prevent the dispossession that led to
their poverty at the start. The Irish famine began the same year that
Friedrich Engels introduced the concept of "social murder" in *The
Condition of the Working Class in England.* The working class of England were dying of starvation, he wrote, a state imposed on them
by the well-off bourgeoise. "The English workingmen call this 'social
murder,' and accuse our whole society of perpetrating this crime per-
petually," he argued. "Are they wrong?"[18]

Today, social murder still claims lives. As my grandfather aged from a
working-class life into a fixed income, he found himself at the mercy
of whatever rehabilitation center that he and our family could afford.
Courtenay Brown relied on Amazon to survive, and so she endured danger on the job. Ellen's grandmother was vulnerable because of her age.

Political choices structure societies. People are made disposable—by the likes of Bezos, or Trump, or their powerful allies. The powerful exploit them, and mostly ignore them, except to sloganeer about personal responsibility or the dignity of work.[19]

That latter phrase is beloved by both major parties, albeit for different reasons, and it says that work confers dignity upon those who accept it. COVID tells us something else. There are two categories of frontline worker, high-wage and low-wage, and while they both faced danger, the latter balanced on a precipice. There's not much dignity in their work; not much of anything except worry. Corporations allowed that condition to fester. Had Amazon deep-cleaned Brown's warehouse, "I wouldn't have felt like a sacrificial lamb," she says.

People who can't work because of illness or age face particular danger. They can be even more isolated than people in the workforce, and they are often reliant on the tattered remnants of the American social safety net. People with disabilities, for example, weren't just biologically susceptible to severe COVID and death; they were much more likely to live in poverty before the pandemic ever began, which made them a twice-vulnerable group in a brutal age.[20] Seniors, too, are prone to serious COVID, as my family and Ellen's would discover. The virus exploited biological weaknesses caused by aging, but socioeconomic factors also exposed many to comorbidities and unsafe living situations. Seniors can at least avail themselves of Social Security benefits, which according to one report from the Center on Budget and Policy Priorities raises around four in ten out of poverty.[21] Yet widespread inequalities persist. Using research produced by KFF, formerly known as the Kaiser Family Foundation, the National Council on Aging concluded[22] that poverty rates are higher among senior women, an outgrowth of the lifelong feminization of poverty, and it is "substantially" higher among Black and Hispanic adults over sixty-five.[23] Well before the pandemic began, older adults who lived in economically disadvantaged neighborhoods were "more likely to have chronic health and mobility issues and die at younger ages compared with older residents in more affluent communities," the Population Reference Bureau reports.[24]

The disposable are not a rarity. They exist in the millions, yet as the pandemic wore on some were inclined to ignore them. Various editorial writers adopted a hopeful tone even as new waves of infection assailed the nation. "At the beginning of the pandemic, we were too slow to adapt to changing circumstances," the contributing writer Yascha Mounk argued in a widely shared piece for the *Atlantic* in February 2022.[25] The U.S. had recorded 60,000 COVID deaths the previous month alone, yet Mounk continued: "Now we are once again in danger of prolonging the status quo more than is justifiable. It is time to open everything."[26] Mounk's argument was an act of misdirection. All over America, bars and restaurants had already reopened to crowds. School districts were attempting in-person classes, though many still had mask mandates in place. The new normal had arrived, even in liberal cities like New York.[27] So Mounk attacked a fantasy rather than the real object of his ire: the cautious individual, who might choose to mask where Mounk would not, who might also experience risks he did not. "Children should be allowed to take off their mask in school. We should get rid of measures such as deep cleaning that are purely performative. Politicians and public-health officials should send the message that Americans should no longer limit their social activities, encouraging them to resume playdates and dinner parties without guilt," he wrote. Without guilt, that's the key. Mounk had oversimplified a complex phenomenon. In 2022, vaccines were available; the risks were not what they had been, and certain limitations were no longer necessary, at least as widespread precautions. But the danger wasn't quite over, either, not for seniors, or for people with vulnerable immune systems. Where did they fit in Mounk's social order? There's no innate harm in looking ahead, but if we do so without acknowledging the dead, and how and why they died, we could repeat an act of social murder. Without that sense of history, people like Mounk look past the disposable to the dinner parties of the future. Capitalism is not a terrible machine, which grinds up human beings and spits out the remains, but a benevolent god to appease. The people that capitalism destroys can only ever be afterthoughts.

The philosopher Martin Hägglund offered the following definition of capitalism in *This Life: Secular Faith and Spiritual Freedom*. "Capitalism is a historical form of life in which wage labor is the foundation of social wealth," he wrote. Nobody is free from capitalism. We all depend on the wealth generated by wage labor, through the exploitation of labor time and the consumption of commodities made for profit. "Under capitalism our collective spiritual cause— that for the sake of which we labor—is profit," he added. Capitalism "does not reflect an original state of nature and does not finally determine who we can be." We need not limit ourselves to what Hägglund called "an inherently alienating form of social life."[28] We can devise better futures for ourselves. But it is only by looking, fully, at the sorrow and the death around us that we can devise a future worth living. An honest accounting of capitalism and its sins would be new for America. We lived with a level of acceptable death before anyone had heard of a new coronavirus in Wuhan.

Now, with over a million dead, the search was on for a villain. Any serious consideration of the pandemic should resist easy explanations for the mass death we endured. Donald Trump was a worthwhile person to blame, but his presidency couldn't fully explain our levels of excess mortality. Though I don't have all the answers, I know we cannot reckon with mass death unless we contend with the role of capitalism. Trump was the willing servant of capital. The horrors we lived through weren't contained to one man. If they were, Biden would have been our savior. Instead, the horror is systemic. To know the lives and premature deaths of America's disposable class is to see the true face of capitalism.

In February 2022, not long after I spoke to Courtenay Brown, Biden offered remarks on the dead. "They were beloved mothers and fathers, grandparents, children, brothers and sisters, neighbors, and friends. Each soul is irreplaceable," he said.[29] In a sea of such death, an individual can become lost. The tragedy is almost beyond comprehension. To reduce the pandemic to numbers is to know how many died, not who they were or what they meant to somebody else. The numbers only tell the beginning of a story. Memory is what the living owe to the dead. Yet working-class death can be less likely to claim our attention. Their lives and their loves pass away with them, as they move from shadow into shadow. But disposable people have something to say.

TWO

AMERICAN SACRIFICE

We cremated my grandfather the week I was supposed to get married. The white dress I bought still hangs in my closet, next to the black dress I brought home with me to Virginia. I'd flown back from New York the first week in September, when he was still alive, when there was still a chance he could stay that way. But we all knew the odds. The black dress was a precaution, and a reminder of how badly things had gone awry. I'd bought it when I still thought I would wear it to work in the summer. But I never did. I never will. The pandemic happened. It's a funeral dress now.

My grandfather died from complications of COVID-19. The last time I saw him I wore gloves and a plastic gown, and put a face shield on over a mask. I stood next to his hospital bed with my family. The doctor warned us not to touch him, but I did, gently, one gloved hand over his. That he should die without touch felt intolerable, a punishment for a man who didn't deserve one. We reminded him that we loved him. My mother told him that the neighborhood bear had returned, that the farmers' market had good carrots. Despite our alien look, he recognized us. The virus was bad, he said, but he'd fight it.

He tried. He lingered for several long days until the virus had its way. From the evening I got the call that he was sick until the moment my mother told us that he'd died, he fought. But he was eighty-six years old, which made him a high-risk COVID patient. His health had been declining, gradually, for months. The virus attacked his lungs, and then his heart. In the end, he was no match for it.

That is a fact. I admit it. I write it out syllable by syllable, a ritual to exorcise grief. But the exercise fails me now, as it's failed me for years, because grief isn't all that haunts me. My grandfather's death, six months into the pandemic, is more than a tragedy. His fate is as political as it is biological. And I am furious.

In the corner of southwest Virginia where my grandfather lived, mask-wearing was far from universal. When I walked into Kroger after my grandfather's memorial service and saw all the middle-aged men without masks on, I almost approached them. I wanted to know: *Did one of you kill my grandfather?* But the men were a distraction. They were taking a risk, yes, and putting others at risk, but they weren't the real problem. That problem is larger than a few men without masks, or the president who encouraged them. The idea that weaklings and moochers must die on the laissez-faire altar is nearly as old as America itself.

Though my grandfather Charles lived in Virginia, he would want you to know he was not from the South. He was from Maine, and only crossed the Mason-Dixon because my grandmother died and he wanted to live near his only child, my mother. He had few relatives living, and none he wanted to speak to; the move to Virginia formalized older estrangements. Born into poverty to an alcholic father and a bright mother, my grandfather spent many of his early years on a farm near the town of Lincolnville. While his father drank, his mother maintained the farm and raised the children and worked, sometimes, as a bookkeeper, though she lacked any formal training. Sometimes his father would take him hunting and fishing. That's how you became a man, my mother told me. At least back then. Though my great-grandmother could track game as well as anyone, she was trapped by her marriage and the responsibilities of home. Freedom was outdoors, the realm of men.

No one had great ambitions for my grandfather. The family sent his older sister to college at the University of Maine for a brief time, until she dropped out. My mother believes he would have been a good tradesman, but that path never materialized. After high school he entered the army as a machinist and shipped out to Korea. The armistice was signed while he was on his way over and he spent most of his time fixing whatever equipment they could pull out of the rice paddies. He spent his adult life in a variety of mostly unrelated jobs, starting at the factory where he met my grandmother.

Theirs was not a love story to emulate. My grandmother suffered from an undiagnosed mental health condition for which she refused all help, and my mother suspects that she was the one who'd pushed for the wedding. Before it could take place, my grandfather's future mother-in-law warned him of danger. "I know you love her, but you're in for some trouble," she told him. Love blinds, and my grandfather tied himself to a woman who verbally abused him, and later my mother, until she died. My grandfather was prone to inertia, which enraged my grandmother, and not always without reason.

She found him work in a shoe store, and again at an estate owned by the heirs of the Curtis Publishing Company, which once produced the *Saturday Evening Post*.

My grandfather kept the grounds. My grandmother cleaned the house. They had followed prior generations into domestic work. My great-grandmother was a "laundress," as my mother put it, and my mother herself cleaned houses to help pay for college. It was better, she once told me, when the families that paid ours didn't try to clean up after themselves—they only made more of a mess.

In my grandfather's spare time, he fished and went to church. Sometimes he carved wood: toys, furniture, and, once, a feeding station for the backyard chipmunks. Mostly he worked, and drove my mother to her music lessons, an endeavor that eventually bore fruit. My mother went to college for music, and became the first person in her family to graduate with a degree. She married another college graduate, and my brother and I would graduate, too, in our own time.

Like my grandparents, I too wound up working for media moguls. But before I became a journalist, I belonged to the D.C. cohort of twenty-something communications professionals. On the day a nonprofit gave me my first salaried job, I printed out the offer letter and drove out to my grandfather's cabin to give it to him. He clutched it in his hands and cried. I would make $50,000, enough to pay rent for one bedroom in a house and to start paying off student loans. It was more money than he'd ever made in a year.

By the time I'd gotten my job, my grandfather had endured years of penury. Not long after my grandmother took early retirement at the age of sixty-two, she was diagnosed with multiple myeloma, a vicious blood cancer. She had no health insurance at first. What little money they did have she spent on clothes and cigarettes. They cashed in their IRAs. Their retirement savings vanished. My grandfather wanted to sell their house. But my grandmother hesitated. Like my grandfather she'd been born into poverty, and she feared they'd never again own anything as decent as the house. They accepted financial help from a local church and visited food pantries and sold off antiques. Once she was eligible for MaineCare, the state's Medicaid program, their financial situation improved.

Their relationship did not. As my grandmother's caregiver, my grandfather had no separation from her worst moods. "She would wake up at two or three o'clock in the morning, start screaming and yelling for him," my mother told me. "And with her very first breath of the day, she'd start verbally abusing him." Twice she took her oxygen cord and wrapped it around her neck. My mother is convinced my grandfather developed post-traumatic stress disorder, and said she wishes she'd recognized it at the time. "I don't know if he ever really got over it. He said he'd wake up in the night thinking he'd hear her screaming for him," she said. My grandmother's death provoked grief and regret and brought with it a kind of peace, too. But the abuse and the poverty were not so easy to escape. When my grandfather moved to Virginia, a widower, his health began to fail. All our hard work—my mother's college education, my job, my grandfather's own efforts—would come to little, in the end.

My grandfather lived just long enough to witness what the think-tank world calls "social mobility." Except our social mobility looked a lot more like stagnation. My mother spent much of her early childhood near the poverty line; decades later, so would I. With time, our financial situation improved. But progress was slow, and the results were fragile. Even after the Affordable Care Act, health-care expenses sometimes threatened to pull us under. My brother and I have a genetic disease. He could stay on my mother's health insurance until the end of the year in which he turned twenty-six. But her own premium had soared to over $900 a month, and she decided to drop her plan and pay for my brother's until Virginia opted to expand Medicaid under the ACA. This privation isn't extreme poverty, which some economists define as life on $2 a day or less, but it's something just as pervasive and persistent: a middle-class life threatened on all sides by catastrophe. Whatever social mobility my grandfather had set in motion now exists mostly as theory, not inhabited reality.

Despite all of his hard work, my grandfather never transcended the state into which he was born. He was disposable, as were his parents and sister. They lingered on the edges, always one blow from absolute misfortune. Real wealth existed in their corner of Maine, but while it provided the occasional job, it never trickled down to families like mine. My grandfather did not complain. A conservative and patriotic man, my grandfather seemed to harbor no resentment toward the country that had failed him. He was fond of Ben Carson, the neurosurgeon turned far-right presidential candidate. Carson's America is a whitewashed citadel where anything is possible and the mobility my grandfather never knew might yet exist for others. It is a splendid and mythological place that captivated my grandfather. It was also under attack, from malicious others he would never quite name. "They're coming for Christmas," he told me once, a sentence I did not quite know how to counter without reminding him that he was speaking to an atheist. We confronted an unhappy fact: Fox News had colonized his brain. Then we stopped paying for the cable package. After that, my mother said he went through something like detox, and normalized.

I don't know what he thought of me or my politics, which were and remain left of his own. Though we loved each other, we saw each other rarely, as we were separated by geography for most of my life. Perhaps the distance made it easier for me to see the whole shape of

his life. From my own vantage, I understood him to be more complicated than he would perhaps admit. What I saw made me angry, and
that anger fed my earliest political questions in turn. Among them:
Why was my area of southern Appalachia so poor? Why couldn't my
family work our way into something like financial security? And why
wasn't everyone as furious as I knew myself to be?

That last question still troubles me. Though COVID still kills
hundreds every week, the deaths make few headlines now. The dead
themselves feel almost forgotten. The other two questions have
firmer answers, rooted in the extractive and exploitative qualities of
capitalism. What happened to my grandfather, before the pandemic
and then during it, can be explained by a ruthless political economy.
My grandfather might not have agreed with me; if he ever doubted
America or questioned the way it ordered itself, there was no proof. I
believe, though, that the evidence is conclusive. My grandfather died
because a virus killed him, but other hands helped him toward his
demise. I blame the almighty free market, and its defenders, and the
inhumanity they have unleashed on millions. My grandfather's life
meant little to the system or to the profiteering class. He was a pair of
hands, maybe. A body to work. Then, nothing at all. Once work was
beyond him, he became detritus.

No amount of good fortune can ward off the indignities of age
forever. So writes the preacher in Ecclesiastes: For everything there
is a season, a time to be born and a time to die. I had the funeral
home print that passage in my grandfather's funeral programs. It was
a reminder that nobody escapes death. But even if money can't buy
you immortality, or inoculate you against COVID, it can buy other
precious things. Like time, or a good death.

• • •

The disposable have always existed in America. Once COVID struck, though, it became so difficult to pretend that American free-market capitalism is anything but brutal that conservatives have largely given up trying. Barely a month into the pandemic, Dan Patrick, the Republican lieutenant governor of Texas, suggested that senior Americans should be "willing to take a chance" on their own survival to keep the economy open for their children and grandchildren. "Those of us who are 70-plus, we'll take care of ourselves, but don't sacrifice the country," he said.[1] The Catholic writer R. R. Reno called wearing masks "cowardice" and warned of "a demonic side to the sentimentalism of saving lives at any cost."[2]

I read Reno's essay when he published it. I even wrote about it, early in the pandemic, and thought of it again at my grandfather's deathbed. I did not feel like a sentimentalist. But I knew that others agreed with Reno, and with Patrick. My grandfather wasn't one of them, but in a sense he got overruled.

What distinguishes a sacrifice from a regular death? Not ceremony, which is present in all funerals. The difference is intent. Sacrifice is deliberate: someone makes an offering in return for a boon, such as a good harvest, a healthy baby, power, love. Sometimes the offering is only prayer, or a voice raised in worship. Other times, it costs the supplicant a bit more. But the effort is supposed to be worth it. The idea: if we appease the gods, or the invisible hand of the free market, we'll prosper.

But people rarely volunteer to sacrifice themselves. When Dan Patrick said seniors should be willing to "take a chance" on their own survival, he was not really referring to himself, with the economic privilege and the top-notch medical care he could count on to protect him from harm. He was talking about my grandfather.

We spent much of my grandfather's last year on earth navigating an elder-care system that was not designed to ensure his survival. My mother became his sole caregiver out of love, but also necessity. We couldn't afford to pay for help, and my grandfather's capabilities were diminishing. In the tiny town where he lived, he would drive. Outside town limits, though, he felt uncomfortable behind the wheel and so my mother would have to drive him where he needed to go. His doctors were spread out over a rural area, and the drives took time. My mother had to cancel work to take him to the doctor or the grocery store. Because the burden of care fell on my mother, her own mental health began to suffer. "I remember one time it really struck me," she says. "I had taken him grocery shopping to Walmart, and he moved very slowly and he's leaning on the cart, and I just looked at him and part of me said, 'My daddy's gone. The physical person he once was is gone.'"

She recalls a former pastor who had very conservative views on the role of women—views she doesn't entirely share. "But he said, I don't have a problem with the woman working outside the home," she tells me before quoting him again: "You've got to realize being in the home is a full-time job, being a parent's a full-time job. Then she's working outside the home. That could be a third full-time job." My mother was buried in work, both the paid work she used to support herself and the unpaid work she performed to support everyone else. "The insurance companies don't exactly give you a lot of help," she adds. "You have to assume the care unless you are very wealthy." We were not very wealthy. We weren't quite poor, either: I made a middle-class living, despite student loans and a move to New York City, and my parents made just enough to cover their needs. Our family occupied a liminal status between true security and absolute poverty, and as such we didn't have much extra for my grandfather's care. My mother would take my grandfather to the doctor or the local emergency room for sciatica and a UTI that wouldn't quit, and this meant there were even fewer resources at their disposal.

My grandfather's care was covered by a combination of public and private insurance: a Medicaid plan offered by the state of Virginia, and UnitedHealthcare's Medicare Advantage plan. In purchasing the Medicare Advantage plan he had fallen prey to a scam. Nobody in my family understood this at the time. Private insurers advertise Medicare Advantage as a helpful way to augment traditional Medicare benefits. The advertising works: KFF reported in 2022 that over half of the nation's 60 million Medicare enrollees owned a Medicare Advantage plan.[3] Millions of seniors like my grandfather now rely on entities like UnitedHealthcare to cover their most desperate medical needs. Often, though, their care gets denied. As journalist Ryan Cooper wrote in the *American Prospect*, the federal government employs "scores of rules and regulations" to hold private insurers accountable. "It's a hugely expensive and difficult undertaking, and it turns out that it basically doesn't work," Cooper observed.[4] "The results have been exactly the opposite of free-market nostrums: worse coverage that costs more."

Medicare Advantage companies often deny care improperly, Cooper added. The Department of Health and Human Services inspector general found that, in 2019, "13 percent of prior authorization denials were improper, along with 18 percent of payment claim denials—or about 85,000 requests and 1.5 million payments," he observed. When the *New York Times* reviewed "dozens" of fraud lawsuits, inspector general reports, and watchdog investigations in 2022, its reporters uncovered a consistent theme. Private insurers "exploited the program to inflate their profits by billions of dollars," reporters wrote.[5] That can affect the care that patients receive. According to the *Times*, four of the largest Medicare Advantage companies—including

UnitedHealthcare, which covered my grandfather—"have faced federal lawsuits alleging that efforts to overdiagnose their customers crossed the line into fraud." Insurers dispute those claims, but the evidence is difficult to ignore. So, too, are the effects on seniors and their families. As Americans age, they become vulnerable not just to illness but to con artists. We could warn him about strangers who wanted his social security number. A health insurance company felt more authoritative—and operated according to rules and regulations that the younger members of his family did not understand. We thought Medicare Advantage would protect him. Instead United-Healthcare became one more predator competing for his time and money.

My grandfather's insurance plan didn't buy him decent care. UnitedHealthcare assumed that the limited home health care it covered would be enough for my grandfather's needs. That wasn't the case, my mother said. "They show up, they're there an hour, then they're gone," she complained. Someone needed to be there for him, she said, and it couldn't be her all the time. Meanwhile his health declined. Twice the insurance company denied him stays in acute inpatient rehabilitation, though my mother believes he'd needed the care. She still speaks of the care we might have gotten for him if only we'd been able to afford it. Someone could have sat with him, and helped with the cooking and the cleaning as his mobility became limited. Someone could have monitored his catheter, which repeatedly clogged with blood clots. Instead, there was only what insurance would cover. His Medicare Advantage plan offered full coverage for only twenty days of rehab at a time; once the clock ran out, a $176 daily co-pay kicked in. For reasons known only to UnitedHealthcare, the company refused to spring for a longer period of care.

Their capriciousness became a problem. My grandfather needed repeat visits to local emergency rooms for a persistent UTI, and a pattern emerged. A hospital would admit him, conclude correctly that he needed rehabilitation, and transfer him to a skilled nursing facility for short-term care. That's when the clock would start. He had twenty days to get better, and if he didn't, he was on his own. In July, one facility nearly sent him home with his Foley catheter still attached. My mother took him back to the hospital, and the clock started all over again.

The emergency room had become my grandfather's safety net. My mother wishes it had been otherwise, especially as COVID locked the country down. She questioned, sometimes, whether the trips were necessary, but my grandfather's pain from sciatica was severe. "There were times I sat in there with that man for hours," she said. She stayed there, surrounded by families who might be ill with a life-threatening contagious infection, time after time. She stayed with him despite her own diabetes and asthma, two conditions that placed her at extreme risk for complications from COVID. She developed a case of shingles and required surgery to remove her gallbladder, but she had no other choice than to accompany my grandfather to the hospital. Exhaustion had set in, and so had the fear: she knew she could contract COVID, and she knew that if she did the possibilities were grave. But my grandfather had no choice, either. His health was so poor that he needed immediate medical help.

Each hospital visit introduced a new chance of infection. So did each stay in rehab. Subject to lax regulation and uneven enforcement, nearly half of all nursing facilities suffer from what one federal report calls "persistent problems" with infection control. In August, my grandfather once again passed through the revolving door between hospital and rehab facility. He spent two weeks in quarantine as a precaution. Then he acquired a roommate with a cough. After he finished a course of antibiotics for his latest infection, he spent a brief interval at home before he had to be rushed back to the hospital. This time, he had COVID.

On paper, my grandfather had advantages, like a loving family and health insurance. But a family's love can't regulate health-care facilities. And no insurance plan can make up for injustices so large they can swallow a person whole. My grandfather was not allowed to stay in rehab for as long as it would have taken him to recover. The lengths of his stays were governed not by his medical needs, in our view, but by UnitedHealthcare's profit margins.

Valley Rehabilitation and Nursing Center, my grandfather's last rehab, became the site of a major COVID outbreak. Around 140 people contracted the virus at Valley before October 2020, and at least thirteen people died. All were seniors, all denied a peaceful end to their decades on earth. Some conservatives may consider this reality an acceptable sacrifice to make on behalf of the economy, but I don't believe that anyone benefits from mass death and suffering. My grandfather's death was an unnecessary tragedy. Toward the end of his life, my grandfather's spirits began to flag. He wanted to go home, but he was never well enough to spend more than a week or two in his own bed. "They're treating him like he's already in a body bag," my brother complained when the insurance company refused to cover a longer rehab stay. Soon enough, it was true.

"I will lift up my eyes unto the hills, from whence does my help come?" asks the psalmist in Psalm 121, the passage we used for my grandfather's funeral sermon. In the next verse, the psalmist answers: "My help comes from the Lord, which made heaven and earth." Without a health-care system that prioritized people over profits, it would have taken divine intervention to keep my grandfather COVID-free. Personal responsibility had nothing do with it.

• • •

Hours after I found out my grandfather had COVID, I watched Trump posture in front of the White House on the last night of the Republican convention, and boast, inaccurately, that America was recovering from the pandemic. The camera pivoted to the audience. I saw Wilbur Ross, the then-eighty-two-year-old commerce secretary, nod off, maskless and comfortable. Eventually the hammer will fall, I told myself. Weeks later it did, when Trump got sick.

My grandfather was dead by then, and I wanted justice, even though I knew a virus wouldn't give it to me. Nobody deserves death by COVID, and in any case, the discrepancy between Trump's material circumstances and my grandfather's meant that Trump was much more likely to survive. "I'm a perfect physical specimen," he said after he recovered from the virus. This is obviously false. Trump's recovery was a testament to the power of money to keep someone going well after their personal habits would have killed other, poorer men. When he got sick, the disparities in how he was treated compared to my grandfather felt like personal insults. A helicopter ferried Trump to the hospital. He had the best doctors. He stayed in a special suite with a real view. He even got to go for a joyride in an armored SUV, to wave to his supporters.

Back in Virginia my mother fumed, and sent me angry messages about the president. She still had shingles, and the anger and the stress so agitated her symptoms that a doctor told her to stop working. She had already lost thousands of dollars in income, a consequence of the months of caregiving she had provided my grandfather and, more recently, of bereavement. I scratched at my legs until the skin broke and scabbed over, then I scratched them again.

Trump got better. My family hasn't, and neither have millions of others. Years after my grandfather's death my mother still lives with regret. While my grandmother was alive she did not speak to my grandfather for years, a distance made necessary by abuse. The relationship only resumed when my grandfather wrote her a letter to say they'd been born again, washed clean in Christ's blood, so everything could be different, and everything was, for a little while. Age did not have to strain their relationship, but under capitalism age turns a person into a burden. Caregiving "made me not as sympathetic, not as empathetic as I should have been, because I was frustrated and tired and wanted a day to myself and wanted time to myself," she admits, a human feeling in an inhumane country. They could've been closer, she thinks, if she'd been able to relax sometimes, if she'd been able to be a daughter. "I remember the day I had to take him to the hospital, and we found out he had COVID," she says. "That day I pulled into the driveway and said, 'Lord, I cannot do this anymore.'" She wanted life for her father, and for herself, too.

Misery is a pandemic in its own right. With more than 1 million Americans dead from a virus that could have been contained, multitudes have plunged into mourning. Black seniors my grandfather's age died at twice the rate of senior whites. Some 14 million people swelled the ranks of the unemployed, and one in three families with children faced food shortages. The cruelty did not end with the height of the pandemic. Four years after COVID first reached American soil, fourteen states with Republican governors declined to run a Summer EBT program for low-income children. The program is a rare extension of pandemic-era aid, and it allotted families $40 a month per child for food. The same Republicans who offered up seniors as a sacrifice to the market opted to let children go hungry. Capitalism has become hyperbolic, the most evil version of itself. That transformation is driven not by the virus but by a top-down emphasis on productivity over humanity. Maybe I am guilty of the demonic sentimentalism that R. R. Reno described, but I worry we are edging ever closer to old territory, where some members of society—the old, the sick, the weak; anyone viewed as insufficiently industrious—are judged unworthy of life.

My grandfather's life was important, and not just to me. He was a human being who deserved the same level of dignity and peace that more fortunate men can purchase. He didn't have to die the way he did, in a small, cold room, separated from everyone he loved. All his hard work, all his responsibility, meant a pittance in the end. There is no justice but a fairer future.

THREE

BODIES ON THE LINE

Anna Mae Morris was born into a family of ministers and died on Good Friday in 2021. A Choctaw and Otoe-Missouria woman, Morris lived in flux, moving from Oklahoma to New Mexico, working a series of mostly low-wage jobs, before COVID cut her down too early at the age of sixty. As a child, she'd dreamed of different fates, her daughter Johnnie Jae told me. "Of course, growing up in a religious family, there's a lot of rules that you follow, a lot of expectations on how you're supposed to just behave in general," Johnnie Jae says. "And my mom was a rebel." Tell Anna Mae she couldn't do something, and that was what she wanted to do. She thought, once, of becoming a collegiate basketball player, even though she stood a mere inch above five feet. "She wanted to be an actress, she wanted to be a singer," her daughter explains, but then she became pregnant with Johnnie Jae at the age of nineteen. Life changed, and so did her dreams, but Anna Mae adapted. For the first seven years of her daughter's life, the family traveled in a converted school bus throughout North America, preaching at Pentecostal tent revival services. There were more babies, and time spent as a stay-at-home mother. She worked as a substitute teacher, and then as a community health worker checking up on elders in her community. Interested in law enforcement, she worked in security, including on the set of the movie *Twister* when they filmed in Oklahoma.

"We grew up really poor and, with four kids, struggled to make ends meet. So, at the same time that she was doing security, she was also working as a waitress at a local Sonic restaurant," Johnnie Jae explains. Anna Mae suffered from alcoholism, and later survived an abusive relationship, and when the family moved to New Mexico, away from her close-knit relatives, her circle narrowed until it began to collapse in on her. After she divorced Johnnie Jae's father, she "took off," and didn't speak to her children for two and a half years. "We would see her in the store, or just on the street, and it was like she didn't know who we were," her daughter remembers. Morris eventually got help, they say, and repaired her relationship with her family. Johnnie Jae is a horror, science fiction, and fantasy fan, and one day, they gave a talk at a convention about how to survive the zombie apocalypse on a reservation. They'd wanted Anna Mae there, but thought she couldn't make it. Then they saw something strange in the audience: someone was dressed as a Wookiee from *Star Wars*. The Wookiee came up after the talk, and a confused Johnnie Jae asked if the stranger wanted a photo. "So I take a picture and the Wookiee keeps posing and I'm thinking, God, this Wookiee is nervy," they tell me. Later, the Wookiee tackled them into a bear hug. "And then I hear my mom laughing and she pulls off her mask and it's my mom," they say. Morris had wanted to surprise them—and it worked, Johnnie Jae tells me.

Morris's health worried her family. She was diagnosed with lupus, an autoimmune disease that would later increase[1] her risk of severe outcomes and even death due to COVID. The disease runs in Morris's family: her sister also has it, and Johnnie Jae was diagnosed with it at age nine. "So as soon as this virus became known, my entire family took it seriously, right from the beginning, because we knew we were at higher risk," they say. The virus found them anyway. Johnnie Jae's cousin and his wife contracted COVID while working at an Indian health center, they tell me; and their aunt Susan would later spend a month on a ventilator. Susan's husband fell ill, too, and died of a stroke as the family prepared to remove him from life support. Everyone wanted to protect Morris from the same fate, but the virus encroached. At the time of her last illness, Morris lived in the same apartment complex as one of her daughters, and often babysat her grandchildren. Johnnie Jae says their sister's partner got sick first. They believe an unmasked coworker passed it on, causing an outbreak that sickened Morris. Her oxygen levels dropped, falling from a relatively healthy 95 percent in the morning to a troubling 88 percent in the evening. The family took Morris to the emergency room, where she was admitted to the hospital. There, Morris was alone, and fragile. She had COVID pneumonia in both lungs, her lupus had begun to flare, and she had previously lost her eyesight due to retinal damage. "She also started getting worse, and we didn't know how much worse, but because she was blind, and because she couldn't breathe, she started having panic attacks, and forgetting where she was," Johnnie Jae recalls. "And so, she would panic in her sleep, or she'd wake up in panic, and she'd rip out her IVs."

The family wanted Morris transferred to Albuquerque or Sante Fe. Her health was too fragile for their rural hospital, they felt. Then Johnnie Jae made a risky decision. Because they were fully vaccinated, and their sister had only had one shot, they would leave isolation in Los Angeles and travel to New Mexico to advocate for their mother. "It was terrifying, but it was also my mom," they explain. Before Johnnie Jae could reach rural New Mexico, Morris's condition worsened. She was put on a ventilator and transferred to a hospital in Albuquerque. In full protective gear, Johnnie could see their mother. Afterward, they scrubbed; sprayed sanitizer onto their clothes and washed their hands so that they could visit their mother without falling ill—passing the virus to anyone else. Despite the dire circumstances, hope endured. Their aunt had survived a full month on a ventilator and made a recovery despite her own lupus and the presence of a pacemaker. Perhaps their mother would also live. She had survived so much already, been tougher than anyone had expected her to be. "We didn't have any reason to believe that she wasn't going to come through this," Johnnie Jae says. It wasn't long, though, before they and their family realized that Morris wouldn't make it. The combination of lupus and COVID pneumonia was too much for her.

A weeping Johnnie recalled the end of their mother's life. They told their sister that she should anticipate the worst. Their mother's skin looked gray; she had sores and was unresponsive. Faced with such a grim reality, the family made the decision to remove their beloved mother from life support. "Once they had everything removed, they started turning off the machines one by one," they say. "We were prepared for it to take a while, but as soon as they turned off the vent, it wasn't even three seconds and my mom flatlined. Her heart stopped beating. And we knew that we had made the right choice." Morris was at rest.

•   •   •

The contours of Anna Mae Morris's foreshortened life map out a familiar America. As an Indigenous woman who'd experienced poverty and disability during her six decades on earth, Morris contended with racism and systematic exploitation. She was fortunate in one sense. Her daughter, Johnnie, said that she had access to health care through the Indian Health Service, or IHS. Chronically underfunded and understaffed, the IHS struggles to meet the needs of Indigenous Americans, who don't live as long as whites on average.[2] Yet the IHS provided Morris with basic medical attention—something many Americans with disabilities struggle to obtain. Americans have no universal right to health care. Disability benefits exist, but they're difficult to attain, and strict asset limits keep people in poverty.[3] In 2022, researchers with the Century Foundation and the Center for Economic and Policy Research reported that Americans with disabilities are twice as likely to live in poverty.[4] It is legal for companies to pay disabled workers a subminimum wage, a double insult in a country that hasn't raised the federal minimum wage since 2009.[5] Antidiscrimination laws have yet to close a "stark" wage gap between disabled and nondisabled workers, the report continued, and among people of color with disabilities, poverty rates are especially pronounced. "In 2020, one in four disabled Black adults in the United States lived in poverty, while just over one in seven of their white counterparts did so," the report said. To have a disability in this country is to be marked out, an inferior class in a stratified place.

Prior to the pandemic, the situation was dire for many. With the advent of COVID, people with disabilities faced an additional threat. For some, it threatened to erase the hard-won gains they'd made.

· · ·

People with intellectual and developmental disabilities live shorter lives on average compared to those without such diagnoses. But in the years before COVID, their lives had begun to lengthen, explained Dr. Scott Landes of Syracuse University's Aging Studies Institute. "In the late 1940s, people with Down syndrome, for example, lived less than twenty years," Landes explains. That's changed, though improvements depend, often, on a person's exact diagnosis. People without comorbidities tend to live longer than those who have them. The persistence of the lifespan gap may indict historical and institutional patterns, Landes adds. People with IDD experience higher rates of death due to pneumonitis in addition to urinary tract infections and dysphagia, which causes difficulty swallowing. "The real question, though, becomes how much of that is preventable death," he says. "A lot of these things that I've just named as causes of deaths, in the general population we would say are highly preventable with the correct care." People with IDD often don't get that care, he tells me. That's the fault, partially, of medical providers who aren't trained to work with people who have such disabilities—who either dismiss their physical complaints outright, or don't know how to communicate with them.

Then COVID struck. Around 20 percent of people with IDD live in congregate settings, according to Landes, which is true of only about 6 percent of adults over sixty-five. Many individuals with IDD were thus uniquely susceptible to a highly contagious disease like COVID. "The spread of the disease seems to have trended between two and a half times higher among people with intellectual and developmental disabilities than the general population case fatality rate," Landes adds. "So once someone gets COVID, their risk of death is been between two and a half and three times higher among people with an intellectual and developmental disability."

In the settings where many people with IDD live, workers often take second jobs due to low wages, Landes points out. A worker could pick up COVID from their second job, and bring it into the group or nursing home setting, where fragile people waited for care. In California, people with IDD who received care at home, rather than in a congregate setting, experienced much lower rates of COVID and lower rates of COVID fatality, Landes said.

As COVID swept through the congregate settings where so many people with IDD lived, it took lives, and left loved ones grieving. Debra McCoskey-Reisert is one such person. She knows she can perform one final service for her older brother, Bobby, and that is to keep his memory alive. On the phone with me, she shares anecdote after anecdote until Bobby nearly felt alive again. He didn't learn to speak until he was around seven and a half years old, she tells me. When he did talk, it was in groups of three. "Mom said he would drive her crazy: I want a cheeseburger, I want a cheeseburger, I want a cheeseburger," she recalls. He lived with a speech impediment thereafter, and Debra, born years later, often mispronounced the words she learned from her brother. Lord land was landlord. Renumber was remember. When he died from COVID at the age of fifty-five, Debra and her family made T-shirts that read "Renumber Bobby."

When a loved one dies, the act of remembrance takes on ritual significance. Memories bring the dead close and holds them there well after the body is no more. But when a death is political this ritual becomes radical. Memory paints flesh on bones some would prefer to keep buried. Memory can, to paraphrase Bobby, number and renumber the dead until loss can be felt in its true enormity. Debra is convinced that Bobby did not need to die, which would make his death an injustice as well as a tragedy. She can trace his last few weeks on earth with precision. At the time of his death, Bobby, who lived with diabetes and an intellectual disability, was living off a meager welfare check in a nursing home. Debra thought the situation was supposed to be temporary until a more suitable spot opened in an assisted-living unit. The moment never came. Bobby's mother, who was responsible for him, believed he was receiving adequate care. There were few other options available. Debra lived states away, as did many of her siblings. She describes her mother as a hoarder, so there wasn't enough space for Bobby to live with her at home. Nobody in the family could afford an apartment for Bobby, or fund the in-home caregiver he likely required. Bobby himself was in no position to pay.

Bobby did thrive in his new environment, Debra said. An outgoing man, he loved to socialize with his neighbors in the nursing home, even though most had decades on him. He sought friends wherever he happened to be: in the Boy Scouts when he was a child, or ringing bells for the Salvation Army when he was an adult. Debra's mind roves over the past. "Neither Bobby or I had talent, we can't dance, our arts and crafts are sloppy," she says. Bowling, however, was an exception: at the Special Olympics, he placed second in the state. He made key chains, too, for people he loved, even when he was in the hospital with COVID. In a story about his life, the Louisville *Courier-Journal* reported that Bobby once asked his brother, Tim, for food money, which he spent on milk and doughnuts for the nearby homeless.[6]

"He was very slow to anger. And if he did get mad, he would stay mad for five minutes and he was over it. I can stay mad for five years," Debra says, a little ruefully. Sometimes anger is justified, even useful. Marshaled by the living on behalf of the dead, anger can even become a power of its own. Though Bobby liked his nursing home, his residency there left him vulnerable at a moment of peril. COVID tore through the nation's nursing homes. By February 2022, over 200,000 long-term-care facility residents and staff had died from the virus, KFF reported.[7] That figure accounted for 23 percent of the nation's COVID deaths at the time. A congregational setting combined with a high prevalence of comorbidities likely contributed to the death toll in long-term-care facilities, or nursing homes. Residents are typically seniors or live with disabilities, qualities that predisposed them to serious complications from COVID. Yet the virus was not all that nursing home residents had to fear.

Faced with COVID's destructive power, some assigned it human qualities. Donald Trump was fond of such rhetoric, calling the virus our "invisible enemy"[8] as early as March 2020. To anthropomorphize a natural phenomenon like a virus is an attempt to exert control. A president can negotiate with an enemy and so can we, with enough savvy. (To fall ill, or die, is to betray weakness.) That capitalist logic underpins a form of social Darwinism, which animated not just the Trump presidency but the ruling class to which he belongs, and the conservative movement that catapulted him into power. Trump, like many conservative businessmen before him, had the grandiose self-confidence to insist that he alone could fix a diseased society. An adherent of the all-American prosperity gospel, he believed, further, that God blesses those who help themselves. Trump and his allies in government and business were willing to let the virus sort the wheat from the chaff.

In 1988, long before he was anything but a brash real estate developer from New York, he told Oprah Winfrey that to be successful, "you have to be born lucky, in the sense that you have to have the right genes."[9] A biographer, Michael D'Antonio, told *Frontline* that

Trump and his family favor "a racehorse theory of human development" and added, "They believe that there are superior people and that if you put together the genes of a superior woman and a superior man, you get a superior offspring."[10] His nephew, Fred C. Trump III, has written in a memoir that after a 2020 meeting with advocates for people who have complex care needs, Trump said, "The shape they're in, all the expenses, maybe those kinds of people should just die."[11] The former president would allegedly go on to suggest that Fred allow his own son, who has a disability, to die as well. Trump did not invent such disdain for people with disabilities. During that first year of COVID, he merely operated within an older American tradition: that of social Darwinism.

Beyond Trump, the American right wing opposed lockdowns and mask mandates almost from the beginning of the pandemic, often in the name of business or sometimes the free exercise of religion. In October 2020, before vaccines were widely available to the public, the editorial board of the *Wall Street Journal* defended the Haredim for protesting New York's restrictions on large gatherings. Then-governor Andrew Cuomo's "rhetoric discredits responsible Haredi leaders who have been urging calm and compliance, even as their communities suffer more than most under lockdown," the board wrote, adding, "It also empowers local demagogues who rouse crowds of teenagers to burn masks and hound disfavored community journalists in the streets."[12] The problem, in their view, stemmed from the restrictions, and from the liberal Cuomo, not from the demagogues themselves. Earlier that year, then-representative Trey Hollingsworth of Indiana, a Republican, said that the medical danger posed by the virus was "the lesser of these two evils" compared to the economic difficulties it could inflict. Also in 2020, Republican senator Rand Paul of Kentucky refused to wear a mask to the Capitol, and in a post on Twitter before it was X, he warned of "people-controls" like mask mandates.[13] Meanwhile, thousands were falling gravely ill—and dying—from COVID.

The pseudoscientific qualities of social Darwinism have faded over time, and so has social Darwinism itself, at least in its classic form. Traces of Darwinian thought persist, and as we assess the pandemic, the basic concept is as relevant now as it was when Richard Hofstadter wrote of it in 1944. The belief that certain qualities, among them intelligence, diligence, and criminality, could be hereditary once inspired a thriving movement in the U.S. and Europe under the rubric of social Darwinism. Called eugenics, it was by definition a movement of elites against the masses. Eugenics would shape a number of state laws that mandated the institutionalization and, later, the involuntary sterilization of those deemed unfit by the appropriate medical authorities. As coined and developed by Francis Galton, a British scholar who was a cousin of Darwin, eugenics held that proper breeding practices could eliminate genetically undesirable traits from the population. "All creatures would agree that it was better to be healthy than sick, vigorous than weak, well-fitted than ill-fitted for their part in life," Galton told supporters in 1904. "So with men."[14] The basic concept tantalized proponents of eugenics, among them progressive reformers engaged in social reform. Here, at last, was the scientific justification for what many already believed to be true about the poor, and the infirm, and the immigrant. Poverty was an individual's moral failing, the product of sloth, they believed. At last they understood the true root of the problem: poor genes made a poor man. Eradicate the qualities that handicapped him, and society would prosper.

Dozens of states would pass laws leading to the confinement and eugenic sterilization of people the state had deemed unfit. Such laws had old roots. "The poorhouse in the early nineteenth century did not simply provide shelter for the indigent," explained the scholar Liat Ben-Moshe in *Decarcerating Disability: Deinstitutionalization and Prison Abolition.*[15] "It was a catchall for all who were deemed dependent, unproductive, or dangerous. This system of warehousing together all the needy populations lasted in various degrees until the 1930s. In addition, during this eugenic era, the category of 'mental defectives' emerged as a way to distinguish those with intellectual disabilities from other 'defectives' and general 'degenerates.'" One Virginia law, passed in 1924, permitted the sterilization of "mental defectives" to improve "both the health of the individual patient and the welfare of society."[16] An early test case concerned Carrie Buck, a seventeen-year-old girl who'd become pregnant as the result of rape. A child of poverty, Buck's foster family, the Dobbs, ended her education after the sixth grade and put her to work. Buck labored in servitude most of her unhappy life. The Dobbses gave her up after her pregnancy, for she had become an inconvenience. Not only did the pregnancy restrict Buck's ability to work, it would produce another mouth to feed. But it was the rape that may have doomed Buck. She had accused a Dobbs relative—a shameful, criminal matter the family was eager to hide along with Buck herself. They had her declared "feebleminded," which led to her forcible commitment at Virginia's Colony for Epileptics and Feebleminded, located not far from Buck's native Charlottesville. There, she would come to the attention of Albert S. Priddy, the colony's superintendent. Priddy found Bell to be "unfit to exercise the proper duties of motherhood" and petitioned to have her sterilized. The case reached the U.S. Supreme Court, where the justices upheld the Virginia statute. The law was necessary, Oliver Wendell Holmes Jr. wrote for the majority, to prevent the nation from "being swamped with incompetence. . . . Three generations of imbeciles are enough."[17]

Holmes, the product of a Boston Brahmin family, had long shared in the eugenic fascinations that then gripped the nation's elite. As Adam Cohen observed in his book *Imbeciles: The Supreme Court, American Eugenics, and the Sterilization of Carrie Buck*, Holmes may have taken up the eugenicist leanings of his father, a physician. "Eight years before Galton published *Hereditary Genius*, Dr. Holmes described the 'Brahmin caste of New England' as a hereditary elite, physically and mentally," Cohen wrote.[18] "They were identifiable, he said, by their appealing 'physiognomy'—slender, smooth-faced, and quick-eyed." Defined, too, by "congenital" scholarly inclinations, the senior Holmes distinguished his peers from the less fortunate in their midst, who had "been bred to bodily labor." The younger Holmes has enjoyed a modern reputation as a progressive. By the standards of his age, his interest in eugenics does not disqualify him from the title; the eugenics movement counted many progressive reformers among its ranks. Their charitable endeavors did not induce in them a respect for the disposable, but rather convinced them to seek out his eradication. In his book *The Path of the Law*, Holmes "put forward the possibility that criminality had a genetic basis," Cohen wrote. "If the typical criminal is a degenerate, bound to swindle or to murder by as deep seated an organic necessity as that which makes the rattlesnake bite," Holmes argued, "it is idle to talk of deterring him by the classical method of imprisonment." For elites such as the Holmes men, Buck represented a horrifying possibility, a young and fertile woman who could bear many children into the poverty that she herself had suffered. According to the view popularized by eugenicists, Buck, and those like her, were more than weights around the slender necks of the more deserving. They were threats. The capitalist age to be born could not flourish as long as the "imbecile" persisted.

The Supreme Court decided *Buck v. Bell* nearly a century ago. Yet the ruling has never been overturned, and the case's influence lingers; eugenic beliefs are not an artifact of the past. Thirty-one states and the District of Columbia have laws that permit the forcible sterilization of people with disabilties, the National Women's Law Center reported in 2022, and outside the legal realm, policy preferences and popular stereotypes combine to inform widespread beliefs about who matters, and who does not.[19] "Lurking beneath the sound and fury of the eugenics movement and its language of defectives, mongrels, and misfits is a set of brutal yet recognizable beliefs about the kind of lives people on the margins deserve," the writer Elizabeth Catte observed in her book *Pure America: Eugenics and the Making of Modern Virginia.*[20] Later, noting that the University of Virginia's medical program had "flourished under eugenicists," and in more recent years had sued thousands of patients for unpaid medical bills, Catte wrote that she wondered if anyone in the school's "modern-day iteration would be brave enough to say that putting healthcare beyond the reach of the poor was just eugenics by a different name."[21] The pandemic did not inscribe eugenics into American society; it peeled back the layers until it became obvious that eugenics and the ideas behind it had never disappeared at all. In the 1960s and '70s, welfare rights activists who were predominantly poor women of color fought against "coerced sterilization," as historian Premilla Nadasen explained in *Welfare Warriors: The Welfare Rights Movement in the United States.* "Welfare recipients, in particular, were sometimes sterilized under the threat of losing their welfare payments," Nadasen wrote.[22] An early 1970s case exemplified the injustice, when doctors in Alabama sterilized two Black teenagers without consent. A lawsuit followed, and a federal district court found "uncontroverted evidence in the record that minors and other incompetents have been sterilized with federal funds and that an indefinite number of poor people have been improperly coerced into accepting a sterilization operation under the threat that various federally supported welfare benefits would be withdrawn unless they submitted to irreversible sterilization."[23] Coerced or forced sterilization still happens today, often to people with disabilities.

When Trump invoked the invisible enemy, he partook in an act of misdirection as his words disguised the real truth of the pandemic. People who are most at risk of serious illness or death from COVID face many enemies, and none are invisible. Their foes are human. The virus generated risks that decision-makers could either mitigate or magnify, and many opted for the latter. With time the pandemic became a crucible, revealing the true inclinations of those in power. As the virus swept the ranks of the disabled and seniors it revealed old patterns of neglect and abuse. The basic social Darwinism that shaped the eugenic regime never disappeared; indeed, it gained new strength in the COVID era. Implicit in Trump's rush to reopen the economy, explicit in Dan Patrick's suggestion that seniors sacrifice themselves for prosperity, eugenic patterns of thought and deed still haunt America and kill. Eugenics created certain categories of person, and set them apart based on what allegedly made them inferior to others. The scientific justification for eugenics has been discredited, but in America, some people are still disposable.

While age and disability made residents vulnerable to COVID, so did chronic negligence, which manifests in overcrowded rooms and understaffed facilities. In Indiana, where Bobby lived, the problem was acute. An *Indianapolis Star* investigation originally published in December 2020 found that, at the time, the state had one of the nation's highest number of deaths per one thousand nursing home residents.[24] More than 20 percent of Indiana's nursing home residents who fell ill with COVID died from it, at a time when the national rate for these deaths hovered around 13 percent. Bobby was one such person: he'd died months earlier, in April.

Bobby arguably did not belong in a nursing home, according to his sister Debra. He had lived independently in the past, until he began to have trouble managing his diabetes at home. He may have been able to retain some independence if he'd been able to find support services in his community, but outside nursing homes, people with disabilities in Indiana often have trouble accessing care and services that they need. "We've been facing a workforce crisis for several years," says Kim Dodson, the chief executive officer of the Arc of Indiana. The state had seen a sharp decrease in the number of individuals who chose to become direct support professionals, working with people like Bobby. People, she adds, "were already struggling to get some of their most critical and intimate needs met, so that when COVID hit, all of that just kind of exploded, because everybody was told to isolate and to hunker down." Isolation set in, stranding people with disabilities away from friends and caregivers. "We have a lot of people with disabilities who already get anxious and suffer from depression," she explains, and the pandemic "made all of that a hundred times worse.

"Families themselves don't always have access to quality health insurance or health benefits and health providers," she says. "So again, at the time of a health emergency, it just became much more evident that we needed to fix some of these problems." The problems Dodson cited are political problems, with origins in public attitudes about illness and disability. Since the era of eugenics, disability rights activists have fought for justice against cruelty and negligence. People with disabilities lacked federal civil rights protections until 1973, when President Richard Nixon signed the Rehabilitation Act into law. The bill contained a key provision, section 504, which states that "no otherwise qualified handicapped individual in the United States shall solely on the basis of his handicap, be excluded from the participation, be denied the benefits of, or be subjected to discrimination under any program or activity receiving federal financial assistance."[25] As the late disability rights activist Kitty Cone explained in an article for the Disability Rights Education & Defense Fund, section 504 "dramatically changed" social and legal perceptions of disability.[26] "Only with section 504 was the role of discrimination finally legally acknowledged," Cone wrote.

Nixon deserves little credit for signing the bill into law: he'd vetoed the legislation twice and only reversed his position after sustained protest from disability rights activists. In New York City, dozens of activists, led in part by Judith Heumann, blocked traffic on Madison Avenue to direct attention to the bill. Section 504 was an achievement, but it required new regulations to work. Such regulations, Cone wrote, "would provide a consistent, coherent interpretation of 504's legal intent rather than leaving it up to any judge who heard a 504 case to interpret what the law meant." The Department of Health, Education, and Welfare, or HEW, was responsible for drafting the regulations, but the agency stalled, so activists again placed their bodies on the line.

Four years after Nixon signed the Rehabilitation Act into law, Heumann and Cone helped occupy a HEW building in San Francisco for twenty-six days. The Americans with Disabilities Act exists not as a congressional act of pity but as a legacy of direct action. Activists staged the Capitol Crawl of 1990 to pressure Congress into passing the bill. Jennifer Keelan, who was then eight years old and who lives with cerebral palsy, pulled herself up the steps of the Capitol to demand passage of the ADA. "I'll take all night if I have to!" she told reporters at the time.[27] Keelan and other activists dragged themselves out of the margins and into the center of public life to demand equal treatment from a society that preferred to warehouse them out of view.

Yet the ADA could not end centuries of discrimination and abuse on its own, and neither could section 504. Problems persisted—the same structural inequalities isolated people with disabilities during the pandemic, that put them in nursing homes where they didn't belong, that created heavy burdens for families who lacked the means to care for their loved ones. Indiana must account for its own wrongs, but it is not a step out of pace with America. True, the landscape has changed. Disability rights activists, like Keelan, have fought for key advancements—and won. But as long as America prioritizes the market over people with disabilities, it consigns millions to precarity.

America taught me my place while I was still young. When a doctor first told me that I had a genetic disease, I suspected I would never truly be free—not of my condition, and not of America. To me, America seemed less of a disinterested party and more of a hostile entity. The moment my diagnosis appeared in my chart, the invisible hand of the market had judged me, and found me wanting. This was before the Affordable Care Act was law. A genetic disease seemed like the ultimate preexisting condition, a chain around my ankles. I had health insurance, but the deductible was so high that it covered almost nothing. There is no simple cure for my illness, which is a red blood cell disorder called hereditary spherocytosis, but there were tests, and emergency room trips for abdominal pain, and visits to a hematologist. I thought back to sixth grade, when my father fell ill with prostate cancer. He sat across from me at a table and counted a pill out onto a palm and told me how much each little white tablet cost. I understood the lesson. I understood why our church sent us financial help, why the rich girls who once bullied me now looked at me with pity. They understood, too, what a man's life could mean. It costs so much to be worth so little.

Hereditary spherocytosis is not fatal and I will live a long time unless some other ailment interferes. Nevertheless, I knew even at twenty-one that I would always need care. I would need a specialist. I would need pain management. I would likely need surgery at some unspecified date to treat the gallstones the condition creates, or perhaps to remove my spleen, which is painfully enlarged. I don't live in a nursing home, like Bobby, but I'm not well, either; I occupy an unenviable middle territory between health and sickness. As a child I learned the story of Daniel, a Jewish prophet who lives in Babylon. The sinful king, Belshazzar, holds a great feast, but he doesn't get to enjoy himself for long. A hand appears, and writes out "MENE, MENE, TEKEL, UPHARSIN" on the wall, and so Belshazzar calls on the wise Daniel to interpret. Daniel, like most prophets, is a bearer of bad news. "Mene: God has numbered the days of your reign and brought it to an end. Tekel: You have been weighed on the scales and found wanting. Peres: Your kingdom is divided and given to the Medes and Persians," he told the king. God had judged the blaspheming Belshazzar, and found him wanting. Someone had judged me, and found me wanting, as if my very existence was blasphemy. Perhaps it was.

I would never be the picture of American health. In the eugenics era, there were contests[28] at state fairs to find the local family with the best genetic hygiene. My family would lose, I knew that, and even in the twenty-first century there was a price to pay for inferiority. We struggled to pay for health insurance. I would set myself benchmarks. As long as I could stand up straight, I would not go to the emergency room for pain. I'd wait, instead, until the pain bent me over, or until it passed. Later, when I went to the UK for a postgraduate program, a hematologist told me that the American health-care system was "barbaric." I couldn't argue with him.

There are gradations to disability, yet regardless of diagnosis, we face the same enemies in America. I never met Bobby, never knew of him until he died and I spoke to someone who had loved him. He is not an object lesson, or an inspirational tale, but a real person, and we shared a certain kinship even if we never knew each other in life. We had both been judged wanting by a political system much larger and more powerful than ourselves. When the pandemic arrived, the ACA had been law for years. I had a steady job and good health insurance. Because I could work from home, I shut myself away in my apartment, not knowing how the virus would interact with my illness. Bobby had no such option. He depended on his nursing home for protection. Debra believes the home failed to do all it could to keep him well, and struggles, even now, with what she perceives to be a lack of transparency around his final illness and eventual death. "This is what they told me," she remembers. "They had a patient that they put in Bobby's room, and that patient had COVID and they died. And then they put a second patient in with Bobby, who had COVID who died." In these circumstances, Bobby's illness may have become inevitable. On April 8, the home sent Bobby to the hospital with COVID, where he stayed for several weeks. He appeared to improve, and the hospital discharged him back to his nursing home.

The next time Debra spoke to her brother, he was not himself. "He just was talking nonsense. And he kept saying, 'I messed up.'" She has two theories. "One is he was having diarrhea and maybe that's what he meant. And the second theory is he might have thought somehow he messed up because he got the virus," she explains. "One of the aides got on the phone with me and she said, 'Get him the hell out of here. Like this place is a shit show.'" She and her family called the nursing home and told staff that Bobby needed to return to the hospital, but in her recollection, the home was less than cooperative, and kept Bobby in his room. "If we had money to cover all of this ourselves, Bobby would have been back at the hospital," she believes. Instead, he died in his room at the nursing home. Debra is convinced he died alone. Later, she lost her mother to COVID, too.

People with disabilities have long fought against the idea that they are disposable. Successful self-advocacy has always been a matter of life and death, a fact thrown into sharper relief by the pandemic. As the virus encroached, it created special risks for people who live with disabilities, due either to their existing health problems or, in some cases, to their living conditions. Melody Cooper lives in a congregate setting, as Bobby once did. She and her husband, Joe, were residents of an assisted-living community in Indianapolis, the city where they'd met and fallen in love. In an interview with me, Melody, an advocate with the Arc of Indiana who also appeared on local television to tell Joe's story, recalls her early friendship with the man who would become her husband. He had worked alongside her at a local Goodwill. Their paths parted when Melody left to work at Meijer, while Joe worked at a library, but she never forgot him. "I didn't see him for a long time, it was about ten years," she tells me. On a trip home to visit her family, Melody spied him in a local park. "I looked, and I looked, and I said, 'Oh my god,' I said. 'That looks like Joe,'" she says. "And sure enough, he was saying the same thing, 'Wow, that looks like Mel.'

And the closer we got it became clear that it was us, and we ran up to one another, gave each other a hug, and there was a picnic table, right there where we were at, and we both just sat down right there at the picnic table." For the two friends, it was as if no time had passed, and over time their relationship deepened. In 2005, Joe proposed. They married in November the same year. "I loved him, I think I loved him unconditionally, Sarah," she insists. "There's nothing that Joe could do wrong." She adds, "I needed someone to love me for me, because I know that I have a disability. I think Joe understood me." Not once in their fifteen years of marriage had Joe ever said anything wrong to her, she explains. "And he protected me, and he wouldn't let nobody hurt me. And he was like, 'This is Mel and you're not gonna hurt her,' so yeah. I think I just loved everything about him. Everything."

The virus ended so many love stories, and it did not spare Melody and Joe. First, it separated the couple for months. The two spent lockdown apart from each other, though Melody would occasionally sneak over to see him. "I'd see him early in the morning, and I probably would see him late at night. I did that all summer, and we would talk through the window," she says. But as that summer faded, a friend in assisted living warned her to prepare for the worst. "She said, 'Mel, I know this pandemic is going on, but please don't keep your hopes up, because if Joe gets it, Mel, nine times out of ten Joe won't pull through.'" Melody could only pray that Joe would not get ill. Soon, though, she received word that he was ill with what at first appeared to be a urinary tract infection. A COVID test came back positive, and Joe, struggling to fight off both illnesses, began to decline. A doctor called and told Melody that Joe would not survive. "I had been crying, and I'm like, 'Okay, I've got to see him. Lord, Lord, I don't know how, but I want to see him one more time,'" she remembers. The hospital called and offered her the use of an iPad, but Melody was desperate to say goodbye to her husband of fifteen years in person. A skilled advocate for herself, she convinced the hospital to agree. She suited up, and walked in the room, although she tells me that she was scared to death of the virus. "And I talked to him like I had been talking to him for fifteen years, I'm like, 'Joe, I got you, I love you,'" she adds. "I know he heard my voice, I know he knew I was in that room." Joe passed not long after Melody said goodbye. His would be her second loss to COVID: her mother had passed from the virus in June. Though she is devastated, she fights on in his memory. "I'm still working for the Arc, but I'm doing a lot of my work here at home," she explains. "So I kept on doing what I'm doing, and I made him a promise that day that I wouldn't stop, and I honored that, I tried, I still to this day, I have honored that promise."

The pandemic created new challenges for anyone who has a disability or chronic illness—whether they live in a congregated setting or at home in their communities, whether they contracted the virus or not. "I was familiar with going to my doctor's appointments," said Linda Beal, who lived with HIV for decades, and who spoke to me before her passing in 2023. With the arrival of COVID, though, her care transformed and she had to rely on telehealth appointments, which were easy to forget. Gone, too, were the in-person support groups that had once sustained her. "Most of us are single people, and going to our groups is when we meet our peers, and we talk, and we show love to each other," she told me. "Without those groups going on, everybody was sad, very sad and lonely, at home alone. And then not knowing what's going to happen. Are we ever going to get together again?"

Beal, then a leader with the advocacy group VOCAL-NY, lost

access to more than the peer support on which she'd come to rely. To protect her fragile immune system, she avoided her loved ones, too. "In the beginning of the pandemic, I took safety precautions by staying away from my family which I'm very close to, my children, and my grandchildren," she explained. "Not only me, all of us, we spent a lot of time alone. A lot of time alone. And being alone and living with HIV, especially, that's not healthy for us." She had a "double fear" that "if I go around a family member, will I get COVID and die? These things were going through my head."

Any pandemic would have added fresh weight to the burdens Beal already carried as a person living with HIV in the United States. "The stigma, in my opinion, is one of the things that holds back from us proceeding and what we are fighting for, because people have their own personal opinions, they look at us in a different way. And we are no different than any other individual," Beal explained. "We're not the disease. We are human beings, who deserve to live a normal life as others do." She added that many people with HIV "would never talk to a news reporter. A lot of us wouldn't do it." Beyond stigma, people living with HIV need policies not forthcoming from people in power. To VOCAL-NY, health care and housing are human rights to which everyone is entitled, a sentiment not universally shared by the political class. When COVID arrived, the cost of such inaction came due. In the absence of widely available, affordable housing and access to health care, suffering proliferated.

Beal spoke to me in December 2021, in between the worst of the Delta and Omicron waves. Within weeks, a sense of exhaustion had set in—and not just among frontline workers. Some Americans, like John, had never taken the pandemic seriously. But liberal energies had begun to flag, too. A longing for normalcy encouraged a sense of recklessness among some. The pandemic was in retreat, David

Leonhardt of the *New York Times* heralded in February 2021. This proclamation turned out to be unduly optimistic, as new waves of infection sickened and killed Americans, but an undaunted Leonhardt would continue to preach in the same vein for months. "By April of the same year, Leonhardt was castigating the 'many vaccinated people [who] continue to obsess over the risks from COVID,'" wrote Jacob Bacharach in the *New Republic*.[29] Bacharach noted that Leonhardt "declared 'Omicron in Retreat'" on January 19, 2021, a day with 3,376 COVID deaths reported in the U.S. alone. The pandemic was not over for anyone, let alone those whose comorbidities made them susceptible to severe COVID.

Beal and others with compromised immune systems continued to live in "limbo," as the writer Ed Yong put it in a February 2022 piece for the *Atlantic*.[30] As society tried to move on, it threatened to strand many behind—an outcome painted by some, like Leonhardt, as a necessity. Though vaccines changed our risk calculus, and the nation couldn't stay locked down forever, the virus remains uniquely dangerous for many, including seniors and people with disabilities. They don't always find much understanding, let alone accommodation. "For those who don't agree that the vaccinated can return to pre-pandemic normal, I ask: What should we all do? Perpetual masking? Forever not dining out, avoiding large weddings & indoor gatherings, etc? Virtually everything has risk, and zero COVID is not a viable strategy," Dr. Leana Wen posted on Twitter in March 2022.[31] Yet there is substantial territory between zero-COVID, a term that refers to the maximum suppression of the virus via lockdowns and other measures, and a false normal that abandons the disabled to hell. "Ramps, accessibility buttons, screen readers, and many other measures have made life easier for disabled people, and a new wave of similar accommodations is now necessary to make immunosuppression less of a disability in the COVID era," Yong argued. The accommodations themselves were not onerous, as Yong noted. "What they do want—work flexibility, better ways of controlling infectious diseases, and more equitable medical treatments—would also benefit everyone, not just now but for the rest of our lives," he wrote.

Yet there was little sign of accommodation as the nation entered its third pandemic year. Masks had begun to disappear from public spaces. In New York City, newly elected mayor Eric Adams urged employers to force workers back into their offices.[32] "You can't stay home in your pajamas all day," he said at one public event.[33] "That is not who we are as a city. You need to be out cross-pollinating ideas, interacting with humans."

People with disabilities know they can't always count on the government for help—if the government even remembers they exist. In 2024, when the Centers for Disease Control and Prevention said that people with COVID no longer needed to isolate for five days, officials said they'd adapted to a changed reality. COVID deaths are declining, and vaccines reduce the likelihood of severe illness in most adults and children. The CDC's recommendations brought COVID in line with other common respiratory illnesses, including the flu. But people with disabilities live with different risks, and some greeted the CDC's announcement with concern. Maria Town, the president of the American Association of People with Disabilities, told the *Washington Post* that her community "has been really left behind and disposable for the past four years," and the CDC's new guidance "fails to recognize how much more contagious COVID is, how it behaves differently and puts many people, especially disabled people and immunocompromised people, at risk."[34]

In the absence of state support, people with disabilities often rely on each other. Out of this reality sprang Mutual Aid Diabetes, a small group of committed activists pooling community resources on behalf of their most vulnerable peers. Speaking to me in 2021, organizers Emily Miller and Zoe Witt told me about their efforts not long after the group first launched. (Witt left the group in 2024.) Their work had begun in the early days of the pandemic, as activists recognized a need to address the situation before it became even deadlier than normal. "I think it's really important to note that this has been a mounting crisis, that it's only been getting worse and worse," Witt says. "I was rationing insulin for most of 2018 and I live in Washington State, which is a state where people think that's impossible." Witt had encountered a coverage gap, where they made too much money to qualify for Medicaid but not enough money to buy private health insurance, and they were in trouble. Insulin is expensive in the U.S. and people can die from rationing it.[35] From 2002 to 2013, prices had more than tripled, CBS News reported in 2018.[36]

Nicole Smith-Holt became an ambassador for T1International after her son, Alec, died from rationing his insulin in 2017. "I think his story definitely highlights the flaws within our health-care system," she tells me. "Shortly after Alec passed away and I started sharing his story, I heard from people all over the world that if Alec lived in the UK or if Alec lived in Australia, or if Alec lived in Canada, if Alec lived in basically any other part of the world, he would still be alive, because other countries and their health-care systems actually puts the lives of people ahead of profit."

The economic circumstances generated by the pandemic—and worsened by the government's flawed response—posed an additional threat to many living with diabetes. When the pandemic hit, thousands lost their jobs, and their employer-provided health insurance, too. "People that are uninsured are the ones that are subject to paying the full list price of insulin usually, so they're definitely the most vulnerable diabetics," Witt explains.

When Witt and Miller first spoke to me, the group had only just established its intake process and begun processing requests for aid. "It's not like we have thousands and thousands of Instagram followers or anything, but we've been able to reach quite a few people so far," Witt says in a Zoom call. That would soon change. The group's reach has grown steadily over time, making it a small but persistent presence in an often-overlooked corner of the internet. To observe the group is to behold the consequences of state abandonment. Deprived of affordable health care, activists work to save their peers from horrors that are uniquely American. Our system did not hold up under the stress the virus applied.

"This pandemic has really opened up a lot of people's eyes to how difficult it is to have health insurance that's related to your employment," adds Smith-Holt. "I think a lot of people have realized that most of us are lucky to have jobs and that we're lucky to have employer-based insurance. But what happens when that luck runs out?" The answer, sometimes, is death.

FOUR

THE WORTHY AND THE UNWORTHY

Americans encounter a pervasive national mythology in school, at work, and on television. The message is largely the same: Here we are rich and free, so free that even the unlucky few in poverty can find prosperity with a little work. This story is key to America's self-image, and it has been reinforced over time by a ruling class eager to quell discontent. When Ronald Reagan described America as a shining city on a hill, as he did in several speeches during his political lifetime, he reinforced this image, and built America up as an exceptional nation that could be an example to a benighted world. The myth suited Reagan, who for ideological reasons sought to paper over the cracks in the American edifice. While he spoke of America as a beacon, he slashed taxes[1] for the wealthy and cut welfare[2] for working mothers, which pushed poor families more deeply into poverty.

The truth of America is more complex and less attractive than the average political speech betrays. There is an underside to the nation, which Richard Proia discovered after a recession tumbled him into poverty. Others never make it to the middle class at all. The U.S. is rich, but unequal. "The rich in the US are exceptionally rich—the top 10 percent have the highest top-decile disposable incomes in the world, 50 percent above their British counterparts," John Burn-Murdoch of the *Financial Times* reported in 2022.[3] "But the bottom decile struggle by with a standard of living that is worse than the poorest in 14 European countries including Slovenia." America is exceptional compared to other developed nations, but not in ways that Reagan would ever admit.

In 2017, Philip Alston, then the UN Special Rapporteur on extreme poverty and human rights, paid a visit to America. His subsequent report observed that the American youth poverty rate "is the highest across" the Organization for Economic Cooperation and Development (OECD), a fact in contrast with the wealth enjoyed by some.[4] The policies of the Trump administration only contributed to this state of drastic inequality. "The United States has the highest rate of income inequality among Western countries," Alston wrote, and added, "The $1.5 trillion in tax cuts in December 2017 overwhelmingly benefited the wealthy and worsened inequality."[5] While the wealthy, including John, prospered in the Trump era, millions more suffered greater and greater forms of degradation. In the years preceding the pandemic, Trump followed Reagan's example by cutting taxes for society's most fortunate, while attacking the social safety net, which was already unfit for purpose by the time he came to power. He chose Seema Verma to lead the Centers for Medicare & Medicaid Services, which sent another warning signal to the nation's poor.

By the time of her nomination, Verma had earned a reputation for cutting health-care costs in the state of Indiana, where her small consulting firm helped craft the state's version of Medicaid expansion. The Healthy Indiana Plan 2.0 provided health-care coverage to almost 400,000 people, most of whom had been uninsured, the Center on Budget and Policy Priorities reported on its website.[6] Yet beneficiaries also said the plan was complicated. According to the *Indianapolis Star*, the plan required participants to pay "up to 2 percent of their income into a monthly Personal Wellness and Responsibility Account, which helps pay for their care."[7] If a person can't make that monthly payment, then, depending on their income, they're "temporarily locked out" of the program or sorted into a different, less expansive Basic coverage tier. CBPP observed that half of the plan's Black beneficiaries belonged to the Basic tier, raising questions about the plan's ability to resolve long-standing racial health disparities. When Verma took control of CMS, experts concluded that work requirements for Medicaid were likely on the way—and Verma would later prove them correct. Once installed as the administrator of CMS, Verma approved state requests to attach work requirements to Medicaid. In Arkansas, the effects were particularly damaging to low-income people. Adults age thirty to forty-nine, with incomes of up to 138 percent of the federal poverty line, "had to report 80 hours a month of work or community engagement activities to the Arkansas Department of Human Services or risk losing their health coverage," a brief from the Urban Institute explained.[8] The state had disenrolled over 18,000 beneficiaries by the end of December 2018.

Heather Hahn, who is the associate vice president for management in the Center on Labor, Human Services, and Population at the Urban Institute, tells me that the plan is "consistent" with "these attitudes toward the poor and this perception that if people are having trouble making ends meet, it must be because they're not working hard enough." Making people work, she adds, can sound like a logical solution, but while it's great in theory, it doesn't address the causes of poverty or solve it. "Even when people can find work, the nature of low-wage and unskilled work is increasingly that it is unstable and unpredictable," she explains. In interviews with welfare recipients, Hahn found that most do want to work, but have difficulty doing so for reasons that are often outside their control. One factor "is when the jobs are not available where they live or they don't have the transportation to get to where the jobs are," she says. An absence of childcare can also prevent the poor from working. "And then there are many people who are dealing with disability issues that aren't serious enough disabilities to let them qualify for federal disability payments, but are disruptive enough that it is difficult for them to do manual labor or to stay on their feet or for various reasons to maintain consistent employment," she goes on. Work requirements for programs like Medicaid penalize the poor for living in the conditions of poverty. A federal judge later halted the Arkansas work requirements.

The Arkansas program was a failure even by its own standards: one analysis from the Commonwealth Fund found that it didn't increase employment in its targeted age group. The court order mostly reversed coverage losses, but people who lost coverage, even temporarily, faced greater barriers to health care than those who were continuously enrolled in Medicaid. By approving Republican-authored plans to gut Medicaid, Verma saw to it that thousands of poor people were ill-prepared for the trials to come. At the same time, she spoke frequently of the need for personal responsibility and innovation. "Every American deserves the dignity and respect of high expectations and as public officials we should deliver programs that instill hope and say to each beneficiary that we believe in their potential," she said in one 2017 speech. "CMS believes that meaningful work is essential to beneficiaries' economic self-sufficiency, self-esteem, well-being, and health of Americans."[9] Later, after Arkansas began kicking people off Medicaid in 2018, she claimed that so-called "community engagement requirements" were merely designed "to put beneficiaries in control with the right incentives to live healthier, independent lives."

Behind Verma's language of self-sufficiency and independence lie old stereotypes about the poor. Because the disposable person lives on the margins, he is suspect, and represents failures that the ruling class attributes to personal flaws rather than structural designs. For America to be a shining city on a hill, the disposable person must be hidden or helped. He is a source of dread to the more affluent. "That the poor are invisible is one of the most important things about them," wrote Michael Harrington in his 1962 book, *The Other America: Poverty in the United States*. "They are not simply neglected and forgotten as in the old rhetoric of reform; what is much worse, they are not seen."[10] Invisibility forecloses the possibility of substantive progress. If the state does offer help, someone like Seema Verma will say it encourages dependency, even sloth. The poor "had come to represent what the middle class feared most in itself: softening of character, a lack of firm internal values," Barbara Ehrenreich argued in 1989's *Fear of Falling: The Inner Life of the Middle Class*.[11]

Viewed this way, a person is poor because of his own internal failings; he must struggle with himself, not with an exploitative state or with the forces of capitalism. After all, help implies the existence of a problem, which must originate either with the disposable or someplace else. The easiest response is to blame the person in poverty.

When America does aid the poor it has done so, often, with provisions that call the morality of the recipient in question. If someone can't make it in America, the reasoning goes, she should blame herself.

Verma, then, was operating in an old and even bipartisan tradition. The pandemic could claim the lives of the poor at such disproportionately high rates because of failures that long preceded it. Though the poverty rate in America had fallen to a record low in 2019, serious failures persisted, and would later shape the pandemic and its toll. More than one in ten American households experienced food insecurity in 2019, the researcher Zachary Parolin of Bocconi University and Columbia University's Center on Poverty and Social Policy has reported.[12] Around 29 million people lacked health insurance that same year, and millions of others said they couldn't afford medical care. Poverty is difficult to define, and Parolin wrote that there is no "agreed-upon" way to measure it, but the data tells a troubling story. COVID was deadlier for people who had preexisting medical conditions, who were more likely to work frontline jobs, who lived in crowded housing conditions, and who had experienced financial hardship, Parolin found. The conditions we associate with poverty predisposed millions to serious illness and even death from COVID.

"The poor," Michael Harrington wrote, "get sick more than anyone else in the society." The reasons are many, and include shoddy housing and infrequent access to medical care. They stay sick longer than the wealthy, which costs them work and places a better future further out of reach. Harrington went on: "At any given point in the circle, particularly when there is a major illness, their prospect is to move to an even lower level and to begin the cycle, round and round, toward even more suffering."[13] Whatever progress America has made over the years has been arrested, in part, by a specious distinction between the deserving and undeserving poor.

Such scapegoating can be catastrophic for the poor. In 2012, the scholar of poverty and social welfare policy H. Luke Shaefer made a troubling discovery: 1.5 million American households, home to nearly 3 million children, subsisted on cash incomes of $2 a day or less. This state of extreme poverty had risen since 1996, the year that then-president Bill Clinton signed the Personal Responsibility and Work Opportunity Reconciliation Act, known better as welfare reform, into law. As the name implies, legislators intended the bill to move welfare recipients into the workforce. Clinton told reporters at the time that it would "transform a broken system that traps too many people in a cycle of dependence to one that emphasizes work and independence."[14] The bill replaced an older form of welfare, the Aid to Families with Dependent Children, or AFDC, with a new program called Temporary Assistance for Needy Families, or TANF. States receive the bulk of the funding for TANF in the form of a block grant from the federal government. Though state governments have significant leeway in how they spend those funds, they're required to meet any one of the four purposes set out by the welfare reform law: assisting families in need so children can be cared for in their own homes or the homes of relatives; reducing the dependency of parents in need by promoting job preparation, work, and marriage; preventing pregnancies among unmarried persons; and encouraging the formation and maintenance of two-parent families, as the CBPP explained on its website. The law assumed welfare recipients inhabit a dysfunctional culture marked by broken homes and out-of-wedlock births; it assumes, further, that the state can help solve poverty by encouraging marriage.

Such beliefs owed more to stereotypes about the poor, especially poor Black Americans, than they did to evidence. Poverty is a multiracial problem, and so is the extreme poverty that Shaefer documented; it was rising most quickly in Black and Latino households, though half of those living on $2 a day or less were white. Nevertheless, welfare reform operated within a deeply racialized context. The law was but another attempt to distinguish between the deserving and undeserving poor—and by the time Bill Clinton signed it, the public associated Black Americans with that latter category. The scholar Martin Gilens has shown that, historically, Americans thought positively of the welfare state, while opposing some forms of welfare for those they perceived to be lazy. Stereotypes of Black Americans as lacking a firm work ethic shaped this hostility to welfare more than a sense of individualism or self-interest. Those stereotypes are old, originating with slavery; slave owners often claimed that the people they owned were deficient in moral character. "In essence, slave owners needed a Sambo; they needed to believe that blacks were lazy, ignorant, happy-go-lucky, and childlike in order to justify slavery," Gilens wrote.[15] In the 1960s and '70s, the media disproportionately illustrated negative stories of poverty with pictures of Black Americans, which likely encouraged Americans to exaggerate the ranks of the Black poor and to consider them undeserving of aid.

Politicians would capitalize on these stereotypes. When Reagan campaigned on shrinking the welfare state, he did so by linking the poor to fraud and abuse. By the time Clinton said he wanted to "end welfare as we know it," the poor Black woman had arguably become the archetypal welfare recipient in the American imagination. "Welfare had become the lightning rod for Americans' anxieties over their work, incomes, families, and futures," wrote historian Michael B. Katz in his seminal work, *In the Shadow of the Poorhouse: A Social History of Welfare in America*.[16] "Poor, young Black mothers increasingly took the blame for violence, crime, and drugs; for the taxes on overburdened workers; and for the rot eating its way through the American dream."

• • •

Long before Clinton and Reagan launched their respective assaults on welfare, public officials exhibited a certain skepticism of the poor. The architects of welfare and earlier poor relief strove to distinguish between the deserving and undeserving, a futile effort that often had terrible consequences for the poor. "The availability of work for every able-bodied person who really wants a job is one of the enduring myths of American history," Katz observed. Writing decades after Harrington described the other America in such exacting detail, Katz noted that in the nineteenth century, before the existence of the welfare state and during the emergence of capitalism, sickness often contributed to the destitution of the desperately poor. Katz added that the problems of the poor only "intensified" with age, a statement that Richard Proia may have agreed with before his death from COVID in 2020.[17] Yet early forms of poor relief sought to assist the worthy, while leaving the unworthy in the cold, where they allegedly belonged. In the nineteenth century, a community might incarcerate its destitute in a poorhouse, a place to shelter, but also to discipline. The poorhouse isolated a person from the world and its moral dangers, and—in theory—rehabilitated the poor by remedying their "intemperance" and sloth, Katz pointed out.[18] The idea was to reduce poverty by deterring the attitudes that theoretically produced it; an attempt to temper generosity with pragmatism. "One lesson observers learned was the incompatibility of deterrence and compassion: the spread of fear and the kindly treatment of decent poverty could not coexist. One or the other always prevailed," Katz wrote.[19] Fear often won out over compassion, which led, arguably, to the popularity of eugenics as a means of separating the wheat from the chaff. Even now, fear dominates policymaking strategies in both parties. Efforts to reduce the welfare rolls reinforce the belief that there is enough work, offered at a living wage, to lift up the American poor. Neoliberals and conservative reactionaries alike still make a distinction between the worthy, who deserve help, and the unworthy, who don't. Before Paul Ryan ran for vice president in 2012 he spoke, repeatedly, of "makers" and "takers."[20] The more recent debate over the Child Tax Credit is instructive, too. In 2022, Senator Joe Manchin, a conservative Democrat at the time, said he wouldn't support an enhanced CTC without a work requirement—as though there were legions of Americans waiting to leech off the state.[21] Yet this is far more difficult than many choose to admit. Poverty is not a moral state, but a condition that can be experienced by anyone. Not even moderate-income households, which we typically think of as the middle class, are entirely safe from America's surfeit of inequality.

My own family learned this threat many times over. Though both my parents had college degrees, and my father even worked at times as an adjunct professor of music, we remained precarious. Doctors who attended our church would see us at discounted rates and send us home with bags of free sample medication. We all knew that even with this charity in place we could not seek medical help until an illness had persisted for weeks. When I briefly studied in the UK, the National Health Service felt like a reprieve. I got my teeth cleaned for the first time in years. I bought new glasses, which would have cost me $400 back home. When a hospital pharmacist nearly let me walk off with my prescriptions without paying, I stopped, and insisted on handing over the paltry sum. But austerity had followed me across the Atlantic. The Tories were in power, and they had the NHS in their sights. Later the prospect of returning to America, where aspects of the Affordable Care Act were then unsettled, pushed me into a severe depression. I'd learned that in the UK, at least, I could go to the hospital when I was sick, and so I did. I went to the hospital instead of trying to die, and later, in the common room of a South London triage ward, I could hear faintly the sounds of a protest. People had gathered in front of the hospital with signs warning of cuts to the NHS. I no longer wanted to die, yet I could feel the walls closing in around me. My life or death no longer felt like matters of agency, but fates determined by entities I did not control.

"In truth, the forces that pushed individuals and families into poverty originated in the structure of America's political economy," Katz wrote. "Some of us are lucky, not different."[22] My poverty was temporary: I'd managed to finish my education, and the U.S. Supreme Court kept most of the Affordable Care Act intact. My first job out of school gave me the best health insurance I'd ever had in my life; the next time I landed in the hospital, this time for a rare complication of my genetic disease, my weeklong stay was nearly free. So I climbed, slowly, into what could be described as a typical middle-class life. Student loan debt weighed me down, but I could afford my basic expenses with a little left over, and my future no longer looked so dim.

For most of us, disposability is either the active condition of our lives or a state into which we can easily fall. "People that are middle-income are often living paycheck to paycheck and face economic insecurity generally," explains Elise Gould, a senior economist with the left-leaning Economic Policy Institute. In the absence of wealth, in the form of assets or investments, middle-income households "just don't have much of a safety net to fall back on." Wealth is key, Gould adds. "You need personal wealth because we don't have the same social safety nets that other countries have, or the same kind of investments that other countries have," she says. "We think about where wealth is used for in this country, or what the safety net does. It provides some kind of economic stability if you lose your job, or in retirement, or if you need money to pay for health care, or even saving for college. Those kinds of societal investments aren't as secure here as they are in some of our peer, high-income countries." What America does have is inequality, and lots of it. "The amount of inequality here means that wealth is very hard to build because most people's income comes from wages," she goes on. "And there's so much wage inequality that for some it's just very difficult to build any kind of economic stability from it." The Federal Reserve reported in 2019 that 30 percent of Americans said they couldn't pay all their regular bills, or lived one emergency away from financial danger.[23]

For some, COVID became that emergency. In Fresno, Texas, Ebony James and her husband, Terrence, had carved out a middle-class life for themselves and their children. They both worked as teachers in the local public school system, and they owned their own home. Terrence taught social studies and founded a program called Leaders of Tomorrow, which Ebony describes with pride. There, he taught them how to tie their ties, how to do place settings, and how "to be a gentleman," she explains. "He took them to the capital to give them an inspiration of what they could be and what they could do, and things like that." The two met at work. When Ebony had difficult students, coworkers urged her to refer them to Terrence, who always knew how to help. He was a fine dresser. "Even though we were in the school system, he wore a suit every single day to work," she tells me proudly. Terrence was a gentleman in every aspect of his life and a balm to Ebony, who had left a difficult relationship before meeting him. "My husband was my friend, not just my husband, not just my lover, I guess you could say, but was my friend," she says. "Terrence and I did absolutely everything together. I would say, when I look back at it now, I think some would probably say y'all were boring, because we did do Home Depot on Saturdays. We did work in the yard on Saturdays. We went to movies together." On weekends, Terrence would wake up early and fix breakfast for the entire family, and took on greater caregiving responsibilities when Ebony began to work longer hours on the job. Terrence would take their son to school, and help with the children's homework, do housework, and cook dinner. Terrence, who also worked briefly as a radio producer, would ride his bike to their daughter's school and carry hers so they could ride back together. He thought she would remember it someday. "And she does. She remembers that," Ebony adds.

Ebony and Terrence had been teachers for decades, and in choosing education, they adopted a profession that had once paved a reliable route to the middle class. Yet prosperity eluded them. They sometimes had trouble paying all their bills. Ebony had come into the marriage with two children before having a third with Terrence. "So you can imagine, three children, we had just bought a house, because at that time, right before, everything was, for lack of a better word, middle-class. We were doing well," she explains. "And so you never anticipate things to drastically change, but that's what happened. There were a lot of things that we just could not do for the kids, because we had to try to keep a roof over our head. We did programs to try to keep a roof over our head. It's pretty difficult, especially newly married. It was hard." To save their home, they contacted NACA, a nonprofit HUD-certified organization that offers counseling and its Best in America mortgage to low- and moderate-income homeowners like Terrence and Ebony. The couple got their payments under control, but they still teetered on the edge of a cliff. With the slightest push, they'd fall—and all they had to count on was a safety net with holes.

Terrence got COVID in 2021, not long after having lunch with a coworker, who would later be diagnosed with the virus. Ebony remembers the day well. Their oldest son was having car trouble, and Terrence went to check on him and the vehicle. Later she noticed that her husband's teeth were chattering, which was odd because he never got cold. It's cold outside, Terrence told her, and she put it out of her mind. The next day he went to the grocery store and returned covered in sweat. Ebony told him he didn't look so good; Terrence replied that he had simply forgotten to eat, and continued to work on his lesson plans for the week.

On Monday, Terrence's school shut down its social studies department because someone else had gotten sick. And then, on Tuesday, Ebony herself began to feel unwell. She went to the school nurse's office for a test, which came back negative. Terrence, meanwhile, continued to worsen. When she came home on Wednesday, he was in bed, and she told him she would take him for a COVID test. He reminded her that her own test had come back negative, but she knew that something was deeply wrong. "I tried all night long, every place was booked. There was nobody doing COVID tests until the next day," she says. "The next day we got up to go take it, and he told me he didn't feel well enough to get up. So I was like, 'Well, we have to go.' We went. Later on that afternoon, it came back positive." Terrence sat in their car and cried. He couldn't believe COVID had happened to him, he told Ebony, who would later fall ill with the virus, too. Because Terrence had high blood pressure and diabetes, he was at higher risk for complications from COVID. Ebony checked his blood pressure regularly. When the readings flashed "error" instead of a legible number, she decided to take him to the hospital.

On the way to Memorial Hermann, Terrence began to sound like he was having trouble breathing, and Ebony, who felt worse and worse as the days passed, would follow him there a short time later. "I can't explain it other than like what it is on the movies, where you see the door constantly stretch out further as you're walking closer. That's what it felt like. And then my chest literally felt like somebody had, I don't know, kicked me in it, because it hurt so bad. And so they admitted me to the hospital, and come to find out I was bleeding internally," she explains.

Despite her own illness, she called and spoke to Terrence every day. As Ebony prepared herself to tell her husband that she, too, had COVID, and was hospitalized on the same floor a few doors away, a nurse came by to introduce herself and said she'd wanted to meet her. When Ebony asked her why, the nurse said, "All your husband does is talk about you and your family. I've never seen a man love anybody like that. I just had to meet you.'" Ebony told the nurse that she and Terrence loved each other. "That's just what it is," she tells me. The virus, though, would soon part them. Terrence still had trouble breathing, so the hospital began proning him to see if it would bring him any relief. It didn't. He suffered a heart attack, and then another on Valentine's Day. Eventually he would have a third. He was intubated, and then removed from ventilation after he seemed to improve. On February 18, Ebony called him in the evening on Zoom. "I said, 'I love you Terrence. Love you. Love you. Love you.'" He told her that he loved her too, which still brings her comfort. When she saw his mouth form the words, she felt hope stir. But Terrence had another heart attack, and although hospital staff revived him, they couldn't keep him stable. He died, leaving Ebony and their three children alone. Ebony has since become an advocate for other Americans bereaved by COVID. She joined Marked by COVID, a national "remembrance movement" led by those who lost loved ones to the virus.

When Terrence passed away, Ebony not only lost the love of her life but her partner in caregiving and the second income that had kept their family afloat. The mortgage company wouldn't work with her. The house had been in Terrence's name, and she had to go to court to be named the successor of his estate, a process that took nearly eight months. Ebony says the mortgage company wouldn't take payments from her in the meantime, and by the time she'd worked out the details of Terrence's estate, they'd filed paperwork for foreclosure. Ebony lost the house they'd fought so hard to keep. Then she lost one of their cars. She was able to keep the other one only because friends chipped in to help her cover the payments. Even now Ebony still struggles to pay her bills. Though she gets social security payments because of Terrence's death, the money isn't enough to replace his income. She's had to place the kids into counseling, which adds another bill to the pile. Now she looks for hope wherever she can find it, though her future looks uncertain. "I guess you could say that me losing the house alleviated that bill, even though it hurt. So we downsized, and that's how I'm able to have a car now," she tells me. "My credit is pretty much . . . It's shot."

The economist William Darity Jr. of Duke University has written of the "subaltern middle class," which he defined as "the more affluent tier of a marginalized community" in a 2020 paper coauthored with Fenaba R. Addo and Imari Z. Smith.[24] Though Ebony and Terrence had owned their own home and pursued professional careers, their socioeconomic status remained precarious and it could not entirely protect them from the socioeconomic disparities inflicted upon Black Americans as a group. Terrence had type 2 diabetes and high blood pressure, two health conditions that are seen in Black Americans at much higher rates than in white Americans. Darity et al. wrote that infant mortality rates remain higher for Black women with graduate degrees than for white women without high school diplomas. Later, citing previous research, he added that "the likelihood of future incarceration is higher for Blacks at every level of wealth compared with Whites." Black families possess less wealth to pass on to their children, and experience less upward mobility.

Even before the pandemic, Ebony and Terrence had needed help keeping their home. When the virus killed Terrence, the fragility of their situation came to the fore. They'd come far, but not far enough. A concerted legal and political regime that has systematically deprived Black households of wealth and prosperity over the centuries arrested their movement up the socioeconomic ladder. No amount of hard work could have insulated Ebony or Terrence from the decisions of policymakers or the absence of racial justice in America.

No one can undo the injustice of Terrence's death, but there are ways out of the system that made him so susceptible to COVID, and which plagued his family so relentlessly after his death. To close the racial wealth gap, "a comprehensive national program will need to be designed and implemented that is aimed directly at removing racial wealth differences," Darity wrote alongside researchers Fenaba R. Addo and Imari Z. Smith. "That strikes us as reparations—the authentic path toward racial justice and authentic closure of the economic distance between Black and White America."[25] That's a project for the federal government. Speaking to me in 2022, Darity put the bill owed at about $14 trillion. "Federal government can spend indefinitely," he says. That could affect inflation, he adds, though he believes there are ways to mitigate the risk. In *From Here to Equality*, Darity and coauthor A. Kirsten Mullen suggest that reparations payments could be released as "less-liquid assets" like an annuity or a trust fund.[26] "But the idea is that ultimately the individual recipients should have full discretion over the use of the funds," he tells me in a phone interview. "And it should not go through some third party or intermediate institution."

A previously existing system of reparations may have helped reduce COVID transmissions among Black Americans—and saved lives. When defined as an "acknowledgment of a grievous injustice, a redress for the injustice, and closure of the grievances held by the group subjected to the injustice," reparations is powerful policy, researcher Eugene Richardson of Harvard University explains. A 2021 paper coauthored by Richardson, Darity, and others based their projections on a program that would have eradicated the racial wealth gap, calculated at the time to be roughly $10–$12 trillion.[27] The 40 million Black Americans who are descendants of enslaved people would receive "monetary payments of $250,000 to $300,000," Richardson adds. Then they modeled how social conditions in the state of Louisiana would have changed had American policymakers made these payments to Black Americans ten or more years before the COVID-19 pandemic took place. "In particular, we focused on how housing would have changed and how the need to participate in frontline work would have changed for recipients of the wealth redistribution," he explains. Researchers found that reparations, both through monetary compensation and the mere acknowledgment of a historic injustice, would have narrowed the racial wealth gap, spread out frontline work across racial groups, decreased the chronic exposure to stress that sickens so many Black Americans, and made changes to the built environment, which would have made it easier for Black Americans to practice social distancing. That last point was particularly important, he adds. "It should not be too far-fetched to understand that both decreased Black wealth and overcrowded housing among Black people are a direct result of redlining, the historical

practice of racial discrimination in housing and mortgage lending,"
he says. "Repairing these legacies would have decreased overcrowded
housing and fostered the ability to social distance." There are limitations, of course, to this research. Even a sweeping national program
of economic and racial justice could not entirely prevent death from
COVID. But it could have provided millions with a layer of protection, a buffer, that they otherwise lacked.

Reparations, then, is more than an abstract theory. A program of
reparations "would not only have saved lives—in particular, by reduc-
ing transmission during the early riskier period of the pandemic where
vaccines were not available—it would have also helped increased subsequent vaccine uptake as legacies of mistrust were repaired through
apology and wealth redistribution," Richardson adds. Households like
Ebony's likely would have been more able to economically withstand
the loss of one income. "It also would have mitigated economic fallout, as it is well known that increased wealth helps buttress how a
family can respond to emergencies such as a global pandemic, a loss
of a job, or a sudden death," Richardson concludes.

Right now, there is little political will in America to pass a program of
reparations as designed by Darity et al., but reparations is an expansive concept, and there may be other paths to justice. In *Reconsidering
Reparations*, the philosopher Olúfémi O. Táíwò proposed an alternative, or constructive view, which looks beyond financial restitution
in America to the restructuring of an existing world order. "If slavery
and colonialism built the world and its current basic scheme of social
injustice, the proper task of social justice is no smaller: it is, quite literally, to remake the world," he wrote.[28] Unconditional cash transfers
have their place, Táíwò argued, but so does climate justice, since that

crisis "arises from the same political history as racial injustice and presents a challenge of the same scale and scope." For Táíwò, reparations is a global project, and it is generational. Even if we begin now, we may not live to see the world we're trying to build.

If we foreclose the possibility of justice, though, we cut ourselves off from a better future. America is a wealthy country, and it could help remake the world just as Táíwò proposed. On a smaller scale, American policymakers could eradicate domestic poverty altogether, as the sociologist Matthew Desmond has argued.[29] Certain pandemic policy decisions offered glimpses of another, more generous country. In 2021, the *New York Times* reported that pandemic aid programs had "cut poverty nearly in half this year from prepandemic levels and push the share of Americans in poverty to the lowest level on record," according to analysis from the Urban Institute.[30] Nevertheless, trouble loomed. "The three programs that cut poverty most—stimulus checks, increased food stamps and expanded unemployment insurance—have ended or are scheduled to soon revert to their prepandemic size," the *Times* observed. Such lapses frustrate economists, including EPI's Elise Gould. "Such an obvious thing was providing paid sick days to people, because we're in a pandemic and people need sick days," says Gould. "We quickly let that erode and we did not maintain that." Paid sick days, she adds, "obviously should be on a menu of policies. But without having that, it erodes economic security. You can't make the kind of investments you want in your future, nor can you really take care of yourself." Changes to unemployment insurance also prevented people from falling more deeply into insecurity as they reckoned with the economic fallout of the pandemic. Yet that too proved to be temporary. "I was optimistic for a long time," Gould explains. "Not that I'm completely pessimistic, but we saw the way to do it and we just haven't acted on it to make them permanent." Action requires an act of political imagination, even bravery. For a moment the pandemic had erased the imaginary line that separated the worthy from the unworthy poor. The government handed out cash with no restrictions on how it could be spent, and in doing so, helped reduce poverty to historic levels. Though these efforts were too late to protect Americans like Richard Proia and Terrence James from their precarity, they still chart the way out of hell. Poverty doesn't have to be a death sentence. Poverty doesn't even have to exist. It is a political choice, and it kills Americans even in the absence of a pandemic. Outdated notions about who deserves help and who deserves nothing aren't just antiquated but deadly.

FIVE

THE CHERRY ON THE FUCK-YOU SUNDAE

Pandemic lockdowns infuriated Ellen's uncle John, who viewed them as an infringement on his tenuous social life in the D.C. suburbs. The few friends he had made were at meetings for his social club and sci-fi fan conventions, but the friendships tended to end with the events themselves.

John believed that Trump was right to try to open the country up by Easter 2020, even as we marked our first 20,000 pandemic deaths. Days after anti-lockdown militias in Michigan stormed the state capitol to protest the state's Democratic governor, Trump announced that he'd wind down a White House COVID task force. A week later, Trump made another announcement: "We have met the moment, and we have prevailed," he said at a May press conference.[1] Americans, he added, "do whatever it takes to find solutions, pioneer breakthroughs, and harness the energies we need to achieve a total victory." Right-wing pundits weren't far behind him. They were ready to move on—and some conspiratorial voices were already speaking of hoaxes and plots. Some on Twitter (now X) believed the pandemic was a "fraud," Sean Hannity said on a March 2020 broadcast of his radio show. "May be true," he added. COVID was a Chinese scheme, said Rush Limbaugh the same month. "Nothing like wiping out the entire U.S. economy with a biothreat from China, is there?" he asked. On Fox Business, anchor Trish Regan speculated that COVID concerns were "yet another attempt to impeach the president."[2]

From John's and Trump's respective vantage points near the Potomac River, perhaps the pandemic didn't look so bad. John was a retired government worker. Had he still worked, he would have been able to do so from home. Medical care was no issue. John's father had recently died in relative peace, age nearly one hundred, in the same Bethesda military hospital where Trump eventually received his own treatment for COVID. From the skewed perspectives of both men, lockdowns, not the virus, had ruined the order of their lives.

Life looked different for eighty-year-old Guadalupe Campos, who lived far away in the Los Angeles area. Like John, Guadalupe lived in a multigenerational home, but there the similarities ended. She had no family wealth and she lived with essential workers, who risked illness and even death laboring on the front lines of the pandemic. The virus was not an inconvenience but a malicious presence in their lives, and it would find them.

Hardship marked Guadalupe's life. Raised in Puebla, Mexico, by her widowed mother, Guadalupe married a man a dozen years her senior while she was a teenager, her granddaughter Kayla Fernandez tells me in an interview. "The tale goes that she was very poor, and she was playing with her siblings when she met my grandfather and thought, 'This man could financially support me, so I'm going to marry him. He can buy me new shoes,'" Fernandez explains. They'd have eight children together, but the marriage was not without trouble. According to Fernandez, her grandfather could be unfaithful and violent to Guadalupe, who struggled to raise her children alone in Mexico after he immigrated to work in American strawberry fields. She would eventually follow him to a new country.

They settled first in the Watts neighborhood of Los Angeles and moved later to South. Guadalupe took whatever work she could find. As a seamstress, she sewed Speedos; later, she worked in laundry facilities throughout the city of Los Angeles, mostly among undocumented workers. "Back in the day, it was a lot easier to gain citizenship, so my family was very fortunate," Fernandez says. Her mother filed for citizenship status as a legal adult, and then her parents did, too. Soon the entire family was documented. Citizenship offered them newfound security, but it did not deliver immediate prosperity. "My family has been pretty poor. Growing up I think you don't realize how poor you are until you go out into the world," Fernandez observes. She, too, grew up in a single-parent home, where her mother made it clear that her two daughters would someday attend college. Fernandez is now a mental health counselor. "But for the rest of my family, that hasn't really been the case," she explains.

Money was scarce, but the family bonds were tight. "My grandmother's primary focus throughout her entire life has always been her family. I don't really recall her having any friends," Fernandez goes on, adding, "It always felt like everyone just . . ." She trails off, remembering, and then gathers herself to add, "She was the kind of person that took you on and made you feel like family, even if you weren't blood related to her." When her husband fathered children outside their marriage, Guadalupe raised one as her own, incorporating her into the family and its traditions. "Every weekend, we'd go to Grandma's house," Fernandez recalls, and Guadalupe would cook for everyone. Guadalupe had her own passions, too: She adored animals, and kept a cheerful menagerie around the house. Surrounded by dogs and cats and parrots and parakeets and budgies like a character out of a fairy tale, Guadalupe became known for her hospitality. Relatives would filter through the house, where Guadalupe would offer them a place to stay—as long as they were open to pets. She nurtured a particular affection for her parrot, who would whistle like a catcaller. She also loved to gamble. Though she had diabetes and her legs would swell, she would drive two or three hours to go to the casino. At the slots, Guadalupe benefited from what Fernandez calls "old lady luck," winning small sums to take home to her family. And for Guadalupe, life was always about family, no matter how hard, or how complicated, the ties of love could be. She'd cut her gambling trips short to care for her husband, as difficult as he could be.

Guadalupe never made anyone feel excluded. Nor was she inclined to self-pity, though she had cause. Fernandez once asked her grandmother if she'd ever been in love, the way people loved on her favorite telenovelas. "She said, 'Oh, no, no. I don't know what that's like.' That always haunted me because her whole life was sacrificial," Fernandez adds. "She gave every part of her to her husband and her children and her grandchildren, every dime she had."

In a cruel irony, Guadalupe's family may have brought COVID home despite taking serious precautions. "She lived with a couple of children and grandchildren and they were both helping take care of her, but she was also helping them with a roof over their head," Fernandez explains. Several worked in nearby Vernon, a place Fernandez calls "a hellhole." Factories and warehouses crowd the landscape, and draw in desperate workers. Several of Fernandez's relatives worked there in frontline jobs with little protection from the virus, but they couldn't afford to quit. "There was no other choice," she tells me. "My mother, she still works in that industry in a warehouse and it was anxiety-provoking. She was exposed to so many people. It's not really like they can work from home, right?" She adds, "You don't have the luxury of cutting down your hours when you have to make ends meet." Nobody wanted to be on benefits, either; they found pride in working, even during the pandemic. Though much of the family worked in high-risk jobs, they tried to protect themselves along with Guadalupe. The family parties ended, and Guadalupe, ever the seamstress, sewed masks in her spare time. One of Fernandez's uncles, knowing he'd been exposed repeatedly to the virus at work, slept in his car until someone got him a hotel room to quarantine in. He'd had headaches and back pain, and though it wasn't clear if he was suffering from COVID, Guadalupe soon began to experience symptoms herself.

The end began with a sore throat on Christmas. Fernandez had called her for the holiday and noted that she sounded congested, a little unlike herself. Fernandez and her mother suspected COVID: it was December 2020, and COVID cases were spiking in Los Angeles County.[3] Fernandez and her mother made soup and stopped at Rite Aid for cough drops, a thermometer, and vitamins to drop off at Guadalupe's home. They drove away, but as they neared home Fernandez got a call from her aunt, who told her that her grandmother wasn't responding to anyone. Her eyes were open, and moving around the room, but she couldn't talk. She wasn't moving. Fernandez told her to hang up and call 911. But hospitals in Los Angeles were under siege, and Guadalupe hadn't yet been diagnosed with COVID. Paramedics were reluctant to bring her to a place where she would almost certainly come into contact with the virus if she hadn't gotten it already. Guadalupe stayed home, but at 4 a.m. on December 26, Fernandez got another phone call. Guadalupe had once again stopped responding. This time, parademics took her to the hospital, and for the next two weeks, they waited. The occasional glimmer of good news did not alter Guadalupe's general trajectory. A doctor prepared them for the outcome they'd all dreaded. "They just let us know that taking her off the ventilator, she was going to die," Fernandez says. On January 14, 2021, each of Guadalupe's children traveled to the hospital to say a final goodbye behind glass. The grandchildren, including Fernandez, scheduled one last Skype call, and they said their goodbyes at two o'clock the same day. At four o'clock, they learned that Guadalupe had passed away. A final injustice awaited Guadalupe and her family: Los Angeles had become such a COVID hot spot that the funeral industry couldn't keep up with demand.[4] Fernandez and her family would have to wait three months to hold a service for her grandmother.

Fernandez says she's still angry at her grandmother's fate—and at people who don't seem to care. "People didn't believe, and it felt like nobody cared. You couldn't even gather with family. I couldn't hug my mom while she was mourning, even though we lived together. I just was afraid," she remembers and adds, "Then seeing people throw these temper tantrums, and I just felt like I wish we could trade places and I wish my biggest problem was feeling like my rights were being infringed upon. That I have to wait three months for a funeral." In her view, families like hers had been "abandoned" by a negligent president. "I felt rage, and when the Capitol attack happened, all I could think of was how disheartened I am now," she says.

•   •   •

Back in the D.C. suburbs, the Capitol attack meant something else to John, whose fury over lockdowns had led him further into far-right message boards in the months between Easter and Christmas. His niece Ellen emphasized that those lockdowns posed no great threat to him. He could have stayed home if he'd wanted to; he was retired and supported himself on a government pension and family money. Essential workers like his mother's home health aides and Guadalupe's children weren't so fortunate. They had to keep working no matter how dangerous the pandemic became, and the consequences could be fatal, for themselves and for the people they loved.

Work has always been dangerous. In the introduction to *Working*, Studs Terkel said that his classic oral history of the working class was about violence "by its very nature." The book, he added, "is about ulcers as well as accidents, about shouting matches as well as fistfights, about nervous breakdowns as well as kicking the dog around. It is, above all (or beneath all), about daily humiliations. To survive the day is triumph enough for the walking wounded among the great many of us."[5]

The pandemic unveiled the harsh bargain most of us strike with our employers: we offer most of our waking hours and in exchange we receive a wage, which may or may not be enough to keep food on the table or a roof overhead. This bargain favors the employer. In the absence of a union, there are few checks on the power of the boss in the U.S. The philosopher Elizabeth Anderson has even compared the American workplace to a communist dictatorship. "Under the employment-at-will baseline, workers, in effect, cede all of their rights to their employers, except those specifically guaranteed to them by law, for the duration of the employment relationship," Anderson wrote in *Private Government: How Employers Rule Our Lives*

(And Why We Don't Talk about It).[6] A boss can dictate the way a worker dresses. He can surveil his workers, as Anderson pointed out; he can also search their belongings and subject them to drug testing. A worker has a protected legal right to organize in response to the conditions imposed by the boss, but retaliation remains common, and the National Labor Relations Board remains underfunded, while workers contend with looming bad actors such as Starbucks and Amazon. By February 2024, the NLRB had issued dozens of rulings to both companies for serious infractions like interfering with workers' rights to organize, and had ordered the reinstatement[7] of workers fired for their union activity.

To be "essential" in the pandemic is to be offered up as a sacrifice. The U.S. stands alone among other wealthy countries in its refusal to guarantee paid sick leave, and with the arrival of the pandemic, sick leave took on renewed importance for workers, their loved ones, and communities at large. But the lower a person's wage, the more likely it is that they lack any form of paid sick leave. The Economic Policy Institute reported in September 2022 that over 60 percent of low-wage workers lacked access to paid sick leave, a long-standing inequity that likely contributed to illness and death.[8] The working class would suffer further during the pandemic. In January 2021, not long after Guadalupe had passed, researchers at the University of California, San Francisco examined excess mortality by occupation in their state during the pandemic.[9] In California the most dangerous pandemic profession compared to past years was that of a line cook, they concluded, part of an overarching trend. Researchers wrote that essential workers experienced the pandemic's greatest effects on mortality, especially if they worked in food or agriculture, transportation and logistics, facilities, and manufacturing. They added that the elimination of COVID depended on mitigation efforts in the workplace.

Though some corporations did offer a limited form of paid COVID leave to workers, these measures often did not last the duration of the pandemic. Amazon, for example, ended its paid COVID leave program in May 2022.[10]

Despite such high stakes, workers couldn't count on the boss to keep them safe. "I don't believe they took it like something serious," Adriana Gopar says of the warehouse that employed her at the start of the pandemic, adding, "First of all they didn't have, like, the essential needs that we need to protect ourselves, like hand sanitizer and masks. They didn't provide that for us." Gopar knew the virus was dangerous, that it was killing people. "I was really scared that maybe it will be the end of me," she tells me. At work, however, little changed. She had to buy masks and hand sanitizer with her own funds, a hardship because her husband's hours had been cut at work. She eventually heard that absent coworkers had fallen ill with COVID, but the company, whose identity I am withholding to protect Gopar, never formally told workers that there were cases in their midst. If she'd gotten sick and asked for leave, she says she would have been fired. Gopar, who is now an activist with the Warehouse Worker Resource Center and worked as a waitress at the time of our interview, still worries about the pandemic. "They send us to, like, banquets. We do quinceañeras and big parties, and nobody wears a mask," she explains. "There's a lot of people and then we are picking up the forks, the plates, like all this stuff from the people. We are exposed."

Melissa Ojeda worked as a baker for Disneyland when the pandemic struck. A furlough kept her home for a time, but not so her relatives; she watched from her home in California's high desert as her father reported to his construction job and her brother worked for Amazon. Soon, Ojeda got a job at Amazon, too. (Though Disneyland brought her back, the job was unsustainable.) "I went back to work there, but everything was completely different. Unfortunately, one of my coworkers there died from COVID. People moved out of state," she says. She'd known the coworker a little; their team at Disneyland was small, and they'd kept in touch off and on during the pandemic. It was frightening to work through the pandemic, she adds, but she had no choice. She needed the money. And Disneyland wasn't paying—at least not enough. They kept switching her schedule around until she faced a three-hour commute home from work. Amazon wasn't a great option, but it was work. At first it seemed as though the company took the pandemic seriously. "But the more you would pay attention, the more they weren't doing," she explains. "The thing that stood out to me the most was that cleanliness. It should have shifted people's mentality with cleanliness." Ojeda was most alarmed by the break room. "First you would see hand sanitizers or sanitizing wipes, and they would give us the opportunity for us to do it. But eventually it just got to a point where none of these things were available and we'd bring it up to our managers and then they're like, 'Oh yeah, we'll see what we can do,'" she adds. "They have air filters around the warehouse, in your workstations, and you can see the filters. They just don't care to change them. And I bring them up and they don't care. It's like the only thing they really care about is the packages because that's what the managers get in trouble for," says Ojeda, who, like Gopar, organized with the Warehouse Worker Resource Center and now works as the organization's communications specialist.

When Sara Fee started working for Amazon in April 2021, the company rolled out its version of a red carpet. "When they onboarded us, there was this big blue carpet and all the managers are out front and they're clapping and music is playing and they're making this big show," she remembers. Like Ojeda, she says the company did appear to take care of workers—but only at first. The company even sanitized its stairwells and handrails, according to Fee, but over time that caution began to disappear. People couldn't practice social distancing in her building, and the company's cleaning efforts became lackluster. Fee once had to clean her workstation with hand sanitizer and napkins. As the winter of 2022 arrived, COVID and the flu had begun to tear through her building again. Amazon did test workers for COVID, she says, but if someone had the flu, they were still expected to work. "If it's not COVID, they're not going to give you time off," adds Fee, who was an activist with the Warehouse Worker Resource Center and now works for the organization. "That we don't have paid sick leave? It sucks. It sucks for everybody. We're not the only ones dealing with that." Amazon treats workers like they're "disposable," she claims.

Companies like Amazon treat sick workers poorly because they can. America doesn't guarantee universal paid sick leave, which makes it an outlier among peer developed nations. Over 60 percent of low-wage workers lacked paid sick leave on the job, the Economic Policy Institute reported[11] in 2022. That year, the issue began to dominate headlines as unions for rail workers debated a proposed contract that did not grant them a single paid sick day. Though sick leave wasn't the only or perhaps even the primary contention rail workers had with the contract as proposed, its absence came to characterize the debate. When the Biden administration first brokered a tentative agreement in conjunction with the leaders of twelve unions, the contract lacked majority support among workers themselves. A group of unions representing more than half of the affected rail workers voted to reject the contract.[12] As a December 9 strike date approached, Congress voted across partisan lines to impose the contract anyway; a separate vote to grant workers seven paid sick days failed to pass the Senate with a filibuster-proof majority. "We carry the country on our backs whether [Congress] realizes it or not," one worker told the *Washington Post*.[13] "That they are willing to force a contract down our throats to keep the railroads from shutting down means we're important. But they get sick days, and we're out here in the snow all day and we don't. It's pretty hypocritical."

Ross Grooters, a railroad worker and the cochair of Railroad Workers United, an interunion solidarity caucus, tells me that sick leave "was a way to elevate our issues and our broader demands." They add, "It was a positive thing that it was lifted up, but it's certainly not going to address all the problems or even the root causes of what's wrong in our industry." Those root issues are inadequate staffing and "a focus on the bottom line, how much profit can we make?" he explains. Nick Wurst, a freight conductor who is also a member of Railroad Workers United, sounded frustrated in our interview. "Sick time has come to dominate the discussion, which I think is kind of unfortunate because I think it has buried in a lot of ways some of the other issues and made it seem like, 'Oh, it's just as simple as giving them a few sick days and then they'll shut up,'" he says. "Which is, of course, how the House Democrats and Senate Democrats positioned themselves, as though seven days off will probably be enough." Wurst believes workers needed more than a few days of paid sick leave. The same scheduling regime that prevents workers from taking paid days for illness prevents them from having much work-life balance. Wurst also points to a meager pay raise, rising health insurance premiums, and the addition of so-called self-supporting pools, which could allow rail companies to decrease the number of jobs overall and force workers like Wurst to be on call more often.

The contract is a bleak footnote to the dangerous and debilitating work Wurst and others perform for the railroads. "When you are working twelve hours on and ten hours off, there's obviously symptoms of exhaustion and buildup that worsens your general physical well-being. You're much more likely to get sick," Wurst tells me. Not long before lockdowns closed much of the country, Wurst began to feel symptoms of the flu partway through a twelve-hour shift. "All I had heard at that point was COVID might feel like the flu at first," he remembers. Wurst later tested negative for COVID, but his boss urged him to call into the company's pandemic hotline to report the test anyway. When he did, they told him to stay home and quarantine for two weeks—unpaid. Wurst says he learned an important lesson. "I shouldn't have been proactive at all," he concludes. Instead, Wurst found himself trapped: by corporate bureaucracy, and an uncaring employer.

"While the specifics of the freight rail workers' plight are unique, their situation is not. Nor is it limited to blue collar workers," journalist Aaron Gordon wrote at *Vice*.[14] "Feeling crushed under the thumb of an elitist management that seemingly has no interest in running a sound, sustainable business at the expense of the people who do the work just so the big shots at the top can buy another weekend retreat is the dominant American 21st Century worker experience." Worker exploitation is far from a new problem; it is the status quo. A decades-long assault on union power combined with unchecked employer greed primed workers for illness and death during the pandemic. As sacrifices to Mammon, the one true American god, workers could not trust the political class for salvation.

If workers have champions in either party, they tend to find them in the Democratic Party. Yet political calculations restrict the party's advocacy. Both parties fail workers, as Congress repeatedly demonstrates. Because of conservatives in their midst, Democrats could not pass the PRO Act during Biden's first term. Should they ever succeed, the act would strengthen collective bargaining rights. As one party dithers, the other understands who it is for and what it is about. Trump was no anomaly but rather a snug fit for a party that prioritizes the wealthy over worker power. The former president's tenure was thus a triumph for business interests and a disaster for workers, as explained by Dr. David Michaels, formerly the assistant secretary of labor for OSHA under President Barack Obama and a professor of environmental and occupational health at George Washington University. OSHA has a blood-borne pathogens standard designed to limit the transmission of HIV/AIDS and hepatitis B in the workplace, but it lacked an airborne pathogens standard, and that presented problems for the agency and workers alike. "During the H1N1 epidemic in 2009 and 2010, it became very clear that the lack of an airborne pathogens standard really made OSHA's efforts quite ineffective," Michaels says, so the agency began the yearslong process of creating a new standard that would help protect workers from airborne illnesses on the job. When Trump took office, those efforts ended.

There were other failures, Michaels adds. OSHA should have promptly issued emergency temporary standards for health-care facilities, and later all facilities after the pandemic began to spread widely. He can still remember tweeting about it in January 2020, not long before the pandemic fully sunk its teeth into America. "It was very clear what was coming," he points out. "And it was clear what was needed, that OSHA could issue an emergency temporary standard, saying this is what employers should do. The Trump administration decided not to do that." Employers, then, enjoyed a great deal of freedom in deciding how they would respond to the risks of the pandemic and, according to Michaels, workers suffered. "In most places, very little was done to properly protect workers," he adds. "I think in health-care facilities where they have a better understanding of infectious disease spread, some efforts were made to ensure that workers were at least given masks, though not necessarily the correct ones." In other facilities, such as meatpacking plants, where there were significant early outbreaks, workers often lacked appropriate protective gear and employers incentivized them to come to work sick. In Cactus, Texas, supervisors at a JBS meatpacking plant reportedly told workers to use hairnets as masks.[15]

Like railroads, meatpacking and poultry processing plants illustrate the danger and discomfort American workers suffered well before the pandemic raised the stakes. Meatpacking and processing work has always been difficult. Although Upton Sinclair's *The Jungle* horrified the American public upon its publication in 1906, and spurred the creation of the Food and Drug Administration to regulate the food that goes into American bodies, the conditions faced by workers garnered less outrage, researchers for Human Rights Watch observed in 2004.[16] That year, the organization reported, American meat and poultry labor still carried "constant fear and risk" despite reforms. Workers—many of whom are immigrants, and vulnerable to retaliation—reported pervasive, and preventable, injuries on the job. Corporate greed helps explain why: fast line speeds increase the quantities of dead animals processed by a plant, but they can injure workers. "Repeating thousands of cutting motions during each work shift puts enormous traumatic stress on workers' hands, wrists, arms, shoulders and backs," researchers explained, adding, "They often work in close quarters creating additional dangers for themselves and coworkers. They often receive little training and are not always given the safety equipment they need. They are often forced to work long overtime hours under pain of dismissal if they refuse." Little improved over time. In 2009, 73 percent of meatpacking workers surveyed by

Nebraska Appleseed, a nonpartisan nonprofit, "stated that the speed of the line had increased in the past year." An overwhelming 94 percent said the number of workers had either decreased or stayed the same, leaving them ill-equipped to safely meet the demands imposed by increasing line speeds. Another 62 percent said they had been injured on the job, and while 91 percent of workers said they knew they had certain rights, "less than 30% thought those rights made a difference."[17] A 2016 report from Oxfam America found that supervisors routinely denied bathroom breaks to workers in meatpacking and poultry processing plants across America.[18] "Workers urinate and defecate while standing on the line; they wear diapers to work; they restrict intake of liquids and fluids to dangerous degrees; they endure pain and discomfort while they worry about their health and job security," the report's authors concluded.

Women suffered greater harms due to the demands of menstruation and pregnancy. "We're human beings who feel, and hurt, and we work the best we can. But it's not enough for them. They demand more and more. . . . They demand more than you can do," one woman said. In 2019, Human Rights Watch revisited the issue. According to data collected by OSHA, "a worker in the meat and poultry industry lost a body part or was sent to the hospital for in-patient treatment about every other day between 2015 and 2018."[19] An average of eight meatpacking workers died because of workplace incidents every year between 2013 and 2017.

A meatpacking worker based in Washington State told me in 2022 that her plant did take some steps to protect workers. "As we came in, they would check our temperatures and they would give us the mask. So they had sanitizers everywhere. And so they were cautious on that part," she said. Some precautions exacted a toll on her and her fellow workers. "They started putting up dividers on our tables where the people cut," she explained. The company later removed microwaves from the workplace, and forbade people from sitting next to each other at lunch—a small thing that nevertheless made the workplace feel isolating and strange. And she wished the company had provided hazard pay to workers. "They could offer more because we put our lives at stake and we still came in," she told me. "You know, we still have our families that we have to support and maintain. So, yes, they could offer us a little bit more just for coming in. Just for being here." She eventually contracted COVID, and believes she got the virus at work. It was the summer of 2020, and there was an outbreak at her plant. "All of us got sick about the same time," she said. "I work in the cold, and I have a lot of layers. I remember that day, just running outside. And I just wanted to take off all my layers that I have on." The worker, who was then a member of the United Food and Commercial Workers International Union, or UFCW, said the virus inflicted emotional as well as physical damage. "I think every day that I would come to work, I was scared because there's so many people that work here. I was just too scared to come in contact with people," she explained. "I don't want to touch the door. I try not to touch a lot of things, you know, and if I do touch something, I just want to run and wash my hands right away." The plant, meanwhile, has relaxed all of its COVID measures. The hand sanitizer stations are gone. The microwaves are back. The vaccines help, she acknowledged, and she thanked God she hadn't gotten sick again, but the fear remained. "We're labor workers, so we have to be out here," she pointed out. "But a lot of people got lucky. And to this day, they're lucky because they got to work from home. We didn't. We had to come out here every day, put our lives in danger." She knows the pandemic was profitable for some. "A lot of people took advantage of that, of all this money that they were getting and not us. We didn't get lucky and we still had to come in and we never got rewarded," she said.

Corporations like Amazon and Kroger posted record profits during the pandemic, while their workers risked illness, or even death, often for wages that barely kept them afloat. A white paper produced by the Economic Roundtable in 2022 found that three-quarters of Kroger workers surveyed are food insecure.[20] Two-thirds said that they couldn't meet basic expenses every month, and 14 percent are either homeless now or have been homeless within the past year. Over one-third say they're worried about eviction, and 90 percent said they will not have enough money to retire. Meanwhile Kroger prospered—and so did its executives. As *Business Insider* reported[21] at the time, Kroger posted profits of $4.1 billion in 2020, and its chief executive officer, Rodney McMullen, made $22 million.[22] Kroger ended its "hero pay" for workers in May 2020, well before vaccines reduced the risks the company expected its workers to take.[23]

The pandemic harrowed America's essential workers and in doing so, revealed just how little corporations care for workers. But some workers, like Eddie Quezada of Long Island, believed their unions helped them. Quezada, who's worked in grocery stores for over thirty years, belongs to Local 338 RWDSU/UFCW. As the pandemic began, the union called him constantly to make sure that he and fellow workers had enough masks and sanitizer, he said. When he fell ill in March 2020, he says the union stepped in. "Besides them blowing up my phone every five minutes to check up on me, they said, 'We're going to see what we can do on our part, see if we can get you a test,'" he explains. The union had a program called Guardian Nurses that provided outside help to members in medical crisis. "They send a guardian nurse with us to speak to the doctor because they said sometimes when you get these kind of health issues, you don't know what they're saying to you. And they're trying to help explain everything for you." The union linked him to an urgent care where he could get a test—no small thing, for tests were scarce at the time. His test later came back positive for COVID.

Unions aren't a panacea. Yet without one, workers are vulnerable to exploitation. They can be fired for nearly any reason and lack leverage over the boss. Most American workers in the private sector lack union representation, the result of a much longer war on labor power. But many workers still fought back. Adriana Gopar said the pandemic led her to the Warehouse Worker Resource Center. "The main thing that got me really interested in it was all the information they had about COVID," she says. "Because for me, it was really frustrating. I would watch the TV and I would see all the information they give you," she adds, but it wasn't good enough. The WWRC was different, she explains. "Since I learned about the WWRC, I knew that they will talk about the workers' rights. And then I noticed that all of our rights were being ignored. That's why I said I need to get involved. Maybe not just for me, but maybe I can help others with that information."

Workers at a McDonald's in Oakland, California, walked off the job after a supervisor gave them masks made from dog diapers. By the time of the walkout four workers had tested positive for COVID and the virus had spread to their loved ones, including a ten-month-old baby.

In 2021, workers at a Buffalo, New York, area Starbucks store voted to unionize with Workers United, an affiliate of the Service Employees International Union, or SEIU. Over three hundred stores would follow. Nabretta Hardin, who works for Starbucks in

Memphis, Tennessee, says that COVID influenced her decision to unionize. When she started working for Starbucks in December 2020, the popular chain impressed her with its COVID benefits and protections. Over time, though, those measures disappeared as the pandemic continued. "They slowly started taking away a lot of those rules that were in place, and the policies that were in place, to protect the workers and started catering more towards the customers, making sure their comfort level was, I guess, better than the workers," Hardin says. Customers took advantage of the relaxed rules. "They have a drink that people call the Medicine Ball, and people legit think that there's medicine in it and that it cures every cold or flu," she explains. A 2022 *Better Homes & Gardens* article urges customers to try the drink, which is a tea that contains lemonade: "The next time you're feeling a little unwell, try ordering the Medicine Ball at Starbucks, and hopefully, you'll feel much more like yourself in no time."[24] If people will show up to Starbucks sick to get their Medicine Balls, that's a problem on its own; as usual, the pandemic made everything worse. "People thought it cured COVID," Hardin tells me. "They were coming up there, with COVID, telling us, 'I just tested positive for COVID and I'm here to get a Medicine Ball.'" When Starbucks relaxed its safety measures, the company only made the situation worse, she adds. When we spoke in 2022, she complained, "There's no barriers anymore. Customers don't have to wear a mask anymore. We can't ask them to wear a mask anymore. There's no hand sanitizer to give to customers. We only have hand sanitizer where we are, and we were just not happy with that at all."

Hardin reached her limit. "A guy came to our store while I was in the drive-through and in the process of handing me his cash, he was like, 'I just tested positive for COVID,'" she remembers. "And I'm thinking, 'I just touched this man's COVID money. I have to put it in a drawer, and hand it out, and then my manager has to touch it, and whoever comes behind has to touch the same money. This guy clearly has COVID, and he's passing it now in my store.'" The store suffered an outbreak of COVID soon after, though it's unclear whether the virus rode in on a dollar bill or arrived by some other means. Hardin didn't get sick—a relief, since she takes immunosuppressants for a medical condition. Instead, she and two other employees worked to keep the store open until their coworkers could return. "And regardless of the workers saying, 'We don't feel comfortable working with people that have tested positive,' they wouldn't allow us to self-quarantine ourselves. We were still required to come to work if you had the vaccine," she asserts. Everyone in her store caught COVID, she adds, and when she asked upper management repeatedly if they could close the store down and sanitize it, they told her no, and that she was fine because she was vaccinated. "It really made me mad and upset," she says. Starbucks managers, she added, didn't listen to her. "So I wanted to change that. I wanted to have a voice and a say in how our workplace was run because of that. That's what really started me to want to unionize," she explains.

The pandemic had a similar effect on Victoria Conklin, who has worked for several Starbucks locations in the Buffalo, New York, area. Starbucks shut her mall kiosk down when the pandemic began and offered her catastrophe pay to compensate for the lost work. Then her manager called her and told her that she was going back to work. Two stores had opened in the Buffalo area, and she had been placed at one of them. But nobody had asked her if she felt safe enough to work. Her lungs are scarred from childhood illness and she feared, too, that she might infect her grandfather, who is immunocompromised. In response, her manager told her that she'd lose her catastrophe pay if she didn't comply. Conklin reluctantly agreed to go back to work.

Starbucks placed her at a store that lacked a drive-through. To attract customers, they set up two tables outside the café with a karaoke mic system. "We had the microphone on our side and a karaoke speaker on the outside, and the door was unlocked, and we would run up to the microphone and call whatever drink out, put it on the table, close the door, and run away from the doors," she says. One time a customer called the store to complain that Conklin had violated the Americans with Disabilities Act and HIPAA because she'd asked the woman's unmasked daughter to wait outside for her drink. "The manager I had clearly felt bad, but there wasn't a lot she could do," Conklin remembers. The woman filed a complaint with corporate, so it fell to Conklin's manager to talk to her about the company's "Third Place Policy." That policy, as Starbucks says on its website, is intended to protect customers and workers alike. According to Conklin, the idea is "that you have three places you feel most comfortable at. And it should be home, work, and the third place should be Starbucks." Partners have to provide "great" customer service, she adds, and in return, they can ask customers to leave if they make workers unsafe. "But they usually just do this to punish partners for not being super cheerful and talking to you for five minutes when you get your drink," she explains.

Conklin's mall kiosk eventually reopened, but she was transferred to a third Starbucks location. She began organizing in January the same year, she says, "because of Starbucks' reaction to the Omicron variant coming back up." The pandemic, she adds, "made it easier for me to walk up to a coworker and be like, 'You deserve a lot better, and I'm presenting you with an option for Starbucks to give us better because they're not going to do it on their own.'" Conklin, like Hardin, says that Starbucks began to strip back the pandemic benefits and protections it once offered workers. When Omicron hit, workers in Conklin's store needed masks, but none were forthcoming from Starbucks. Conklin approached Workers United for help. The union gave her boxes of KN95 masks to distribute to her coworkers. The underlying message—that the union would do for workers what Starbucks would not—was persuasive. Conklin's store later voted 7–4 to unionize.

Starbucks has constructed a progressive brand image. It offers workers some health coverage and college benefits, and in 2017 reporting tipped the company's then-CEO, Howard Schultz, as Hillary Clinton's choice for secretary of labor.[25] When the pandemic began, it implemented paid COVID leave for workers, and the company also raised its starting pay to $15 an hour in 2022—a decade after groups like the Fight for $15 and a Union began organizing around the minimum wage. But Conklin and Hardin have seen another side of Starbucks. The company fired the outspoken union supporters in the middle of the pandemic. First, Starbucks accused Hardin of store safety violations. She wasn't alone, either. "I'm a part of a group of baristas called the Memphis Seven and we're the first set of firings during our unionizing campaign," she explains. Hardin believes that she and her fellow workers were set up as "examples" by Starbucks: a warning to other would-be union supporters. Starbucks fired all seven workers on the same day in February 2022, which sent a statement. Hardin said it was the first time she'd been fired from a job. "I've always been an exemplary employee in any job I go to, I always work hard, I pull double shifts. I'm very helpful," she insists. She was shocked to hear Starbucks accuse her of being "a threat" to her coworkers. Later, in June 2022, the company fired Conklin for arriving twenty minutes late to a shift—her first late arrival in almost five years as a Starbucks worker.

Starbucks maintains that it did not fire Hardin or Conklin due to their labor activity. Nevertheless, Workers United filed unfair labor practices with the NLRB, alleging that they'd been illegally fired for protected organizing activity. In August 2022, a federal judge ordered Starbucks to reinstate Hardin and the other members of the Memphis Seven. (Starbucks appealed, and the U.S. Supreme Court agreed to hear the case in 2024.[26]) Conklin also won her unemployment case. In February 2024, an NLRB administrative law judge concluded that Starbucks had illegally fired her and nine others and ordered their reinstatement with back pay.[27] Other union supporters have accused Starbucks of similar illegal firings; at the same time, the benefits that once distinguished the company from its competitors now look precarious. Starbucks ended its paid COVID leave in October 2022, though the pandemic was ongoing, and in June 2022, Bloomberg reported that the company threatened workers with the loss of trans-inclusive health-care coverage if they unionized.[28] Starbucks denied the story, yet its opposition to the union is not in doubt. The corporate narrative never shifts: workers don't need a union, say Schultz and others. The pandemic taught workers a different story.

In at least one respect, Conklin and Hardin have been fortunate. When I spoke to them, neither had contracted COVID at work. For others, though, COVID has been fatal. Eric Winston still thinks about his coworker Consuela. They started working at a Durham-area Cracker Barrel at the same time. Over time, he came to know her well. "I worked with Consuela and her husband for about two years, the first time I was at Cracker Barrel. I left that job and came back. When I came back to Cracker Barrel, I worked with them again for eight months. I had already known them and loved working with both of them," he explains. Conseula and her husband both worked as dishwashers for the popular chain restaurant, and Winston says that they were a very good team—until COVID broke the team up.

Consuela and her husband both contracted the virus, and though he lived, she did not. Though it can be difficult to know exactly where a person contracted COVID, Winston believes she got it at Cracker Barrel. Management let her passing go mostly without comment, he says. Nobody told the remaining staff that Consuela had died from COVID; Winston "did his own digging" and talked to their families to find out the truth. "All my coworkers were terrified. They were really scared," he tells me. He later started a petition to try to unionize the Cracker Barrel location, and then he, like many workers in his position, experienced retaliation. Cracker Barrel slashed his hours until he could no longer live on the wage he received. Winston has since moved on from Cracker Barrel and works two full-time jobs that he said he prefers to his experience working for the chain. Yet the memory lingers, and it has helped transform him into an activist: he joined Raise Up, the southern U.S. branch of Fight for a Union, which is affiliated with the SEIU.

Winston wasn't the only worker whose pandemic experiences turned him into an activist. For Derrick Bryant, the pandemic was the backdrop to his descent into ever-deeper poverty. On the phone with me, Bryant tells me he can't complain—it is "another day, another dollar," he says gamely—but the truth is that he has the right to complain, a lot. The year is 2022, the pandemic is ongoing, and he is working at Panera Bread while living in his car. He had been living in a Red Roof Inn, where he worked until he was fired and lost his job and his home in one day. "Long story short, it was unsafe for me, and if it was unsafe for me, it was unsafe for the customers," he explains. The work was hard and varied, and in return he received low wages and no respect. "I did all types of things throughout the day and night. I wasn't paid for it and it wasn't on my check. I went through wage theft there. I went through racial discrimination there and daily, just no respect at all," he asserts. Bryant had wanted to rent an apartment, for which he needed pay stubs. "But they didn't give it to me at all until the day they fired me," he complains. "That was pretty hard, man." Supervisors expected him to do most of the manual labor in addition to his regular cleaning tasks, and he suspects this had something to do with the fact that he is a Black man. "When I wake up in the morning, I get all types of looks throughout the day and night. But I'm the guy that you call whenever you need help. That bothered me a little bit," he says. Bryant finally got tired. His younger brother belonged to Raise Up and invited Bryant to a meeting. There, Bryant found a sense of solidarity. He spent most of the pandemic on bedrest with an illness he blames on the work he'd been doing: landscaping, mostly, with some factory work on the side. "Being the underpaid worker, trying to be a father, trying to be a family man, trying to live out my hopes and dreams, all that breaks down your body," he tells me. When he did return to work, he found that the pandemic had a radicalizing effect on him. "You see all your supervisors are gone, or the people that run the company, they're not there. But the every-day employees were in there with masks," he points out. "They say six feet, but how can you be six feet away from someone if you're working on an assembly line? I can't be six feet away from people." He adds, "That's what the pandemic did for me. Pretty much it's the cherry on the fuck-you sundae."

In November 2022, Bryant and Winston joined dozens of other Raise Up members to launch an ambitious and distinctive new organizing effort: the Union of Southern Service Workers, or USSW. "Our demands are that we demand equal treatment. We demand health and safety. And when I say health and safety, we want safety on the job," one worker, Mama Cookie Bradley, tells me. "We demand fair scheduling. We demand fair pay, and we demand a seat at the table."

Bradley knows she's earned that seat, and more. A grandmother who organized her first workplace protest at the age of nineteen, Bradley worked two jobs in fast food and home health care to support herself. Her day began early in the morning when she left for her home health care job to fix a client's breakfast, and then, at nine, she started working in fast food to feed everybody else. At three thirty in the afternoon, she left the fast-food restaurant and went back to home health care to check in on her clients and make sure they were ready for the evening. "I'm chilling today, but the majority of the time my day ends at nine or ten o'clock at night," she told me before her retirement. It was a long day for a sixty-three-year-old woman who was constantly on her feet. Bradley worked in home health care seven days a week, and received no benefits. "I don't have anything to supplement, so I have to struggle the best I can," she explained. "My sons help out, but I don't want to depend on them. I just want to depend on myself, and to be working all these years and I still can't take care of myself alone, that's sad." In USSW, Bradley sees a chance at a different future. "We as workers have to take a stand. If we don't take this stand now, nobody will ever hear us," she said.

The USSW aims to reverse a long-standing legacy of the Jim Crow South: the exclusion of Black and Brown workers from labor protections. The system doesn't want Black and white workers to organize together, Bradley said. "We've had enough of that," she added. "They passed laws to make it harder for Black and southern workers to organize. It excluded the backbone of the southern service industry, and this industry was powered by the labor of Black and Brown workers." The USSW, she said, will be different. Powered by Raise Up's decades-long organizing efforts in the South, the union is open to workers from a variety of low-wage service sectors, and it isn't waiting to be recognized by the NLRB. At a November summit in

South Carolina, where union density hovers under 2 percent, workers signed membership cards and outlined their vision for victory.

Worker organizing won't bring back the dead, but it could save lives. Organizing is often born of anger, whether it takes place at work or in the streets. Optimism then propels it forward. At work, where I'm a shop steward in our union, I've learned that organizing can be sensitive and difficult work. There are detailed spreadsheets, and long meetings, and patient conversations. It would all be hard to sustain if our union hadn't agreed, collectively, that ours is not only a fight worth having but a fight we can win. When Mama Cookie Bradley first began to organize, she similarly did so out of the conviction that she could change her circumstances if she fought. She operates within a long and successful history. Had American workers not organized centuries ago, workplaces would be much more dangerous than they are today. The pandemic reminded us that there's still work to be done. For the disposable who risk their lives on the job, organizing can win protection the boss would otherwise never offer. There is still power in a union, strength in the collective refusal to accept degradation and pain. "We have found a new way to come for them and they can't handle that," Bradley said. "They're not going to be able to handle it, because we ready."

SIX

THE TWO PANDEMICS

"What you are now, we once were; what we are now, you shall be." Those words on the walls of an ossuary in Rome are meant to encourage introspection and perhaps repentance in the reader.[1] Americans might read in them a material truth along with the spiritual lesson. Someday, if we're lucky, we're going to grow old. Before we turn to dust, we'll have needs—but our needs aren't equally met under capitalism. American seniors know that well. By the time COVID reached our shores, experts knew the virus posed a special risk to seniors. Age made their bodies vulnerable to severe illness and death, but age was not all that endangered many of them.

American seniors without means lose security as they age. Many must remain in the workforce, obligated to give up their final years. In 2022, Gallup found that Americans were retiring later than they had in the 1990s.[2] Americans retired at age fifty-seven on average in

1991; in 2022, that average had risen to sixty-one. Higher medical expenses and costs of living likely contributed to the trend, argued one report from CNBC.[3] Though some economists have argued that Americans should work longer, others say there are significant drawbacks for seniors. "Working longer means giving up well-earned rest in old age," wrote labor economist Teresa Ghilarducci of the New School for Social Research in her 2024 book *Work, Retire, Repeat: The Uncertainty of Retirement in the New Economy.* "For some, working longer means aging more quickly and dying sooner," she added. "For most people, the only way working longer boosts retirement finances is grotesque: when they finally retire, they are closer to death." According to Ghilarducci, "nearly half" of American families lack retirement savings, which can deprive them of financial security in old age and force them to keep working. Though some seniors—around 11 percent, Ghilarducci wrote—work because they choose to, she added, "Over twice as many older workers are working because they have to, and the majority of elders aren't working and are living on income living below their pre-retirement standard of living, even after accounting for reduced transportation and other work-related expenses."[4] The American poor tend not to live as long as the wealthy.[5] A person who is disposable may have little time to rest before the end—if they can rest at all. Their experiences and their contributions can't buy them a dignified old age.

Cast out, the disposable stay on the fringe. They land, often, in nursing homes of dubious quality. There they find their status relatively unchanged by age: as workers, they were sites of profit, and as bodies in beds they are sites of profit still. In the *New Yorker,* Yasmin Rafiei reported in 2022 that private equity investment in nursing homes had grown from $5 billion at the turn of the century to $100 billion.[6] Cost-cutting measures can be deadly for seniors, as private equity squeezes profit out of human life. Data collected by University of Pennsylvania economist Atul Gupta and a team of researchers revealed that "when private-equity firms acquired nursing homes, deaths among residents increased by an average of ten percent," Rafiei wrote. Seniors died in the name of economic efficiency as private equity firms cut nursing staff to save costs. Though private equity firms own only 11 percent of nursing homes, Rafiei reported that 70 percent are run for profit, which subjects seniors to similar cost-cutting efforts. The more a nursing home relies on Medicaid to fill its beds, the likelier it is to provide poor quality care, according to KFF Health News.[7] Understaffing is a consistent problem. KFF went on to report that although the average five-star home has the staff it needs to provide 5.4 hours of care a day per resident, seniors who live in one-star homes can expect a mere 3.0 hours of care a day. "At the best-staffed homes (five stars), only 4 of 10 residents are on Medicaid, meaning the remainder of residents are more lucrative for those facilities. At the worst-staffed homes (one star), 7 of 10 residents are on Medicaid," KFF added. The quality of a resident's care depends not only on their ability to pay but on their proximity to wealth.

Still others age at home, and rely on friends and family for community and support. Without wealth of their own, however, their circumstances can be difficult. The arrival of COVID isolated seniors, whether they lived in nursing homes or their own private residences. Haunted by the prospect of a cruel and untimely death, seniors and their loved ones had to make complicated decisions about their care. Some soon discovered that the love and respect they'd earned over their long lives could not protect them from facility mismanagement, political malfeasance, or the virus itself.

In a phone call, Alexa Rivera starts with the basic facts of her mother's life, which means we began with a death. Ana Celia

Martinez was seventy-eight at the time of her passing: a mother, a grandmother, a recent great-grandmother. Rivera's sister, Vivian Rivera Zayas, tells me that Martinez and her siblings had a difficult life in Puerto Rico. After they lost their parents, they became "mini-adults," which "instilled in them a very hard work ethic," Zayas says. The surviving siblings became a little closed off to the world, even to other family members. Zayas adds that when she and her sister try to talk to their surviving uncles, it can be like "talking to a brick wall, because they became so close, such a tight nucleus after their parents died." Sometimes she compares them to the Knights of the Round Table. Two siblings eventually died, one in a diving accident in Puerto Rico, which bound the survivors even more closely to each other. The survivors came to the mainland United States to work, and while some eventually returned to Puerto Rico, Martinez stayed behind in New York City. She liked to sew, and to cook and to bake. Though she had rheumatoid arthritis, she was otherwise strong, and Zayas said her mind was sharp. But over time, her arthritis gradually sapped the independence she so prized. Her daughters, Alexa and Vivian, became her main support.

Vivian remembers how the end began. Ana rehabbed from knee surgery in Vivian's home, and began to complain of back trouble. Then she developed a massive cyst on her thigh, which Vivian promptly showed to Alexa. The sisters decided the hospital was their best option and took Ana in for care, but she didn't return home. Doctors sent her to a short-term rehabilitation facility instead, a dreary place that made her miserable. Vivian removed her from the center, and shortly thereafter she developed nausea and suffered from a poor appetite. Later, Vivian took her back to the hospital, and Ana soon found herself in another rehab facility on Long Island. At first, she did well. But trouble circled her: the pandemic had arrived. The rehab center "sent a letter to my sister saying that they were going to close the facility and that we were only going to be able to say goodbye to her on March 11," Alexa adds, checking with her sister to make sure her dates were correct. Vivian concurs. The sisters "scrambled" to see their mother before the facility shut down, Rivera explains, and Vivian made it, leaving Ana with puzzles so she could amuse herself as the lockdown dragged on. Alexa visited later the same day. When she got off work and was able to visit her mother, it was around 8 p.m., and Ana was already in bed, reading. "So I said goodbye to her, I told her we would see her in a couple of weeks, and that was the last time my sister and I saw our mother alive," Alexa tells me.

"We kept calling, we wouldn't get through to her," Vivian adds. "Every time we were calling and wouldn't get an get answer, nurses would tell us that she was okay and she didn't have a fever. We weren't asking if she had a fever or not, but that was always the response." They later learned that COVID had already entered the rehab center, but at the time, they called in ignorance. "I didn't even know that COVID was in the facility, especially since I get a letter that says that they had taken all precautions in place, and nowhere in the letter did it say, 'We have two patients which are in isolation,'" Vivian complains. "I didn't even get a follow-up letter or follow-up call. And I found it interesting because I remember March nineteenth of 2020. I'm calling my mom, I'm calling, calling, calling. And when I don't hear anything, I called the social worker, I called the person who's in charge of discharge, and I called the head nurse." Vivian wanted her mother out of the rehab center. Upset, she waited days until center staff called her back to tell her they would help her bring her mother home.

The sisters feared bringing her back to Rivera's apartment in Brooklyn, where COVID was spreading throughout the neighborhood. But

Ana was in tears. "She wanted to get home. And that's what we were trying to do, get her home," Vivian explains. Though the sisters were afraid of catching COVID themselves, or of exposing their beloved mother to the virus in one of their homes, they were determined to free her from the facility like she wanted. Vivian even acquired an electric wheelchair and prepared her mother's apartment for her to come home on Monday.

On Saturday, a cousin called her to tell her that her mother didn't sound like herself. A desperate Vivian managed to get her mother on the phone, but the call wasn't reassuring. "My mother, when she talked, she was garbling all her words. She was like, 'Rawr, rawr, rawr.' It sounded like a little monster on the phone, because I could not understand. I couldn't understand anything she said," Vivian says.

Both sisters say that their mother's rehab center didn't tell them that COVID had entered the grounds. Vivian explains that she learned later that an infectious disease specialist had identified her mother as a possible COVID patient days earlier, and no one had told either of her daughters. "At that point, I was really worried," Vivian remembers. "I told my husband, 'I don't know if I should go there with a police officer.'" Her mother's exact condition remained unclear. A nurse told Vivian that Ana didn't have a fever, and because neither Vivian nor Alexa knew that COVID was in the center, they reassured themselves that their mother had a cold.

On Monday, the day Ana was supposed to come home, they called her, and received no answer. The sisters decided they'd had enough. A nurse suggested that Alexa speak to the director. When she finally reached him, he told her that her mother was in respiratory failure. He offered to send her home, still, but with an oxygen tank. Alexa refused, pointing out that her mother hadn't been on oxygen when she'd arrived at the rehab center. The facility performed an X-ray, and the director told Alexa he'd send her mother to the hospital. "Now, I'm talking about this was about ten o'clock, quarter maybe to eleven in the morning," Alexa says. "My mother didn't get to the hospital until about eleven o'clock that night." The hospital told Alexa that they'd signed off on COVID testing—and that everyone in her mother's ward was being treated as a suspected COVID patient. The next time Alexa called, the hospital informed her that her mother's lungs had collapsed in the middle of the night, and they'd intubated her and moved her into the ICU. "From there, my mother was doing a little bit better," Alexa explains. "She was responding to the antibiotics at first; they said they put a tube in her chest to drain fluids. By the next day, my mother started to have kidney failure." The hospital called again, seeking permission to perform dialysis, but within a half hour, Ana had died.

The devastated sisters were so afraid of catching COVID, and of seeing their beloved mother strapped to the machines that were keeping her alive, that they both declined to see her one final time. "I'm thinking if I see her dead on a table, strapped with stuff, and things in her mouth, I just didn't know how I was going to react," Vivian says. "And then to have to be by myself for fourteen days in my basement or in a hotel just really put me over. So I also declined to go." She pauses. "Sometimes I'm not sure if that was a good decision or not, because you could have said goodbye, you know?" she adds. "But we didn't get to say goodbye because we didn't know she was going to die, number one. So that blindsided us. Here we are, three days prior, fixing her apartment because she was coming home. And three days later, we are talking to a morgue, and I have to tell my husband to talk to the morgue because I just couldn't."

Alexa and Vivian remain furious with the rehab facility: for not telling them COVID was there in the center, and for delaying their mother's final trip to the hospital. They soon learned they weren't alone with their complaints. "I actually posted on the page of the nursing home," Alexa tells me. "I posted a picture of my mother and I said that they knew my mother was sick and didn't inform us, and that we were lied to, and that they essentially killed my mother." The center took the post down, but Rivera kept posting it back up, and a woman later contacted her to tell her that she'd had a similar experience. "We did our first protest in front of the nursing home on Mother's Day," she says.

By May 1, a full month after their mother had passed, the sisters had launched their own website: VoicesforSeniors.com. The sisters told me their Facebook group now has around 4,300 members, many of whom lost loved ones to COVID. Others survived it, but had questions or concerns about their treatment. Though the group has members from several states, the sisters focused much of their ire on Andrew Cuomo, then the Democratic governor of New York. Vivian and Alexa even excoriated him in respective editorials for the *New York Post*.

Cuomo had transformed into a national celebrity with televised COVID briefings that played up the contrast between the Democratic governor and President Donald Trump. For a while, Cuomo was difficult to avoid—even for people who didn't live in New York. Fans dubbed themselves Cuomosexuals: there were T-shirts, and mugs, and other regrettable pieces of kitsch. The Cuomo industrial complex would break down in a fashion so dramatic that it claimed his brother, former CNN anchor Chris Cuomo, too.

The primary reason for Cuomo's fall was his propensity for sexual harassment. Underneath that scandal, however, another brewed. In the spring of 2020, as the pandemic sank its teeth into his state, Cuomo issued a controversial advisory. Nursing homes could accept patients who had, or were suspected of having, COVID, he directed. They were further prohibited from testing medically stable patients for COVID. Cuomo critics worried that the advisory would fan the spread of COVID among an already-fragile population. By August 2020, people in nursing homes and other long-term-care facilities accounted for 26 percent of the state's COVID deaths.[8] There are likely many reasons for that statistic, beyond Cuomo's directive: seniors are biologically susceptible to severe COVID, congregate living arrangements can make quarantine difficult, and sick staff members helped drive the spread of COVID in nursing homes.

In a July report, the state health department concluded that the directive hadn't contributed to an increase in nursing home deaths from COVID. In January 2021, though, the state attorney general, Letitia James, accused the Cuomo administration of undercounting nursing home deaths by the thousands.[9] People who'd died after being transferred to a hospital weren't counted among the death toll. Months later, in March, the *New York Times* reported that senior Cuomo aides had interfered with the health department's report, rewriting portions to hide the true death toll—all while Cuomo pitched a book based on his handling of the pandemic.[10] Cuomo received $5.1 million to write the book, called *American Crisis: Leadership Lessons from the COVID-19 Pandemic*. A 2022 report by a law firm later found that Cuomo had improperly used state resources to sell, and then write, the book.[11]

Vivian and Alexa had asked to meet with Cuomo, but "obviously he didn't want to meet with us," Zayas says. Though Cuomo is no longer in office—his resignation the product of his own vices—Vivian and Alexa blame him still for actions at odds with his lofty rhetoric. "My mom was expendable. His mom wasn't, but mine was," Zayas adds.

Cuomo did not say that some seniors belong to a disposable class of person. Few would. But millions live in poverty, and will die in poverty as Richard Proia did. Medicare, meanwhile, "doesn't cover the long-term daily care—whether in the home or in a full-time nursing facility—that millions of aging Americans require," *Vox* reported in 2019.[12] Seniors or their families then have to pay out of pocket for care, and costs are steep: According to Genworth Financial, "the median yearly cost of in-home care with a home health aide in 2019 was $54,912, and the median cost for a private room in a nursing home was $105,850."[13] That's far more than many can afford, which means family members must often step into the breach. Eldercare can be difficult to navigate even when a family can afford the care their loved one needs.

When Krista Ziegler's mother died, her ninety-three-year-old grandfather lost his primary caregiver. The family rushed to find help while her grandfather, who'd fallen and broken his hip, recovered in a rehab facility. "They were like, graciously, 'We can offer you a couple extra days to get things set up, but other than that, he's got to get out,'" she says. She felt her grandfather needed a longer stay, but he is "stubborn," she said, and had convinced the doctors he was ready to leave. The facility, she adds, was only too happy to free up the bed. "We talked to the social workers at the hospital. We called all of the town numbers. He's a veteran, so we called the VA. And basically all we ended up getting from everyone was a stack of pamphlets and this sort of understanding from them that there's very little help available," she tells me. Facilities had few staff members available to help, and she discovered, quickly, that there were often arcane rules on the location a service would cover or the sort of care that could be provided. "It ended up that me and my uncle and my aunt were all on the phone just dozens of hours a week, making and returning phone calls to try to see what was even available," she says. They did have one benefit on their side: money. Her grandfather had enough savings to cover the services of a home health aide.

Faced with high costs and a labyrinthine eldercare system, many other families struggle to cope without much of a safety net. The National Alliance for Caregiving and the AARP reported in 2023 that nearly one in five Americans are now unpaid caregivers for a loved one, and a third of that number have left their jobs in order to provide care full-time, according to data collected by the Rosalynn Carter Institute for Caregivers.[14] Meanwhile, the pandemic saw a sharp decrease in the number of nursing home staff nationwide, which shifts additional responsibilities onto families and creates extra risks for seniors. The result is an eldercare crisis. "Eldercare in capitalist society has always been in a state of crisis, both because of the devaluation of reproductive work in capitalism and because the elderly are seen as no longer productive, instead of being treasured, as they were in many precapitalist societies as depositories of the collective memory and experience," the feminist scholar, Silvia Federici, has written.[15] In our society age can make a person expendable, just as Vivian and Alexa feared. Dignity is not innate, but rather a commodity a senior must purchase.

That's visible in the nation's nursing homes, where patients often suffered subpar care before the pandemic—especially in homes owned by private equity. One report found that nursing staff hours per patient day fell by 2.4 percent following a private equity buyout. Staff quality declined, too. "The quality of care declines after the private equity buyout, which seems to reflect staffing cuts," one researcher told the *New York Times*.[16] Nursing homes in general are chronically understaffed, yet the Centers for Medicare & Medicaid Services "has failed to set minimum staffing requirements, despite repeated calls from advocates and experts," Human Rights Watch reported in 2021.[17]

A 2020 report from the Government Accountability Office found that "most" nursing homes had infection control deficiencies before the pandemic took place, and around half had "persistent" violations. "Infection prevention and control deficiencies cited by surveyors can include situations where nursing home staff did not regularly use proper hand hygiene or failed to implement preventive measures during an infectious disease outbreak, such as isolating sick residents and using masks and other personal protective equipment to control the spread of infection," the report explained.[18] Though the deficiencies weren't all classed as severe, experts say the report is proof that nursing homes were ill-prepared for a public health crisis on the scale of COVID.

"We have pretty good standards in this country for nursing home care," said Richard Mollot, the executive director of the New York–based Long Term Care Community Coalition, or LTCCC. "But the problem is that they're not self implementing. And so if they're not actively enforced, then they're really not very meaningful, and that has always been the case with infection control and prevention." The deficiencies documented by the GAO set up future catastrophe, he added. By June 2021, nursing home residents accounted for nearly one-third of the nation's COVID deaths. Dr. Mark Lachs, a geriatric internist based at Weill Cornell Medicine, wrote of "two pandemics" in a 2021 piece for *Nature Aging*.[19] While New Yorkers clapped and cheered nightly for health-care providers in hospitals, the bravest heroes, he said, worked "without fanfare or applause" in facilities where "another pandemic entirely was playing out, one of carnage." In nursing homes, providers often lacked protective gear. One colleague told Lachs that she and her staff had to wear ponchos instead of gowns.

Seniors aren't the only class of person to be consumed by ageism. Like childcare, senior care is in demand, but workers command little respect or material compensation. Debased for their proximity to disposable people, they're underpaid and suffer from low staffing levels, especially in nursing homes, explained Robert Oronia, a certified nursing assistant and a member of SEIU 2015, which represents nearly 450,000 long-term-care workers in California. The pandemic greatly exacerbated older problems at his for-profit skilled nursing facility in Chatsworth, California. "Not all the equipment worked correctly," he tells me. "Wheelchairs and beds were broken. Lousy pay all around." When the virus struck, nobody wanted to work, he adds. Nobody wanted to get sick on the job, or carry the virus home to someone they loved. But Oronia felt he had no choice but to report to work. "It was horrible," he remembers. He worked nights, and sometimes there were only two or three NAs to cover the entire shift. Protective gear was scarce. Oronia and his fellow workers once ran out of gowns and, like Lachs's colleague, wore poncho-style raincoats in a desperate attempt to protect themselves. "People will say, 'Oh, we made do,'" Oronia says. "Problem is, you shouldn't have to make do." Fear saturated the place. "I can only imagine if I were one of the residents, I'd be afraid," he adds. "I'm there alone. Nobody was allowed to visit." People began to die, victims of a strange disease they'd only just heard of and barely understood. In 2020 Oronia got sick on the job and spent around three weeks in the hospital with COVID. When we spoke in 2023, he still needed an oxygen machine. While he struggles to breathe, workers at his facility are struggling, too—for decent pay on the job. The facility offered a $35 daily bonus to care for COVID patients. To Oronia, that's not high enough. In 2022, he joined other members of SEIU 2015 on an informational picket line to call public attention to low pay, high staff turnover, and understaffing at the facility.[20]

Jesus Figueroa Cacho—a CNA who also belongs to SEIU 2015—
shares many of Oronia's concerns. Staffing levels at her for-profit facility plummeted so low the National Guard stepped in to assist, she
tells me. After the Guard arrived, the facility started to bring on staff
from other states to try to keep the home afloat. But no amount of
staffing help could blunt the trauma of working in a nursing home
during a pandemic. Figueroa Cacho recalled one special patient. He'd
planned to move into a retirement home after receiving short-term
rehabilitation care at Figueroa Cacho's facility. She brought him a
hot chocolate every morning as her night shift ended, but she knew
that he was lonely. With the arrival of lockdown, he didn't get to see
friends and family, or even his beloved dog. When Figueroa Cacho
returned from a day off, she asked for him—only to be told he'd
passed away from COVID. "It just breaks my heart so bad," she says.
"His life just went away, with all his visions and dreams." She wishes,
still, that she could have fetched his dog, or comforted him in his
last hours. Her position on the frontlines of the pandemic created a
"devastating" situation for her, she adds. "I worked sixteen hours and
I was tired, but you know, if nobody shows up, what can you do? You
got to continue working," she says. Her circumstances have improved
in the years since early lockdown, she adds, but the facility was still
understaffed in 2023.

The pandemic tested Nancy Leon, a CNA and member of SEIU
2015 who works with Figueroa Cacho. Work was hectic well before
the pandemic, she tells me; patients in her behavioral unit need assistance in nearly every aspect of their lives. "We clean them, we love
them, we care for them," Leon says. "We comb their hair, we change
their briefs, we shower them, feed them. We're complete caretakers."
She likes to make her residents laugh, but that was difficult during
the height of the pandemic, when she worked in the COVID unit.

A "mass panic" struck the facility, she explains. The workers would rotate, two days on and two days off, so they wouldn't get sick. Inside, the virus stalked her patients. "It's just that I wasn't expecting so many deaths," she says. "It was a nightmare." Some nurses couldn't handle the chaos, she remembers. Staff could only spend a set amount of time in each patient's room, so "you couldn't show them love. And they were so scared." A woman came in with her husband, married for many years; "old hippies," Leon calls them. "She started to die and she was crying," the CNA remembered. "And I remember holding her and not giving a crap whether I got it or not at that point." Because of COVID regulations, the woman's husband couldn't see her and her world shrank to the four corners of her room. The staff were all the residents had, according to Leon.

For all the suffering the staff had endured, they received no recognition from the administration. "They didn't spit at us, but they treated it like it was no big deal. Like what happened to us was nothing," she says. A bit of extra pay can't make up for what they experienced. Leon's pain is personal. She didn't just lose patients to the pandemic: while she labored away in a COVID ward, the virus killed her mother. Leon could not see her before she died.

The experiences of CNAs, overworked and underpaid on the frontlines of horror, speak to deeper problems with senior care in the U.S. "Coronavirus exposed so many things to the larger world that we gerontologists already knew; ageism, a chronically broken and underfunded system of long-term care, and the lack of expertise in geriatric medicine to name a few," Lachs wrote. Though the pandemic also created new research opportunities that could benefit seniors, Lachs feared they "will be lost as the nursing home pandemic fades from memory."[21]

Jessica Lehman speaks to me while she is still the executive director of Senior and Disability Action in San Francisco, California, and tells me that the group's members faced mounting obstacles to a dignified life in the years before the pandemic. "Even when there was so-called affordable senior housing, it often wasn't affordable enough for so many seniors on very low incomes," Lehman says. "And when there were very affordable units, it's always nearly impossible to get in because there are so many people that need them." SDA works often with seniors in single-room-occupancy hotels, where elevators rarely work and bedbugs and roaches abound. In SRO hotels, cooking facilities can be "a mess," Lehman explains, and the rooms themselves are small, with barely enough space for a bed and perhaps a mini-fridge. Home care is another area of concern. Seniors sometimes don't know the options they have at their disposal, and even when they do, they can't always afford the care. In San Francisco, she adds, transit also worries her members. Older people in the city "really had to fight to make sure that bus stops don't get eliminated," she says. "Similarly, we fought to get the crosswalk time increased because somebody would get halfway across the street and if they couldn't move quickly enough, they wouldn't make it across safely."

Seniors must also fear displacement from gentrification. The city was once a place where people lived for decades, and formed communities that were integral to a comfortable old age. Apartment buildings were places where neighbors got to know each other, and as a person aged, residents might help with groceries or provide support after a surgery. "Now that more and more people are getting pushed out, and of course, especially Black people and other people of color, you lose that sense of community," she explains. "So if an older person is lucky enough to not be harassed and pushed out and displaced out of their own unit, then a lot of the people they've known for decades may be gone. And you lose that natural support network."

Through SDA's work, seniors challenge a society that wasn't built with their comfort or security in mind. Lehman and SDA's members imagine a more inclusive city, where seniors and people with disabilities are integrated fully into community life, and where their needs aren't dismissed as fringe concerns. That city does not yet exist. Society in its current form exploits many seniors until the end and makes their suffering invisible. The true level of danger that seniors endured during COVID may not even be known. Nursing homes became sites of carnage, as Lachs, the doctor, put it, but the situation could be even worse in assisted-living facilities. "I am really, really, really concerned about what is going on in assisted living," says Richard Mollot of the Long Term Care Community Coalition. "As bad as nursing homes tend to be, we have a lot of data on who's in them, who's providing care in them, and what is going on with them. In assisted living, we have no idea." Mollot adds that assisted living residents often have needs similar to their peers in nursing homes, but data about their lives can be scarce. In assisted living, rooms aren't set up for patients to receive care, and the facilities themselves are focused on social activities, which means the potential for viral spread is high. "We still don't know to this day the extent to which assisted living has been hit because of the absence of any federal safety standards or any federal monitoring or even requirements about who can provide caring services or who is providing oversight," Mollot explains.

The federal government may have closed its eyes, but seniors can't. COVID has inflicted immense damage on this aging population. The figures are near-apocalyptic. To date, the virus has killed hundreds of thousands of seniors, and it is killing them still. In February 2023, the *New York Times* reported that seniors over sixty-five accounted for three-quarters of America's COVID dead.[22] Though hospital admissions have declined, they "remain more than five times as high among people over 70 as among those in their 50s," the *Times* added. Fewer than half have received a bivalent booster, and in nursing homes the numbers aren't much better. Only 52 percent of residents and 23 percent of staff were up-to-date on vaccinations, according to the *Times*.

For seniors the result is a narrowing world. Even outside the confines of nursing homes, assisted-living facilities, or rehab centers, seniors who live at home faced dangers of their own. Elissa Matross still worked as a public school teacher in San Francisco's Chinatown neighborhood in her seventies when the pandemic shut everything down. She'd noticed signs of trouble early. "I don't remember what I was hearing, but working in Chinatown, families were very aware of health precautions and actually had been masking for a while based on what they were hearing, I think, from China," she explains to me. Some parents even offered her a mask before classes went remote. Teaching became a challenge, she said, as poor families struggled with technology. The school principal stepped in when the city did not, setting up hot spots and getting computers to families that lacked them. But work wasn't the most difficult part of the lockdown for Matross, who lives at home with her husband. "Just the loss of my former life," she says. She went for walks with her husband, but that was nearly all she could do. A "sense of dread" haunted her. She listened to the news out of New York City and imagined what might happen to her own city and to the people she loved.

Her husband is two years older than her and lives with a variety of disabilities that placed him in extra danger from the virus. "It was a concern," she explains. They'd been told by medical professionals that their age and medical conditions could mean trouble. They stayed inside, and waited, and relied on the generosity of friends and family for groceries and other needs. Here, Matross and her husband were fortunate: they had a community willing to step in and help. Friends of their daughters went shopping for them. "These friends, who were in their thirties, were just invaluable, and they were doing the same thing for their parents and they just added us on. And that was a real gift," she tells me. To fight their sense of isolation, they stayed in contact with their daughters, with other relatives. There were Zoom calls with college friends and, she conceded, a lot of television—distractions from the precautions that she and her husband were obligated to take. They masked carefully, though all they had were flimsy blue surgical options at first. They washed their hands, and wiped down their milk cartons and produce for a while during lockdown. When we spoke in 2023, Matross and her husband had remained virus-free. She doesn't know whether that's because of their caution or unnaturally good luck. They've taken some chances, especially after two grandchildren were born during the pandemic. "It just felt like we needed to see these new babies," she adds. "And that meant flying to London, that meant getting to Sacramento." In the UK, she says, they felt like the only people wearing masks. People seemed eager to move on, a tendency that worries Matross. She belongs to Senior and Disability Action, and as an activist, she'd urged public agencies to continue to mask.

"We are in hearings every week with local health departments, local transit agencies, the state health department," she explains. Some people think they're overly cautious, but Matross believes the evidence is in her favor. She spoke to me just hours before joining SDA for a 2023 die-in at the Alameda County Public Health Department. A nurse or doctor will mask, but nobody else will have to. She could find herself in a waiting room filled with unmasked people.

"It makes no sense to us," she says. Masking "is a small sacrifice to keep the most vulnerable people safe," she adds. Everything seems so dishonest now, she tells me, and the world was moving in directions she could not follow. She knows that vaccinations have become so deeply politicized that some now question vaccines for dangerous childhood illnesses, like mumps. She finds them selfish. But she does give thanks for her blessings, she says. She has a house. Many don't. And thanks to the teachers' union, she has a strong pension. "Who would've thought that being a teacher would've been my salvation in my old age?" she asks. She has family and friends. But in a later email, Matross describes a somber mood. "As it becomes clearer that there is no end in sight I become gloomier than I was 3 years ago," she writes. "Hopes and dreams seem more out of reach and as I head toward my 76th birthday I just feel old. A lot of my friends express the same feeling."

As the nation moves on, it may leave seniors like Matross behind. "We certainly have some members who are really glad to be back in person and who are not so concerned about COVID anymore," says Lehman. "But we have a lot of people who are very concerned, especially people who are immunocompromised." The group has "more than its fair share" of members who are preparing for surgery or living with chronic illness, she adds. "In some ways, it's gotten even harder to stay connected and to not be isolated because of everyone else's behavior," she explains. A cavalier attitude toward masking can increase the isolation that seniors already endured during COVID. Many SDA members refrain from taking public transit or from going to San Francisco City Hall because the building no longer requires masks. Members have to ask if events are going to be inside, or if they'll require masks. Often the group has "to take ourselves out of the picture because of that." The group's members struggle for basic respect, she tells me: "There is almost a scorn, a suggestion that we're overreacting or that we're being stubborn, that we get blamed for self-isolating for our own safety."

Faced with state abandonment, members of SDA organize for survival. They have set themselves against a society that is not indifferent, but hostile to the vulnerable. In France, the Village Landais houses adults with memory-care needs and "is part of a movement to make memory-care units less like hospitals and more like small neighborhoods," Marion Renault wrote for the *New Yorker* in 2022.[23] That movement extends to the U.S., but there aren't many places like the Village anywhere. Over a hundred people with memory-care issues live in sixteen group houses, where they enjoy an unusual degree of autonomy. Residents, most of them seniors, can walk the grounds as they please. Many garden, and enjoy the arts. "As long as they *can* do, we must be able to leave them the liberty *to* do," said Nathalie Bonnet, a staff psychologist. Two-thirds of the Village's funding comes from "public coffers," a collective investment in its radical model, Renault explained. Policymakers could heed economists like Ghilarducci, who has outlined what she calls A Gray New Deal for seniors: robust pensions, a lower Medicare qualifying age, plus the enforcement of antidiscrimination policies that protect older Americans, among other measures.

Everyone will age, unless death intervenes. Senior life is therefore a public concern. If we abandon seniors, we abandon ourselves, too. When the pandemic arrived, exploitation and the fragility of age created a nightmare for many seniors. The pandemic winnowed them, and left trauma and grief in its wake. Vivian and Alexa say that during their years of advocacy, they've come to believe that "a web" is to blame for the dangers facing America's seniors. Legislators heed lobbyists for the nursing home industry, while the legal system is difficult to navigate, and justice remains out of reach for many. The sisters heard that police departments don't investigate nursing home abuses. And they want cameras in nursing home rooms to catch abuse or neglect, which unions oppose. Years after their mother's death, they miss her acutely, and are determined to make sure no other family experiences their pain. With Voices for Seniors, they've lobbied for federal legislation that would have guaranteed family caregivers limited access to their loved ones in nursing homes and other publicly funded congregate settings during public health emergencies. Caregivers would have to wear protective equipment and be subject to the same COVID screening requirements as facility staff. The sisters believe that if they'd been able to see their mother, they would have caught her decline, and could have advocated for her. The Essential Caregivers Act of 2021 has not passed, but Vivian and Alexa haven't given up. They're determined to fight for families like theirs. "We're still trying to figure out how our mission is evolving," Vivian tells me. All COVID did was show "the extent of the neglect and abuse and poor treatment that our seniors get" on a daily basis, she adds. Their loss was "deep and painful," she adds. "We're hoping that other people don't go through the same thing."

SEVEN

HOW THE FRINGE CAPTURED THE CENTER

Earla Dawn Dimitriadis sought beauty in life and looked for it on her deathbed, her daughter, Jennifer Ritz Sullivan, said. No stranger to ugliness, Earla wanted the happiness that others had often denied her. "She grew up in a poor household with a lot of abuse at the hands of her parents," Jennifer explains. At the age of fifteen, her parents forced her out of school and into a marriage that turned abusive. Jennifer hates the word "resiliency," she tells me; she believes it's not a gift to be resilient, but a necessity, created of pain and survival. "My mom was a warrior," she adds. There was much to admire: A determined Dimitriadis earned her GED when she was in her thirties and attended night classes at a local community college before getting a master's degree from the University of Phoenix at age fifty-eight. She worked hard at a variety of jobs, but she especially loved working with children as a teacher's assistant.

"This woman was beyond creative," Jennifer remembers. Give her a toilet paper roll and some construction paper and Earla could create anything. The master of elementary school boards, costumes, and play scenery, Earla taught herself to make jewelry, and learned woodworking and pottery. For Halloween, her children always had handmade costumes. She had a lively spirit, Jennifer adds. "My mom would go to shows with me a lot, and we'd be rocking and dancing and singing and just in the moment, and not worried about what anybody's going to say," she says. When she came out as queer, Earla wore a rainbow pin to support her daughter.

In 2020, when the virus immobilized the nation, Earla took her health seriously and rarely ventured out. She got sick anyway. From her hospital bed in the ICU, she posted regular Facebook updates along with photos of bedazzled butterflies and dragonflies: small joys in a bleak place. But her prognosis was never good. "By the time she got there, there was damage done to her lungs and she had pneumonia set in," Jennifer says. "So she wasn't able to talk due to the lack of oxygen." She and her sister arranged a final, devastating call with their mother. For fourteen minutes, Earla made a gurgling, almost suffocating sound in between gasps of conversation. She told her daughters that she didn't want to be on a ventilator, that she was in too much pain, and that she was ready to be done.

There was more to say and not enough time. "She told us that she loved us, that she had a gift waiting for us, and my mom and my sister and I just stayed on the phone until she couldn't do it anymore," Jennifer continues. Her daughters told her that they loved her. They remembered shows, and family trips, and Earla's famous lasagna. They thanked her for helping them break the cycle of abuse.

Dimitriadis died of COVID on December 5, 2020.

She left behind a community united in appreciation for her life. "When she passed, I had two different people tell me that she helped them in domestic violence situations. And my mother, with all the abuse she experienced, was very aware of other people's circumstances," Jennifer says. "I had somebody post the other day that they had the artificial Christmas tree my mom gave her twenty-five years ago, because she had come over to the house and commented on how beautiful the tree was and her and her kids didn't have one. And my mom packed it up and gave it to her. She still has it. And that's just how she was."

Jennifer believes she knows who to blame for her mother's death. Dimitriadis was careful during the pandemic, keeping close to home to protect herself, but home would not stay a sanctuary: according to Jennifer, a Trump-supporting relative who refused to wear masks brought the virus to Dimitriadis. Jennifer says that even after Dimitriadis passed away, that relative still did not believe that COVID was a major threat. Right-wing rhetoric fostered a delusion immovable even by Earla's death.

Jennifer is still angry. Not only did the politicization of COVID contribute to her mother's death, it complicated everything that followed. "I don't think people realize behind every COVID death, there's this catastrophic grief that is often interlocking with so many different things because we're complex human beings," she explains. While she mourned her mother, she feared for her husband, an essential worker who stripped at the back door every day because of the possibility he'd spread COVID. When a death is political, grief is a territory to defend. "People fat-shamed my mom in her death, and I've been called a crisis actor. I'm like, 'Why would I fucking put myself out there knowing the hatred that's going to be spewed at me, and the comments?'" Jennifer wonders. Melissa Powers, who lost her mother, Deborah Smith, to COVID, says she encountered a similar hatred. "I just started dropping people off my Facebook friend list and blocking people out of my life, because they'd be like, 'COVID's a hoax, and it's all overblown, and only people that are old and frail are dying.' Talking about people like they don't matter because they're old," she adds.

Melissa and Jennifer stare down a conservative movement convulsed by the pandemic. For the right, so skeptical of experts, government intervention, and collective action, the pandemic was a political problem. Their solution was an active and collective neglect. A real response would have shaken the movement to its foundations. Trump, then, could only intermittently endorse public health measures. Meanwhile, conservative activists and intellectuals cried out against lockdowns, masks, and vaccine mandates to provide the president with the cover he needed to retreat and, later, to undermine his liberal successor. They couched their words in the language of liberty and populist fervor. Patrick Deneen, the post-liberal academic, once said that "elites" favored lockdowns in opposition to the "masses." Quoting Christopher Lasch, he said that the masses understand "inherent limits on human control over social development, over nature and the body, over the tragic elements in human life and history."[1] R. R. Reno, the editor of *First Things*, tweeted that "mask culture if [sic] fear-driven" and that "it's a regime dominate [sic] by fear of infection and fear of causing of infection. Both are species of cowardice."[2]

The right cared nothing for either Jennifer or Melissa, or for their mothers. Their pain only made them targets in a broader conflict. The American right wing revels in a war on the public sphere. As the writer Matthew Sitman put it in an essay for Gawker, "The right benefits from people becoming more isolated, hunkered down, wary of others, and doubtful that a better future can be built. It is to such people that the reactionary message appeals: the best you can hope for is to hoard what you have, and attack the shadowy forces and alien others that you're told imperil you and your livelihood. Solidarity and generosity are turned into risky wagers not worth taking."[3]

Jennifer is more than a target to the right. Once an activist for the group Marked by COVID, she remains an advocate, speaking out about her mother's death and pushing for a COVID remembrance day in her home state of Massachusetts. She is therefore a threat. By asking the public to remember the dead—and why they died—she defies a plot that stole her mother's life.

In Trump, the right discovered a mouthpiece for ideas it had always harbored. The former president's hostility to public health uncovered a hostility to the public, period. "I think wearing a face mask as I greet presidents, prime ministers, dictators, kings, queens—I don't know, somehow I don't see it for myself. I just, I just don't," he once meandered. Maybe masks are good, he said that August, "maybe they're not so good." To dismiss masking was to accept Trump's view of a virus that he deemed a nonevent. "It's going to disappear. One day—it's like a miracle—it will disappear," he insisted in February 2020.[4] By the end of March, the virus had shuttered New York City.

Morgue trucks waited outside overflowing hospitals, and as my husband and I fought off a mysterious respiratory ailment at home, we listened to sirens, all day and into the evening. The virus was no longer abstract; it was sickening and killing our neighbors. But denial persisted, even flourished. As we filled prescriptions for our inhalers, Trump fretted over the economy and dismissed the dead. "You have suicides over things like this when you have terrible economies. You have death. Probably—and I mean definitely—would be in far greater numbers than the numbers that we're talking about with regard to the virus," he said at a March press conference.[5] Spurred not only by Trump but by the spread of conspiratorial thinking, COVID denialism captured the base. Lockdown protests were attended by diehards like John, who considered masks an assault on his personal liberties. After Trump repeatedly attacked Michigan governor Gretchen Whitmer for requesting emergency medical supplies, thousands of conservative activists packed the state capital for an April protest against her stay-at-home order. "We know this demonstration is going to come at a cost to people's health," Whitmer told press at the time. "That's how COVID-19 spreads."[6] In May, a protester carried a doll resembling Whitmer, with a noose around its neck, to the state capitol.

Most Americans supported lockdown measures and mask mandates at the time, just as most American voters had rejected Donald Trump at the ballot box in 2016. Though Trump liked to call himself a man of the silent majority, he only ever represented a febrile minority. Yet that minority inflicts real damage on themselves, and on bystanders like Dimitriadis. As COVID spread, conservatives weren't merely disruptive; they were trying to break society apart. Conspiracy theories foretold collapse; now the fringe was forcing a war. In the process, the far right found common cause with conservative intellectuals, the so-called mainstream. A skepticism of democratic institutions has given way to pure authoritarianism. In previous decades conservatives were more willing to work within democratic means, but the pretense is over. The right fractures old bonds to make way for a new order—one they aim to control.

COVID denialism is a rejection of society, which has always been more than a grouping of relationships. Society is an idea, and during COVID, an egalitarian ethos clashed directly with an antidemocratic view. There were casualties, including Dimitriadis. To the right, their deaths are an acceptable loss. A disposable person has no innate rights, no meaning beyond the profit they can generate for others. The right's new order would make more people disposable, with little say over their working conditions let alone the trajectory of the nation.

The right's war on democracy manifests in various cruelties, like its feud with social programs that support the poor. This is most stark when attempts have been made to guarantee health care for those who can't afford it. Although it's difficult to imagine the United States without Medicare now, conservatives opposed the program when it was introduced. Medicare would open the gate to socialism, they claimed. "If you don't [stop Medicare] and I don't do it, one of these days you and I are going to spend our sunset years telling our children and our children's children what it once was like in America when men were free," Ronald Reagan said in 1961.[7]

A few years later, in 1964, Barry Goldwater imagined new horrors. "Having given our pensioners their medical care in kind, why not food baskets, why not public housing accommodations, why not vacation resorts, why not a ration of cigarettes for those who smoke and of beer for those who drink?" he asked.[8] Why not indeed? Give the people bread and roses, the socialist says. To liberals, that's a fantasy; to the right, that's a threat. The right's class loyalties lie with the rich, so its policies empower the wealthiest and immiserate the poor. Reagan's workfare program, which he inflicted on the people of California as their governor, had no success "in discouraging people from applying for welfare or in getting those already on the rolls to go off and find normal employment," wrote the *Washington Post* about a report from the state's Employment Development Department in 1981.[9]

As president he cut welfare and lowered taxes for the wealthy, and pushed poor families deeper into poverty.[10] If Reagan's goal was to reduce poverty, then by any objective measure he failed. If his goal was to reduce welfare, however, he succeeded—and this explains why he remains such a hero to the right. He entrenched a hierarchy that the right has always sought to protect, with the rich at the top and the disposable at the bottom. Because the system forces the disposable to take its evils upon themselves, they become a sacrifice, and it is through their suffering that others may experience true material security and, subsequently, true freedom.

A direct relationship exists between the right's war on welfare and its attacks on public health measures during the pandemic. Welfare and public health interventions offer egalitarian possibilities, a direct threat to the right. In response the right falls back onto rage, even conspiracism, to bind its coalition together.

To understand the right's reaction to COVID, look to its past. Though we may associate "crunchiness" with the left, there is a long history of medical skepticism and "crunchy" thinking on the right, and on the far right in particular, as the historian Kathleen Belew noted in a piece for the *Atlantic*.[11] "Consider Coeur d'Alene, Idaho, the home of the white-separatist compound Aryan Nations," which simultaneously appealed to "environmentally inclined leftists attracted to the scenic lakes and mountains," she added. "Scholars have spent ample time on other alliances between neighbors in this period—such as the way the white-power movement radicalized its rural neighbors affected by the farm crisis of the 1970s." Both groups can fixate upon "ideas of purity, an interest in survivalism, and a deep distrust of the government," albeit for different reasons, and water fluoridation emerged as a point of agreement. Some progressive environmentalists believed fluoride threatened human bodies and ecosystems alike. Libertarians opposed fluoridation on individual-rights grounds. To members of the John Birch Society, fluoride was a communist plot to poison red-blooded Americans. White nationalists consumed by thoughts of a coming race war "worried that fluoride would make people docile, such that revolution against the state and race war would be harder to accomplish," Belew wrote.

"I often think of the far right as the people who beta test talking points and moral panics, so they beta tested the fluoride thing," explains Seth Cotlar, a professor of history at Willamette University who has studied the right. That fringe antifluoridation message gained some traction, he adds. "When we talk about fluoride as this evil conspiracy to sap you of your bodily purity, people's ears perk up and they hear it. They respond to it, and they'll show up at city council meetings and get really angry about it. It becomes a way to just throw a monkey wrench in public interest governance, which is what these fascists are angry about." For the far right, antifluoridation also looked like a means to transcend the fringe and earn the mainstream consideration they otherwise lacked. "They learn that a very small number of very dedicated people, who show up with a barrage of what looks like scientific information, can pretty easily circumvent what feels like an emergent consensus, so they do it and they push it," he says.

The right's antifluoridation tactics capitalized upon the public's Cold War fear of communism. Many were openly anti-Semitic and white nationalist, eager for a way to popularize their racist ideals. Although activists were prone to overstate their influence, they were able to dissuade some locales from fluoridating water supplies despite the clear public health benefits of doing so. Matthew Dallek, a political historian at George Washington University and the author of Birchers: How the John Birch Society Radicalized the American Right,

sees echoes of old Bircher obsessions in today's conservative movement. In addition to the suspicion that communists would use fluoride to poison an unsuspecting American public, "there's a somewhat
milder version of it, which is basically that this is government trying
to control our lives." Birchers latched on to the belief that too much
fluoride would yellow the teeth as proof it was dangerous for human
consumption. "But again, they sort of latch onto this as the rhetoric of
'it's a choice.' It should be a choice in the same way maybe the vaccines should be a choice for small kids. And so that, I would say, has
been a significant through line in modern times," he adds. "You can
draw a line, I think, between the conspiracy theories about fluoride
and the vaccine and mask denialism." Dallek sees further echoes in
the Society's promotion of laetrile, an extract found in fruit seeds
such as apricot that could, proponents claimed, cure cancer. One
Birch Society leader, a urologist, prescribed the extract to a patient
with cancer, who later died; the family sued. "The reason I think this
story is relevant is that there are even doctors and dentists who are
supposedly scientists or people of science who engage in this kind of
public health denialism and conspiracy theories," Dallek says. "It's not
alternative medicine, it's really a denialism. It's not thinking about
yoga or meditation to calm anxiety, which is a legitimate field of
study, or psychedelics to treat depression. These are things that just
have no real basis in scientific reality." Though membership in the
John Birch Society would decline over the years, its conspiratorial
ideas persisted.

Beyond the John Birch Society, the right wing's commitment to
public health denialism goes back decades and even centuries. Dr.
David Gorski, a surgical oncologist who is the managing editor of the
website Science-Based Medicine, and who has monitored the anti-
vaccine movement for nearly two decades, tells me that there has

always been a rightward tilt to vaccine skepticism. At anti-vaccine protests in the 1800s, you'd hear familiar messages about the tyranny of vaccine mandates. Though there are "enclaves" of left-wing vaccine resistance in places like Marin County, California, he says, "beginning sometime around the rise of the Tea Party movement, I started noticing the shift. Even then, some of the most prominent anti-vaxxers were conservatives."

In 2007, the state of Texas offered a glimpse of alliances to come when a coalition of right-wing organizations and parents formed against then-governor Rick Perry, who'd issued an executive order requiring the Gardasil HPV vaccine for girls ages eleven and twelve. The vaccine, which was created by Merck, protects against some cancer-causing forms of HPV. Many conservative groups, particularly Christian right groups, went on the attack. To the Eagle Forum, Perry's order represented unforgivable governmental overreach—especially for a Republican politician. In one 2007 editorial, the late Phyllis Schlafly attacked Perry, citing reports that his reelection campaign had received $5,000 from Merck's political action committee.[12] Not only had Perry been bought, she insinuated, his order "would force the vaccine on good girls who don't engage in premarital sex and don't need the vaccine." (Bad girls would have to suffer.) Texas legislators overrode the executive order, but Perry defended his decision until a presidential campaign event in 2011, when he admitted he hadn't done his research.[13] "I always thought that it should have been the parents' choice," said Tonya Waite, the director of the East Texas Abstinence Program, in a 2011 interview with NPR.[14] "I was upset that there wasn't more time for me to get my facts together so that my schools and educators were comfortable, and we were all on the same page." Yet on the grassroots level, it was the right that attacked the Gardasil vaccine, using the language of parental rights and government overreach—slogans that would come to saturate the right wing's attacks on other vaccines and public health interventions.

Gorski also cites the example of former representative Dan Burton, an Indiana Republican and proponent of the debunked belief that a mercury-based preservative used in some medicines and vaccines contributed to a rise in autism. Before Burton's retirement in 2013, he "held at least 20 hearings examining the potential link between the two during three terms as chairman of the Oversight and Government Reform Committee and one as head of the panel's subcommittee on Human Rights and Wellness," his office told Roll Call in 2012.[15] Burton was a member of the Tea Party Caucus, a group that, nationally, started building alliances with anti-vaccine activists during its rise. "Around that time, maybe 2011, 2012, anti-vaxxers started appearing on Fox News. Not as regularly as they do now by any stretch of the imagination, but they did start to appear on Fox News with credulous interviews," Gorski says.

Within a few years, a legislative battle in California would "turbocharge" the anti-vaccine movement's shift to the right, he adds. In 2015, Jerry Brown, then the Democratic governor of California, signed SB 277 into law, which removed most nonmedical vaccine exemptions for schoolchildren.[16] "During the debate over that law and the passage of that law, the anti-vaxxers first got organized. Second, they really started harping on anti-government regulation: 'Government can't tell me what to do,' a government overreach theme which appealed to conservatives" even if they weren't yet anti-vaccination, Gorski explains. That attitude made conservatives sympathetic to conspiracy theories about public health. The longer conservatives stayed in that milieu, he says, the more they absorbed its pseudoscience and conspiratorial thinking. In time, they became true believers.

Likewise, as that fringe crept toward the center of the conservative movement and Republican Party, those conspiracists became valuable to the right's larger war. Eager foot soldiers, their paranoia could be directed not only against certain public health interventions but against government action in general.

Dorit Rubinstein Reiss, a professor of law at UC Law San Francisco, tells me that historically, the resistance to vaccines and vaccine mandates was not really partisan. SB 277 began to change that, she notes. "We've seen a growing partisan trend with anti-vaccine activists successfully tying opposition to vaccine mandates to the language of liberty," she explains. The year SB 277 passed in California, Donald Trump announced his candidacy for president, an unhappy coincidence that would have ramifications for the popularity of conspiracist thinking in the conservative movement. Trump ran alongside Republican primary candidates such as Senator Rand Paul of Kentucky, who'd long pandered to anti-vaccine and anti–public health sentiments on the right using the same language of personal liberty. Gorski also cites the growing influence of the parental rights movement, which gained energy during the Trump presidency over not just the subject of vaccines but over hysterias like the alleged teaching of critical race theory in public schools and "grooming" moral panics centered on the existence of LGBTQ teachers and trans student athletes. In 2019, when California attempted to pass a new law that would have made it more difficult for parents to exempt their children from vaccines on medical grounds, Gorski says far-right militias marched alongside anti-vaccine activists.

When the pandemic hit a year later, there had been "a marked shift to the right" in the anti-vaccine movement, Gorski adds, which Republican politicians embraced. As they promoted fear to their followers, "the anti-vaccine movement had pretty much fused with the anti–public health movement, which was pretty much a wholly owned subsidiary of a larger, more global populist right-wing movement," he explains. Anti-vaxxers, he added, "are like the dog that caught the car." Once they'd won over conservatives with their emphasis on freedom and parental rights, they found themselves "subsumed" into a larger movement where they were no longer in charge, he says.

Anti-vaxxers have become useful tools for the right, partly because they share tactics and goals. "Disaster capitalism and disaster spirituality rely, respectively, on an endless supply of items to commodify and minds to recruit," wrote Derek Beres, Matthew Remski, and Julian Walker in their book *Conspirituality: How New Age Conspiracy Theories Became a Health Threat.*[17] Beres, Remski, and Walker showed that the fusion of conspiratorial spirituality and right-wing politics promoted COVID denialism to millions. A member of the anti-vax fringe may cite a spiritual or medical rationale, but as they rail against an elite cabal, they can sound like any far-right congressman. These days, the congressman may welcome the help. Anti-vaxxers have done much of their work for them. Vaccines are the product of a top-down war on the common man, or so opponents claim. The right can then tap into the same language, the same fears, and disguise its pro-business loyalties. So Republicans raged against lockdowns, and following Trump, minimized the pandemic's destruction. Conservatives might argue they protected the public sphere from overzealous health officials. But by undermining public health measures in the face of a pandemic, they sacrificed the public to the virus, in the name of the business interests and their profits.

With time, conservative and libertarian think tanks professionalized the task of COVID minimization and, sometimes, outright denial. The libertarian American Institute for Economic Research organized the Great Barrington Declaration, an open letter named for the Massachusetts town where the institute is based. Signatories claimed that lockdown measures were "producing devastating effects on short and long-term public health" and that normal life should resume for most. As an alternative, it advocated for "focused protection," which would, it claimed, "allow those who are at minimal risk of death to live their lives normally to build up immunity to the virus through natural infection, while better protecting those who are at highest risk."[18] Released in October 2020, before vaccines had become available, the medical and scientific communities largely condemned the Declaration as dangerous pseudoscience, but it found sympathetic ears in the Trump White House.

The *New York Times* reported in October 2020 that two senior administration officials had cited the Great Barrington Declaration in a phone call. Trump's Health and Human Services secretary, Alex Azar, and COVID task force adviser Dr. Scott Atlas, also met[19] with Great Barrington Declaration signatories,[20] many of whom went on to found a new libertarian think tank, the Brownstone Institute for Social and Economic Research. The Declaration appears to have influenced the Trump administration's messaging on COVID. "We heard strong reinforcement of the Trump Administration's strategy of aggressively protecting the vulnerable while opening schools and the workplace," Azar tweeted.[21] Great Barrington signatories, including Dr. Martin Kulldorff, who later became senior scientific director at the Brownstone Institute, claimed they weren't pushing a "herd immunity" strategy. In an email to BuzzFeed News in October 2020, Kulldorff claimed that "we will reach herd immunity sooner or later, just as an airplane will reach the ground one way or another," and "The key is to minimize the number of death[s] until we reach herd immunity, and that is what the Great Barrington Declaration is about."[22] Experts disagreed. "Based on simple math and past experiences and outbreaks, and emerging evidence from this ongoing pandemic, this claim is quite honestly a fantasy," Dr. Ravina Kullar of the Infectious Diseases Society of America told BuzzFeed at the time.[23]

Though the Brownstone Institute and its spokespeople put forward an apolitical face, the group has deep ties to the organized right wing. The Brownstone Institute's principal founder, Jeffrey Tucker, is formerly the editorial director of the American Institute for Economic Research. Though he told MedPage Today that the think tank "in no way sponsored or backed Brownstone," it's hard to deny that the Declaration, and later the institute, put forward similar right-wing arguments that lacked scientific or medical support.[24] Members of the Brownstone Institute have become useful to right-wing politicians like Governor Ron DeSantis of Florida as they worked to restrict or end mask mandates: *Mother Jones* reported in 2022 that "almost all" the members of DeSantis's newly formed health advisory panel had ties to Brownstone.[25] Don't expect the DeSantis panel to tout vaccines or masks: the "benefits of widespread masking, evidence about how lockdown restrictions flattened the curve, and COVID vaccines' high efficacy rates are not readily accessible on the Brownstone website," MedPage Today observed.[26] To DeSantis, who has repeatedly cast doubt on the necessity and safety of COVID vaccines, Brownstone provides an authoritative cover for unscientific views.

As Brownstone partnered with the far-right DeSantis administration, it let slip another partisan trend as COVID minimizers make alliances with the right-wing. Prominent vaccine skeptic Robert F. Kennedy Jr. ran for president as a Democrat before he dropped out of the race and endorsed Trump. Gorski points out, "I can't distinguish him from the right-wing anti-vaxxers anymore." CBS News reporter Robert Costa tweeted that far-right Trump ally Steve Bannon had been "encouraging" Kennedy to run "for months," and thinks the candidate could be "a useful chaos agent" who could "help stoke anti-vax sentiment around the country."[27] Since Kennedy announced his run, he's made appearances on right-wing media outlets like Republican billionaire John Catsimatidis's *Cats Roundtable* podcast.

Dr. Vinay Prasad, a hematologist-oncologist who once wrote frequently for the Brownstone Institute, has described himself as a progressive. In his writings, however, he sounds exactly like the conservative public health skeptics Gorski describes. "Post-COVID we need to seriously talk about setting restrictions. But not on people," Prasad wrote in a 2022 piece for Brownstone.[28] He went on: "We need to place restrictions on public health and things done in the name of public health. We cannot allow individuals who are poor at weighing risk and benefit and uncertainty to coerce human beings, disproportionately the young and powerless (waiters/servers) to participate in interventions that have no data supporting them, for years on end."

Gorski believes that Prasad's turncoat qualities are becoming more common among COVID minimizers and anti-vaxxers alike, as the right offers them a public platform and lucrative professional opportunities. "He's parroting right-wing tropes about the pandemic and vaccines and likening public health intervention in late 2021 to incipient fascism," Gorski says. "There is this whole bunch of COVID minimizers and deniers and anti-vaxxers who claimed that they are or were left-wing or progressives who sure as hell do not sound like progressives or left-wing anymore and haven't for some time. And that's been a puzzling phenomenon to me."

The conservative movement has by now overtaken much of the anti-vax fringe. Since SB 277 passed in 2015, Reiss says that when states propose vaccine mandates, a partisan divide emerges. Opposition to vaccine mandates has, for years, also had the backing of some entities in the conservative legal movement, she observes. In 2016, Michigan nurse Tara Nikolao sued the director of the Michigan Department of Health and Human Services and several other state officials.[29] After nurses urged her to vaccinate her children, she claimed they violated her religious freedom rights. Beyond hearing a vocal plea, however, Nikolao suffered little injury. She sought, and received, a religious exemption from the state's vaccine mandate for school-age children. Representing Nikolao was the Thomas More Law Center, a right-wing Christian legal organization. (The courts rejected Nikolao's complaint.) After the pandemic began, the National Federation of Independent Business sued OSHA to stay a measure that employers with a workforce of at least one hundred people must require that workers receive the COVID vaccine, or wear a mask and subject themselves to weekly testing. The NFIB is conservative, Reiss points out: According to OpenSecrets.org, its PAC donated to Republican candidates over 98 percent of the time from 2021 to 2022.[30] The U.S. Supreme Court eventually sided with them and stayed the OSHA rule. "Similarly, the challenges to the other federal mandates were often brought by state attorneys general that were openly conservative, and I think they were very clear that they were doing it in part for conservative views," Reiss adds. The professor has also noticed a growing emphasis on religious freedom as activists claim public health measures infringe on their First Amendment rights. So claimed musician and minister Sean Feucht. As COVID killed thousands in 2020, Feucht drew crowds of devoted worshippers in cities across the nation. All believed themselves victims of a malicious anti-Christian conspiracy. "The church will not be silenced!" Feucht once tweeted.[31] Offline, reality was favorable to the right. In many states, exemptions allowed houses of worship to meet even during the height of the pandemic. Feucht himself faced no serious legal repercussions for his tour.

False as the right's claims may be, the movement's leading figures know how to spin a powerful tale. Fear is the glue that binds the movement together: the fear of threats from below, and the fear of lost power. To the right, the public sphere is a threat; democratically accountable institutions are the enemy. Considered superficially, there's no link between the right wing's opposition to basic public health interventions and its war on public education, but in both cases, the word "public" is a tell. A fixation on individual rights provides a thin disguise for anti-government views that can quickly veer conspiratorial, as it did when the right took on fluoridation. "The idea is, look, if people want to take fluoride, fine. Give your kid fluoride pills. But putting this in the water forces everybody to do it whether they want to do it or not," Cotlar says. Some far-right activists would try to wage a campaign against the polio vaccine, albeit with far less success.

Viewed from the right, democratic institutions intended to safeguard the public's good merit suspicion and, ultimately, control and destruction. The right's renewed obsession with parental rights thus reminds Dallek of the Birchers. "The arguments are basically identical," he says. Robert Welch, the society's founder, urged followers to "take the war to the communists in their communities, and one of the best ways to do that was to take over their local school boards." Welch, who was convinced that the United States, and indeed freedom itself, was threatened by secret communists embedded in the U.S. government, believed that public schools "were indoctrination camps, in a sense," Dallek explains. In one infamous case, the Birchers took issue with a public school teacher in Paradise, California, who'd taken students to a Quaker conference. By exposing students to different political views, to liberals as well as conservatives, the teacher sought balance. Such pedagogical methods infuriated the Birchers, who whipped up a harassment campaign against her. A committee in California investigated it, and the teacher was exonerated, but hounded out of her job, Dallek tells me. The Birchers had won.

The society faded from the spotlight, a casualty of its own internal divisions. But it is not dead yet. Though the American Conservative Union blacklisted the group from the Conservative Political Action Conference, better known as CPAC, in 2012, the Birchers reportedly had a booth at the event in 2023 and 2024. David Giordano, a field coordinator for the group, told the *Atlantic* in 2024 that Trump made the Birchers seem mainstream.[32] COVID, he added, woke him up further. "I've been a member since 1994. And I said to my wife, 'I wonder if this new world order will come in my lifetime,'" he said. When the pandemic struck, he decided that the "new world order" had indeed arrived. He has never been vaccinated, and refused to wear a mask. As conspiratorial fears of a new order spread, some on the right have begun to sour on democracy altogether. At CPAC the same year, Twitter troll and conspiracy theorist Jack Posobiec welcomed attendees with an alarming message. "Welcome to the end of democracy. We are here to overthrow it completely," he said. "We didn't get all the way there on Jan. 6, but we will endeavor to get rid of it."[33] He later claimed that he was being satirical. "We're not destroying all of democracy, just their [Democrats'] democracy," he said, which isn't much of a distinction.

The same year, *Texas Monthly* profiled billionaire oilman and Republican donor Tim Dunn, who purportedly believes that the right is locked in a holy war with "Marxists."[34] To Dunn, a conservative evangelical Christian, society should resemble a beehive. "When everybody does what they do best for the hive, it prospers," he told members of his Sunday school class. Too often, politics lacks the harmony of the hive, he said. People aren't serving where their gifts direct them. Dunn's is a fundamentally antidemocratic perspective, as the *New York Times*'s Jamelle Bouie later wrote in his newsletter.[35] Read within the context of Dunn's avowed Christian nationalism, the oilman's longing for the beehive is "the perspective of a man who does not believe in democratic freedom—a freedom rooted in political and social equality—as much as he believes in the freedom of the master, which is to say the freedom to rule and subordinate others," Bouie argued. Dunn's definition of freedom is "tyrannical" at heart, a vision of "overlapping hierarchies" shaped by the belief that there are natural masters and servants in the world. Dunn believes a person will "find freedom within your role, and nowhere else," Bouie wrote.

Dunn, Posobiec, and figures like them adhere to the same basic triad of conspiratorial thinking, anti-communist rhetoric, and a hostility toward public institutions. In practice that triad can feed a form of social Darwinism. Not every bee can be the queen, and worker drones must labor. In April 2020, Dunn coauthored a letter urging Trump to reopen the economy, though vaccines were not yet available. An "indefinite shutdown" would "steer the country toward socialism," he and his fellow writers claimed, and Americans should proceed as they individually saw fit.[36] "Let vulnerable populations continue to self-isolate with all the support their communities can provide," they wrote. "But also let our economic activities resume in order to restore business and consumer confidence quickly." Market demands took priority over COVID mitigation, no matter the human cost.

As Dunn fights with his pocketbook, conservative activists like Chaya Raichik of Libs of TikTok wage war on other fronts. The triad that compels Dunn is visible in Raichik's efforts, too. On her popular social media accounts, Raichik drums up constant outrage over the supposed excesses of trans and queer people, framing them as unique threats to the well-being of children and society itself. She's also indulged frequently in COVID denialism and has attacked efforts to mitigate the pandemic. On her Libs of TikTok account, Raichik has said that masks don't work and railed against lockdowns; on her personal Twitter, she has said that she would be "terrified" if she were vaccinated against COVID.[37]

Raichik's obsessions represent a coherent worldview. She, and conservatives like her, are hostile not just to science, or medicine, or education, but to the notion of secular communal life in the United States. "Secular" in this case does not mean atheistic but neutral, a society that welcomes religious Jews like Raichik alongside the LGBTQ people she so despises. Raichik and her allies oppose such egalitarianism. On a Tucker Carlson appearance where she first revealed her face, Raichik bragged of getting about a dozen teachers fired and referred to the LGBTQ community as "this cult." Raichik isn't interested in coexistence. Nor is Carlson. Nor are their allies. They seek the elimination of their enemies in a bid for total political control. As the groups they harass bid for equality, Raichik, Carlson, and other conservatives reassert a hierarchy with themselves at the top.

The conservative project can also be deadly to its adherents. A 2022 study published in *Health Affairs* found that "counties with a Republican majority had a greater share of COVID deaths through October 2021, relative to majority-Democratic counties," NBC News reported at the time.[38] A working paper from the National Bureau of Economic Research also found that excess deaths in Florida and Ohio were 76 percent higher among Republicans than Democrats. Conservative rhetoric and policy manifested in greater vaccine hesitancy among Republicans and a partisan reluctance to comply with mask mandates and other public health interventions, which may have contributed to the deaths.

Nevertheless, Republican politicians—and their supporters—appear increasingly committed to vaccine skepticism alongside COVID denialism, and the attitudes that cost Earla Dawn Dimitriadis her life are gaining strength. On Twitter, Representative Thomas Massie of Kentucky, a Republican, has called COVID vaccine mandates "immoral and unethical" and demanded an end to them.[39] Although Florida governor Ron DeSantis once endorsed vaccination, as the pandemic dragged on he said he wanted to ban all vaccine and mask mandates for the state's public schools, prohibit businesses from enforcing masking, and block employers from making hiring or firing decisions based on a person's vaccination status. DeSantis had signed a series of similar measures in 2021. As a Republican presidential candidate, DeSantis spoke often of COVID overreach and maintains ties to COVID denialists. The Florida Department of Health inspector general has investigated DeSantis's state surgeon general, Joseph Ladapo, for altering a report, which falsely claimed that the Pfizer and Moderna vaccines may increase the risk of cardiac-related deaths in young men.

Conservative agitprop could weaken public faith in vaccines, particularly within the movement's own base. A 2022 poll from KFF revealed that seven in ten adults thought that healthy children should be vaccinated for measles, mumps, and rubella before they can attend school. That's down from 82 percent who said the same in a 2019

Pew Research Center poll. "Among Republicans and Republican-leaning independents, there has been a 24 percentage-point increase in the share who hold this view," KFF noted.[40] COVID denialism is now a mainstream conservative position. DeSantis ran on it, and in January 2023, then-speaker Kevin McCarthy appointed Representative Marjorie Taylor Greene of Georgia to a House subcommittee investigating the U.S. government's response to COVID. Greene, a far-right Republican, is prone to various conspiracies. (In 2024, she also gave an interview to the *New American*, the Birchers' magazine.) Greene once speculated that a space laser controlled by a mysterious cabal ignited a wildfire in California—a conspiracy theory with clear anti-Semitic undertones. COVID conspiracies, then, are a natural fit for the congresswoman. Twitter suspended her personal account after she repeatedly violated its policies against COVID misinformation: she suggested that the virus was not dangerous, railed against vaccine mandates, and tweeted, falsely, about alleged deaths due to the COVID vaccine.[41] Now Greene is nearly mainstream. Twitter is now X, and it's owned by Elon Musk, himself a vaccine skeptic. Her account is back, and her position in Congress appears secure.

Vaccination rates in America remain high, and outbreaks of vaccine-preventable diseases can still occur in liberal areas.[42] Partisan politics can't explain everything about the return of measles, for example, or tell us why some parents are hesitant to vaccinate their children. Conspiratorial thinking is not limited to the right wing. There is evidence, though, that some conservatives are beginning to question vaccines and vaccine mandates alongside other commonsense public health measures. Officials in Union County, North Carolina, voted to ban water fluoridation after an activist with the conservative Moms for Liberty group falsely told them that the chemical lowered IQ.[43] As STAT reported in 2021, Republican opposition to vaccines, and specifically vaccine mandates, is growing among legislators.[44] One Idaho lawmaker "introduced a bill that would define vaccine mandates—of any kind—as a form of assault," the health news outlet reported. Another lawmaker, in Florida, has called for the state to review "all vaccine requirements," including those for polio, measles, mumps, and rubella. A partisan divide has even become apparent in public attitudes about the flu shot. Democrats are 24 to 25 points more likely than Republicans to get, or plan to get, the vaccine, according to two polls from Axios/Ipsos and KFF. In March 2024, the Republican-controlled New Hampshire House passed a bill that would lift a requirement that parents show proof of vaccination before enrolling their children in childcare. If the bill ever becomes law, childcare providers could no longer ensure that children are vaccinated against diseases like polio and measles.

Ideas may wax and wane and the fringe can exchange places with the center, but the right's lust for dominance remains the same. The goal is to protect an old order from progress, and to keep the disposable person in their place. The greatest harms of the pandemic have been borne by people on the margins, and the right wants to keep them there. Trump was merely an avatar of older ideas, and the right, including the Christian right, saw much in him that it recognized. "The key bulwark of faith-based Trumpism is the prosperity gospel— a movement rooted in Pentecostal preaching that holds that God directly dispenses divine favor in the capitalist marketplace to his steadfast believers," Chris Lehmann, the author of *The Money Cult: Capitalism, Christianity, and the Unmaking of the American Dream,* explained in an editorial for the *Washington Post.*[45] To adherents of the prosperity gospel, wealth is proof of a man's faith.

These views can inflict a body count, as the nation learned anew during COVID. Earla Dawn Dimitriadis was one such victim, and there are so many others that even the Biden administration has largely stopped commemorating them. Trump achieved a number of conservative goals during his time in office, but among the most consequential may have been to undermine public trust in the government during the worst pandemic of the last century. The liberal Biden has done little to repair the damage. "The fact that these deaths were politicized, there needs to be work done for healing for us because there's no trust in the government," Dimitriadis's daughter, Jennifer, says. "They allowed this to happen and they continue to. This is a policy choice, just like gun violence. These deaths continue to be preventable."

There can be no reckoning without accountability for the perpetrators. Blame Trump, certainly, but the score doesn't stop with him. The former president fit easily into a reactionary movement that is hostile to progress, beholden to wealth, and committed to the destruction of a democratic public sphere. Liberals speak, sometimes, of reasonable conservatives. The U.S. needs a strong Republican Party, Nancy Pelosi once said, meaning one not in thrall to extremism. A saner GOP would be a boon, but even Trump's conservative critics should reckon with their complicity in mass suffering. The movement's various factions may disagree on tactics or the finer points of policy. They may even disagree on vaccines or the necessity of a strong Centers for Disease Control and Prevention. They are aligned, however, on their larger political goals. A small government could not meet the country's public health needs during a pandemic.

Should conservatives get their way, the disposable are at further risk. People like Earla, who relied on others—and their commitment to the public good—to stay alive. The conservative project always served the demands of capital, not the needs of the disposable. Now the movement's recent turn against public health threatens them with fresh militancy. The results have already been deadly: for Earla, and for others whose names we might never know.

EIGHT

EXPOSING BEDROCK

Whether the target is public education or public health, an attack on a collective good is an attack on democratic life itself. Allies of an unrestrained free market take services that are lifelines to a disposable person and destroy them. The debris they leave behind is no use to the disposable or to anyone else. The public sphere shrinks along with the government and democracy looks more like a mirage. This is by design. In the life and the often-premature death of the disposable person, the effects of a hierarchy are visible. Wealthy and typically white, top households hoard most political power for themselves and exploit the classes beneath them. Capitalism isn't just universal: to these well-off white households it is natural, even easy. The disposable see and feel what they do not. Prosperity can be a door at the end of a hallway that lengthens with each step; the scenario is deeply unnatural. Freedom exists somewhere outside, in a world the disposable can glimpse but only sometimes touch. A racial hierarchy results.

At the bottom of this hierarchy there are working-class Black and Brown men and women, who contend with racism along with the exploitation of their labor. Condemned historically as welfare queens or worse, they watched their fortunes expand with the arrival of pandemic-era social democracy, only for Republicans and conservative Democrats to force a regression. They had even fewer allies after Republicans regained the House of Representatives in 2022. The war on big government is now a war on "wokeness," itself an assault on multiracial democracy. The *Washington Post* has charted the rising influence of former Trump aide Russ Vought, who circulated an influential budget proposal among Republicans in 2023.[1] America, Vought wrote in the proposal, "cannot be saved unless the current grip of woke and weaponized government is broken. That is the central and immediate threat facing the country—the one that all our statesmen must rise tall to vanquish." So cut Medicaid by $2 trillion, he suggested. Cut another $400 billion from food stamps. Cut the Labor Department in half. Unwoke government, as Vought would have it, is a government so small it only works for the wealthy. No one else could withstand the loss of Medicaid services, or food stamps. Vought and his allies would push the Black and Brown working class further away from prosperity, and this is no accident. There is a racial hierarchy to protect and preserve. Vought's use of "woke," a term the right has stolen from the Black vernacular, is one more insult.

Vought's America is petty and cruel. In that America, the disposable person has no place but in the shadows. Yet all men are created equal, or so we learn as children. Men wrote those words for themselves, not for women, or for the people they'd enslaved. In the centuries since, it has often been the work of the disposable to apply those words to himself: to insist upon his inclusion in our dreams of equality. The disposable person knows how brutal this country has been, can still be, and may become. Sometimes he sees, too, the potential for something greater. Nowhere is that clearer than in the life—and death—of Florcie Yves Chavannes Versailles.

Florcie was driven, her son, DJ Arsene Versailles, remembers. "Force of nature," he says, proudly. A "saint," even. Born in Haiti, she moved to America seeking new opportunities for herself and her family. She spent some time in Florida and New York City, but one city became her true home: Boston, where she went for a one-week vacation in 1967 and never left. There, she found new connections in the city's Haitian community and among like-minded people. Her community loved and respected her, DJ tells me. She wanted what was best for others, he adds, and "would go to the moon and back, as the expression goes."

To support herself, Florcie worked at Filene's Basement in the cosmetics section and spent her free time volunteering at Rosie's Place and Women's Lunch Place, two Boston-area women's shelters. She found meaning, too, in the struggle for affordable housing in gentrifying Boston. Her son speaks with pride of her "instrumental" role in the fight to build a mixed-income housing complex in her neighborhood. DJ said she met the famed Boston civil rights leader Mel King, and in time she became an activist in her own right. On the same site twenty years prior to the building's construction, hundreds of mostly Black residents had organized a sit-in to protest a planned parking garage. Their neighborhood didn't need more parking or luxury apartments, they argued, but rather housing they could afford.

Activists occupied the space for four days in tents and wooden shanties in a complex called Tent City.[2] The protest lingers in Boston's memory. Built in 1988, the housing complex that Florcie dreamed of still bears the name Tent City.

Their family of two lived in Tent City when DJ was a child, but their fortunes declined, and Tent City evicted them. They lived without a permanent home for years in the late nineties, relying heavily on extended family as well as the same shelters and food pantries where Florcie had once volunteered. When DJ was ready for college, the pair struggled to find him transportation to class. But they managed, and DJ now has a bachelor's degree in sociology. Yet times were still hard. As Florcie aged, she went repeatedly to the ICU, sometimes against her will. One event traumatized her for years.

Florcie and DJ had gone to a bank to withdraw funds to pay back rent. While there, Florcie began to feel ill. She went to the bathroom, and didn't come back out. She didn't feel well enough to leave. "Then the bank manager called for an emergency medical response and the police and paramedics showed up," DJ says. "And I remember it was quite the scene. The police were trying to arrest my mom for trespassing and were just oblivious and not concerned that it was a medical emergency that my mom was clearly in." According to DJ, part of her face "had slanted a little," perhaps evidence of a stroke. Florcie was confused, but she did know that she didn't want to go to the hospital. "There was a lot of thoughts and emotions running through me. It was just such a shock," DJ adds. "So one of the paramedics ended up sending my mom to the hospital against her will, even though she didn't want to. And I remember my mom was just so confused and upset and she was saying that she wanted to drop dead and she was upset with just how the police were treating her and the fact that she had to go to the hospital." A few days later, she suffered two cardiac arrests. Though she lived, her health had entered a steady decline, and she spent the last several years of her life in a succession of nursing homes in the Boston area. DJ believes she caught the virus in her last facility. "I know that she was tested for the virus twice and the first time it came back negative, and then the second time it came back positive. And I remember the nursing home didn't want to release the results of the findings to the family, which I don't know why that was," he remembers. "I remember she had stopped eating a week before she would end up passing. And I knew that wasn't good." She passed away a week later, at 1:15 a.m. on May 30, 2020. She was seventy-eight years old.

Losing his mom was a blow on its own. The manner of her death made matters even worse. "I didn't feel good about the care in the nursing home in 2020," DJ explains. He's spoken to the press in the past about the disparities his mother encountered toward the end of her life. He belongs to Marked by COVID and has called for a COVID-19 Remembrance Day in Massachusetts.[3] "I had mentioned how there were just certain facilities, certain nursing homes and certain ethnic backgrounds that were just getting better care than others," he says. "That was a big problem. And I felt like my mom certainly could have got a lot better care, top-level care, and that could have kept her alive a little longer, for sure." Some incidents stand out. "There were clothes that my mom had," he adds. "Some of them were brand-new dresses and somehow they went missing and were never found. And I don't know somehow if they got lost or if someone took them, if they got stolen somehow. But that was certainly disappointing because there was a lot of money that was paid for those dresses by my mom's sister. So that's one that comes to mind, that her belongings and clothes weren't protected." Another occurred on her birthday, when a staff member spoke harshly to his uncle on the phone. He felt they were more concerned with administrative affairs than the significance of the day to his mother. "Administrative items like Medicare, and making sure there's enough money in there, and then talking to us about whether to put my mom in hospice or not," he continues. At times, he asserts, it seemed like the doctors were ready to rush her into the grave. "Just wanting to just give up, throw in the towel, and they would say, 'Mom doesn't really have much of a quality of life. Why keep her alive? If she's declining, why not keep her comfortable until she goes?' And my family felt that she wanted to live and wanted to hang in there," he says. To help his mom, he acted as her power of attorney and health-care proxy, but he soon found it difficult to balance his responsibilities with his job. He decided to transfer both roles to his uncle, only to be disparaged by nursing home staff. "I remember I just was so frustrated and upset with the conversation that I had with them and I felt like their opinion was I wasn't a good son. And just the way that they were talking to me, it's certainly something I remember for sure," he tells me. He doesn't recall any of his mother's three nursing homes with particular fondness, and he lives, still, with questions. What if the bank hadn't called the police on his mother all those years ago? That wouldn't have happened if his mother had come from "a different ethnic background," he believes. "And then in 2020 with COVID, if there was just warning about how dangerous the virus was and if it was taken more seriously, then she would still be here today. So it's always a difficult thing to grasp, for sure," he says. "I feel that my mom should definitely still be alive and that I wasn't able to really say goodbye, either, and have that time with her. It was tough."

· · ·

Like so many before and after her, Florcie had come to America seeking opportunity. She made a family with DJ, whom she adopted at birth. She found meaning in a righteous fight. She also discovered a divided country.[4] There are real opportunities in America, but they are not equally distributed. A racial hierarchy persists, propped up by centuries of legal and social discrimination. Florcie's housing woes are a case in point. Boston was never subject to Jim Crow, but it is a highly segregated city nonetheless. "Of the country's 51 greater metropolitan areas with large Black populations, Boston ranks 15th for segregation," Catherine Elton reported for *Boston* magazine in 2020, the year Florcie died.[5] Elton added that as of the 2010 census, "the so-called index of dissimilarity for the racial distribution of Black and white people in Boston was 69, meaning that 69 percent of Bostonians would have to move somewhere else within the city for it to have an even racial distribution of Black and white people (any city with an index over 60 is considered highly segregated)." Blame public and private actors alike for segregation in Boston, and elsewhere. Though the New Deal expanded opportunity for many, it shut out many Black and Brown people from its reforms and thus denied the promise of a more equitable future. Housing is one such area. The Federal Housing Administration, created in 1934 by President Franklin Delano Roosevelt, did not insure mortgages in or near Black neighborhoods, a practice we now call redlining.[6] Color-coded maps ranked neighborhoods from most to least risky—and the "riskiest" neighborhoods usually happened to be mostly Black. By linking race to the notion of risk, the federal government did more than directly enforce segregation; it helped spread a discriminatory idea to the public, where it endures. Although the Fair Housing Act bans discrimination on the basis of race, it is still rampant: a 2021 working paper from the National Bureau of Economic Research found that property managers are less likely to respond to Black and Hispanic rental applicants.[7] In 2022, the real estate website Zillow reported that renters of color paid security deposits more often than white renters, and that, among those who paid a deposit, the median amount for renters of color was $750; white renters paid $600. Some landlords, Nikitra Bailey of the National Fair Housing Alliance told CBS News, still adhere to practices "rooted in this unfounded association between race and risk."[8] According to census data, Black Americans accounted for around 13 percent of the American population in 2019, but 40 percent of people experiencing homelessness are Black, said the U.S. Department of Housing and Urban Development's 2018 Annual Homeless Assessment Report.[9]

Florcie experienced an ugliness in her adopted country. As a Black woman, barriers helped prevent her from finding secure housing. Her troubles didn't end with shelter: she was much less likely to receive equal pay for equal work, and more likely to have a negative, even dangerous, encounter with the police. DJ's fears about the care she received in her nursing homes are based in evidence, too. Nursing homes with high numbers of Black and Hispanic residents were more likely to report one or more COVID deaths, KFF reported in 2020.[10] According to Justice in Aging, a nonprofit advocacy group for seniors, that's because Black seniors are more likely to live in subpar nursing homes. A 2018 study cited by the group found that "80% of Black patients were admitted to a subset of only 28% of the nursing facilities; similarly, 80% of Latino patients were admitted to 20% of the facilities." The care was typically not good. "Poor quality—as measured by rehospitalization rates, discharge-to-the-community rates, and Medicare star ratings—was more prevalent in facilities with higher percentages of Black residents, although 'associations between quality indicators in [Latino] majority facilities were more complex.'" Another report found that Black seniors were less likely to be admitted to high-quality nursing facilities, "and the disparities were not completely explained by financial and clinical status," according to Justice in Aging.[11] Because of her race and her class, Florcie was less likely to find humane care in her elder years.

The pandemic did not create the disparities that so oppressed Florcie. Rather, it expounded upon them. The same nation that denied her the right to a dignified life also denied her the right to a good death. The pain that the pandemic generated did not spread equally, to all; in the early months especially, it was borne disproportionately by people of color. "Everyone in the U.S. is at the mercy of the coronavirus; it doesn't discriminate by race or class or gender or age," wrote Patrice Peck in the *Atlantic*.[12] "And yet, from the very beginning of the pandemic, the virus has exposed and targeted all of the disparities that come along with being Black in America." "I think it is abundantly clear that this pandemic has had a disproportionate impact at almost every level on communities of color," says Dr. Rohan Khazanchi, an internal medicine and pediatrics physician in Boston and a health services researcher at Harvard University. "And this is not just seen in the case and death counts that we've observed throughout the pandemic, but it's also seen in the ripple effects, the economic effects, the impact on families, the impact on children, that are not just directly related to the virus itself, but really how it's reshaped our society over the last several years." Khazanchi tells me that he was particularly disturbed by the number of children who'd lost a caregiver to COVID. "The fact that that impact has fallen disproportionately on families of color tells me that these impacts are not just on the generation that's here with us now, but really it's going to be an intergenerational impact of children that are now growing up without a caregiver. I think that's just devastating," he explains. As of March 7, 2021, Black Americans had died of COVID at 1.4 times the rate of whites, according to the COVID Racial Data Tracker from the COVID Tracking Project and the Boston University Center for Antiracist Research.[13] Approximately 178 per 100,000 Black Americans had died of the virus by that date; so had 172 per 100,000 American Indian or Alaska Native people. In August 2022, KFF reported that according to age-standardized data, Native Hawaiian or Pacific Islander, Hispanic, and American Indian or Alaska Native people "are at about one and a half times greater risk of COVID-19 infection than White people," and "Black people are about twice as likely to die from COVID-19 as their White counterparts."[14] Start looking for the inequality, and before long, it becomes visible everywhere. A team of researchers at the University of Utah found that racial disparities in COVID deaths could be partly explained by the fact that Black Americans were more likely to work in high-risk "essential" positions during the pandemic.[15] Non-Hispanic Black workers "disproportionately occupied the top nine occupations that placed them at high risk for contracting COVID-19 and for potentially infecting their households," the researchers wrote. Their findings, they added, "confirmed our central hypothesis that COVID-19 mortality was highest among" non-Hispanic Blacks, compared to non-Hispanic whites, because non-Hispanic Blacks held "more essential-worker positions." They added, "Although our findings revealed state-specific occupational differences in states with denser" non-Hispanic Black populations, "they consistently showed that disparities" in non-Hispanic Black-white "mortality were high not only in COVID-19 hotspots but also nearly everywhere across the United States."

Those findings had implications for the push to reopen the United States. Reopen too early, and the risks may be borne by the very same people who'd suffered the greatest harms during the worst of the pandemic. "We suggest that policymakers must first recognize the economic harms that structural racism has caused for [non-Hispanic] Black families across the country," they said. But would anyone listen?

The disposable can and do speak. When they organize, they can even change the order of the world. They must organize because only through numbers can they penetrate a conspiracy of silence. The disposable person by definition fulfills a purpose, a niche, like an essential job during a pandemic. The people who depend on their labor, who require their marginalization, are thus motivated to ignore the danger the disposable are in. Politicians and business leaders eager to reopen the country pursued reckless policies in the name of profit, never caring for the disposable. In this way America behaved largely as it always had, risking the same populations it had always risked, reinforcing a social order that kept the disposable at the bottom. The resulting disparities clamor for recognition, and demand not just sympathy, but action. Had America been a freer and more equal place before the pandemic occurred, the disposable might have fared better, if such a class even continued to exist at all.

Throughout the pandemic, medical professionals have been in a unique position to see these disparities in action. Racism leaves a physical mark. "The first thing I'll just say is my view is that the root cause of racial disparities in COVID-19 is structural racism," says Khazanchi. "And I say that because I think we were set up for this to be a disproportionate pandemic. We had communities that already were struggling with access to basic resources, access to health care, and maybe had less trust in the health-care system. And so when you have something like a sweeping pandemic that is completely reshaping public policy and discourse almost overnight, it's understandable that some of these communities were going to be harder to reach." Not only did people of color often perform the most dangerous work during the pandemic, they suffered from long-standing inequities that exacted an extra toll as the virus took hold. At the Navajo Mountain Community Health Center in Navajo Mountain, Utah, nurse manager Revina Talker faces special challenges as she provides care to the rural local community. "All we have out here is housing, so there's tribal housing and individual homes. We don't have a gas station or a grocery store, or anything of that matter," she explains. "But the biggest town is Page, which has a Walmart, that's about an hour-and-a-half drive one way. So, there's other grocery stores there. So, hope you understand that we're really isolated out here. That's number one." By the time of our 2021 interview, she oversaw around a dozen staff members, who provide primary and urgent care services to the community. There's a lab, an X-ray machine, and a podiatrist that comes in once a month. Talker can't provide ultrasounds, and the nearest hospital facilities are an hour and a half to two hours away. "If there's anything urgent, either I need to call for an ambulance or fly them out. Anything traumatic needs to be flown out," she says. The isolation, she adds, means that "people have to travel a ways to go anywhere, to go shopping, to do anything. We take it for granted. Just simple banking, or you crave a fast food, is it worth driving an hour and a half to two hours to get it?" She tells me, "That's one major problem that we've had before the pandemic, the rural-ness of this area is definitely a challenge. So, getting people in and out for care, having people come to the clinic can be a challenge at times just because of the distance." Poverty and unemployment are high, she continues, and many homes lack electricity or indoor plumbing. Medical providers would tell people to wash their hands, and they'd ask, "'Okay, how am I going to do that? I have to haul it in.' They have these huge fifty-gallon tanks." She adds, "You have to have a good vehicle, a truck to haul that in, you have to go to the nearest place that you can get water from. So, those are challenges they had before COVID, and it was even more so after COVID."

After a March 2020 church revival in nearby Arizona, cases began to appear in Talker's rural community. Later that spring and into early summer, the Navajo Nation experienced a dangerous surge in cases. "I think that COVID, because families live together, it spread really fast on the reservation," she speculates. "And I think once people kind of understood that, they did adhere to that stay-at-home order by the tribal president and try to wear their mask and have hand sanitizers when they traveled." Preexisting disparities made the situation much more difficult, she adds. "The disparities of just basic stuff, like electricity and indoor plumbing," she says. "Not having to live with other family, but you have to here. And because they did, I mean, the exposure rate doubled and tripled. The fact that a lot of people had to lose their jobs because of COVID. We have a lot of people that work off the reservation. I know a lot of people, they weren't able to work. So, that I think had an impact." The area's isolation only compounded the dilemmas locals faced. "I have an employee that was telling me, and this really opened my eyes, she said because she helps take care of three families she travels to Page to get groceries. And when you go into Walmart, this was last summer, they limited how much food you'd get," she explains. "So, a package of ground beef was only allowed one per family. She was wanting to go to get for all three families, and she couldn't do that. I know they limited tissue, toilet paper. There were more limitations I saw on the border, we call them border towns, than you would see in the bigger cities. Like say when I went to Salt Lake or Provo, they had no limitations, which is interesting, right?"

Health disparities also made people more vulnerable to the virus. "The disparities are high rates of diabetes, hypertension, obesity that in and of itself makes it hard, too, because you already have a group of people who already have a lot of health problems and then you bring COVID in," she says. "And you're trying to explain to them not having a lot of medical literacy." There were bright moments, though, she goes on. "What I am impressed with the tribe and what I appreciate is that we have a lot of Navajo-speaking professionals," she said. "So, on radio and social media, Facebook, they would post videos in Navajo explaining COVID, explaining quarantining, wearing your masks. So, we did a lot of that early when this pandemic started, and they continue to do that. And I think that's helped quite a bit, trying to explain." Once vaccines were available, Talker and her staff worked hard to get them to locals in need. The *Salt Lake Tribune* reported in February 2021 that the remote clinic had helped make the area among the most vaccinated in the state. "Statistically, with their population, they're probably the most vaccinated community in Utah, or around there," Byron Clarke, the chief operations officer for Utah Navajo Health System, told the *Tribune*.[16]

In Navajo communities and other communities of color, the pandemic amplified old inequities and illustrated the extent of their reach. Inequity is so entrenched that it complicated important research during the pandemic, Khazanchi tells me, as communities of color were underrepresented. In an editorial for STAT, Khazanchi and coauthors Jennifer Tsai and Emily Laflamme observed that rampant data deficiencies marred the reporting of racial and ethnic disparities in COVID testing, diagnosis, disease severity, treatment, and vaccination. "A whopping 56% of confirmed COVID-19 infections were missing race and ethnicity when first reported in July 2020," they wrote. "In a systematic review published in 2021, researchers had to exclude one-fifth of cross-sectional studies looking at COVID-19 disparities because data on race/ethnicity was missing for more than 20% of cases."[17] This can amount to data genocide, a term they borrowed from the Urban Indian Health Institute. The absence of health surveillance data as it relates to Indigenous groups makes it difficult to perceive the true horror experienced by that community. "To miss this disproportionate impact in reporting, where some states were not even including Indigenous populations on their data dashboards or disaggregating their racial and ethnic data enough to actually represent the magnitude of disparities impacting Indigenous populations, we were completely missing that part of the story," Khazanchi says. Communities of color weren't just excluded from health surveillance data, either. "There were studies that were not ours that looked at the composition of clinical trials and did find that on average across the many COVID-19 therapeutic trials that were ongoing, it seemed like there was an underrepresentation of racial and ethnic minority groups in COVID-19 clinical trials," he explains. That's not a new problem, he adds. "Clinical trials in this country have had a long-standing problem with recruiting patients of color for a multitude of reasons, ranging from where those trials are housed all the way to how they're actually doing that interpersonal recruitment and building trust with the communities they're seeking to serve." A study he coauthored discovered that "geographically speaking, the clinical trial sites ended up not being close enough to our Indigenous communities and our rural communities." That wasn't all. "I think the other finding that's really pertinent about our study is Black and Hispanic populations on average live closer to clinical trial sites than other groups. So what that tells me is geographic access was not the problem," he says. "They're near our hospitals, but it's a matter of doing these other things like building trust, doing high-touch outreach instead of high-tech outreach, and so on and so forth to ensure that these new innovations, like clinical trials or, in our other study test, to treat with access to new antivirals, are really being delivered directly to these communities in a way that they can access them." When communities of color aren't included proportionally in clinical trials, he adds, it can be difficult to know that public health interventions work for everyone as intended. "And in order to do that, we need to have a diverse representation of populations across many different demographic characteristics," he explains. "It's not that I think people are biologically different based on their race, rather it's that I recognize people of color are facing a variety of other barriers to care and may have some aspects that are biologically different, either as a result of environmental influences or specific biological characteristics that have higher prevalence in particular demographic groups."

When researchers picked apart pandemic inequities, their findings had far-reaching implications for public health. LaShyra Nolen, who is the first Black woman to serve as the student council president of her Harvard Medical School class, worked on two papers that explored the extent to which health and racial disparities influenced COVID outcomes. The first, a literature review published in *Nature Reviews Neurology*, examined inequities in neurological care during the pandemic.[18] "And what we found was that because individuals were having challenges with some systemic inequities, such as proximity to a hospital and also having a primary care doctor or having neurological care connection in the first place, they then were not able to get adequate care" for COVID-19 or their neurological symptoms, Nolen says, adding, "I think the large summary of the piece is that if we don't address systemic inequities that exist in society, we're not going to be able to do things in a better way when we are in an emergency such as COVID because we don't have a good safety net, we don't have a good foundation, and it's really just going to exacerbate all of the issues that we've seen patients experiencing previously in terms of equity." The second paper, which was published[19] in *Nature Medicine*, focused on the long-term neurological consequences of COVID, for example in patients with symptoms of long COVID.

"The pervasive segregation of resources and power perpetuates structural barriers that limit our understanding of the true breadth of neurological problems associated with COVID-19," wrote Nolen and her coauthors. The inequities were profound. "Among people surveyed after discharge from 38 Michigan hospitals for the treatment of acute COVID-19, one in five had not received follow-up care within 60 days of hospital discharge, with 60% of the patients who received no care identifying as Black and 5% as Latino," they observed, citing an article previously published in the *Journal of Post-Acute and Long-Term Care Medicine*. "The same study showed that people of color who had COVID-19 were most likely to report lack of health insurance and moderate to severe financial effects, with the majority using up their savings and being unable to cover the cost of health-related supplies." Without access to adequate and consistent care, the neurological symptoms of COVID can linger without relief, and data can remain scarce.

To Nolen, the implications were clear. "I think that what it tells us is that we still have a lot more work to do," she tells me. "And I think that it also tells us that if we don't start to have race-conscious approaches to policy, then we're going to continue to see inequities that emerge among the lines of race. Or, for example, if you look at the disproportionate rates of COVID-19 deaths and also infections, you'll see that most of the individuals who got those infections identify as Black, Latino." The papers are evidence, she adds, that "tells us that we are not able to adequately reach those communities in a way that they're getting the care that they need, they're getting access to the medications that they need, or that they feel comfortable to get access to those things when it comes to the history of medical racism and how those individuals have been systemically left out or taken advantage of." The systematic exclusion of some populations from consistent and adequate medical care would eventually influence their decision-making processes regarding the vaccine. "I think that my challenge with saying that it was vaccine hesitancy is that it puts it on the individual rather than the system itself," Nolen argues. "This is something that I've had to grapple with and learn to conceptualize, but instead of thinking of it as mistrust among those who didn't want to get the vaccine, thinking about the trustworthiness of the medical institution. If the medical institution now wants individuals to go and get a vaccine, but still people are being mistreated when they come into the medical clinic or still there hasn't been a reckoning with medicine's history of racism, and then moving forward to figure out how they're then going to rectify and approach those things, I think naturally people are not going to trust getting something like a vaccine." Nolen points to the rarity of Black physicians as a contributing factor. "Only 5 percent of physicians identify as Black, but yet about 13 percent of the U.S. population is Black. So if you don't have providers who are racially concordant with those patients, then perhaps you won't get that benefit of 'Oh wow, this person looks like me, they're from my community. They understand some of the struggles that I have with recognizing the medical institution as being trustworthy,'" she explains.

Black Americans weren't alone in their mistrust of the government, says Juliet K. Choi, the chief executive officer and president of the Asian & Pacific Islander American Health Forum. "We work together in coalition with Black, Latino, Native American, and other community groups. The cultural relevancy is really, really important because it's overcoming the trust factor," she adds. "Can you trust what the government is telling you?" Historical crimes, like the internment of Japanese Americans during World War II, can linger in a community's collective memory. It's important, she tells me, to make "sure information is provided in a linguistically accessible way, in a culturally relevant way, but also that there are messengers who are trusted by the community. And certainly during the Trump administration, when you pretty much saw Caucasian male leaders as speakers, that's not going to bode well with communities of color." Information about the virus and, later, vaccinations wasn't always available in the languages spoken by Asian Americans, Pacific Islanders, and other communities of color. "What I have tried to do through my organization to walk the walk is when we have community tool kits. We actually invest the time and the dollars to provide these tool kits in over twenty-five Asian, Native Hawaiian, and Pacific Islander languages," she says.

Nolen founded the project We Got Us to encourage Black Americans to get the vaccine. She had the idea at home during a break from school. "I kept on seeing all of these media stories about Black folks being vaccine hesitant. I saw that the first person to get the vaccine in New York was a Black nurse, and they were kind of trying to use images of Black people as a way to get Black people to want to get the vaccine," she says in 2023. "But no one was really talking about forms of current everyday racism, why the medical institution might not be worthy of Black folks' trust. I thought if we think about that and the fact that there's a paucity of Black physicians, it was kind of setting up the situation where Black folks were going to be very disadvantaged." Once she secured funding for We Got Us from the American Board of Internal Medicine's foundation, she began reaching out to students in high school, college, and medical school. Together with the students, who came from marginalized backgrounds, Nolen hosted "empowerment sessions" for community groups, "where we would then go over the history of medical racism, how the vaccine was made, and then just create a safe space for people to ask any questions that they might have about the vaccine," she explains. "As things started to open up, we went from just doing the Empowerment Sessions for different community groups and organizations to doing in-person meet and greets with folks at farmers' markets, at community parades, different community events, and then also doing door-to-door knocking to try to get people vaccine appointments through collaboration we had with the Boston Public Health Commission." They conducted about thirty sessions in total and helped over one hundred people get vaccinated. "From the beginning, our pillars were first to empower through education. The second was to convey, not convince. So we always want to convey information about the vaccine, but we never set out to convince anyone to get the vaccine. Then the third was to put public health first," she continues. "That we knew that, at the end of the day, we needed to make sure that we were promoting the idea that public health infrastructure is what would've prevented a lot of these inequities."

Dr. Nicte Mejia Gonzalez, an associate professor of neurology at Massachusetts General Hospital and Harvard Medical School, not only collaborated with Nolen on her papers; as a physician, she witnesses the consequences of inequity up close. Because Mejia Gonzalez is fluent in Spanish, she joined the hospital's Spanish Language Care Group to translate and provide care during the pandemic. "It was humbling just to see, well beyond the language, the poverty and the marginalization," she tells me. She recalls one patient who reported severe insomnia. "As a neurologist, there's many reasons why people cannot sleep, but when I showed up, this person spoke Spanish, and they had tried all sorts of medications, they had tried all sorts of interventions that hadn't worked," she remembers. So she listened. "And it was just really heartbreaking because they had a younger child, their spouse was alone at home, and it was the very beginning of the pandemic," she says. "The baby didn't have diapers, their wife couldn't figure out how to go to the pharmacy and be safe, and the rent was coming due, they couldn't figure out how they were going to meet the rent. That was the reason he couldn't sleep." The medically indicated intervention, she adds, was to "get a social worker, let's try to figure out how to help his wife get diapers for the baby, let's figure out if they can get a letter so that when rent comes due, there's a way to help them navigate this."

She recalls another patient, a Spanish speaker in the ICU who'd been calling out for help, only to find that the staff member at the front desk could not understand her. "I think that the pandemic has added so many additional layers of trauma, of mental health needs, of socioeconomic needs," she explains. "The health-care system has never been okay, but it's, I think, hurting worse than ever." Another patient reported to the hospital with migraines; Mejia Gonzalez learned that she was homeless, living in a hotel with one young child and another young adult child who had cancer. "She and her kids hadn't had access to food for a week," she says, and that had caused the migraines. In her work, she sees broader lessons about health equity in the U.S., disparities the pandemic forced into the light. One study showed that Black people who suffered strokes in conjunction with acute COVID were twice as likely as non-Black people to die, she tells me. "When you try to tease out why, these patients had ended up at hospitals where there was no acute stroke care, or standards of care like thrombolytics, clot-busting medications, or interventional approaches to get the clot out through catheters," she adds. The place where a person receives care is determined, often, by factors like segregation. The pandemic was particularly difficult for the uninsured, who tend to be low-income and face greater barriers to health care. "I think if you ask me what prevents people from having insurance, my answer is structural racism in many ways. It's just the way that the system is created and perpetuated, where some people have access to resources, while others don't," she says. "And it's the rules that go through all sorts of decision-making by people with power who perpetuate not giving access." Go back to history, "and see how people came together and advocated for Medicare," she continues, many of them "health-care workers, nurses, and doctors marching really to create access to this program."

"I think it's in the power of our society, our country, to say, 'We've done something like Medicare and it didn't take decades,'" she adds. "We have the power to say, 'We will make Medicare better, and potentially expand it to everyone.'" Mejia Gonzalez is a member of Physicians for a National Health Program, and a supporter of single-payer health care. "I've been a proponent of single payer well before the pandemic, but it's really magnified and amplified disparities and inequity," she explains. Look at who is uninsured, she says, and you'll find that it's mostly people of color. "At the beginning of the pandemic, there was this whole movement across the country, an anti-racist movement that I think has fizzled away in many ways," she argues. "But I would say the pandemic was this moment, especially when it intersected with this anti-racist movement, where people actually opened their eyes and listened." She believes that was an opportunity: "We know that this system has been created in a way that benefits some and not others. We know that that system has always had inequity, but here's this broader inequity that we're all facing, and that affects all of us, even if you're not that person who got sick, even if you're not that person who lost the job. As a society, this will affect all of us for decades to come."

There can be solidarity across race and class lines. Solidarity is less vapid than pity and more potent than sympathy; it is conviction, the commitment to a shared struggle against common foes. No better future is possible without solidarity, yet where it exists, it is always under threat from the agents of racial hierarchy. The year 2020 was a time of revelation, not only for the pandemic but for the uprising that it produced. The murder of George Floyd by the Minneapolis police provoked a multiracial reckoning in the American streets—if little formal accountability. A jury convicted Derek Chauvin for the murder of Floyd. Nancy Pelosi kneeled in kente cloth. The police, meanwhile, greeted this multiracial movement with customary violence. Yet for a moment the streets promised new life amid mass death. The uprising had not occurred in isolation; in the broadest sense it followed centuries of assault and in a more immediate sense it followed painful governmental failures.

The CARES Act introduced a measure of belated relief, but as the product of bipartisan consensus it could only staunch the bleeding while it left the country's deeper wounds untouched. It is possible, the writer Tobi Haslett observed in *n+1*, that Floyd's murder "reverberated so painfully because, under the delirious conditions induced by the pandemic, whole sections of the middle class seemed to walk through the political looking glass."[20] Haslett added, "In an instant they were poorer and even more insecure, their noses bluntly rubbed in their disposability to capital. Left without a livelihood by callous fiat in a moment of crisis, they were treated to that peculiar mélange of state control and state neglect—the punitive abandonment that paints the lives of the Black poor."

The George Floyd uprising threatened America's violent racial hierarchy and at the same time exposed how powerful that hierarchy remains. Despite a climate of racial reckoning, communities of color endured disproportionate COVID harms that were centuries in the making. Choi, of the Asian & Pacific Islander American Health Forum, notes that laws targeting Asian immigrants date back to the 1700s. The combination of COVID and the openly racist and anti-immigrant Trump had a "double effect" if "you were a mixed status family or an individual who had immigration status issues," she adds. "While you were legally entitled to seek care, we had so many in our community who would not seek care out of fear of deportation." That's a "tragic situation," she says, and it further complicated the efforts of first responders and health-care providers. "It just creates an added snowball burden because health-care providers are looking to connect with folks where they can provide care, but they're frustrated because the undocumented individuals or mixed-status families will not step out to seek the care that they're entitled to." Some conservatives, including Trump, emphasized the national origins of COVID and contributed to a rise in anti-Asian bias and hate crimes. That, combined with Trump's immigration policies, led to a hostile environment for many Asian Americans. Choi explained that she heard from community members that it was difficult to get a vaccination appointment. "When they stepped out of their homes to go walk to their doctor's office or CVS or Walgreens or your grocery store, people were physically attacked because of the anti-Asian hate, literally physically attacked," she tells me. "Of course, that news spread like wildfire. Folks said, 'I know I should go get my COVID vaccination, but I'm not going to step out, out of fear of the physical violence.'" She adds that language barriers, anti-immigrant sentiment, and a lack of health insurance could also make it more difficult for Asian Americans to access vaccines. "For an immigrant, especially, whether you don't speak English well or if you are undocumented, that ended up being a very challenging transaction to navigate," she says. "We heard stories of harassment, of people being told, 'We're not going to give you your vaccination unless you provide proof of identification,' which the law of the land was you did not have to provide proof of identification." According to Choi, "Some providers will say, 'Well, if you can't give me your insurance card and I've got like two to three hundred people standing behind me, you're just going to have to step out of the line.' And nine and a half times out of ten, these individuals who are trying to navigate that with limited English-speaking abilities and their immigration status, I mean, you can guess what happened. They dropped their heads and they just walked away and they went home and they didn't get their vaccination." When a white man murdered eight spa workers, most of them Asian women, in 2021, "that really was just a culmination of COVID, the anti-immigrant agenda, the Asian as perpetual foreigner, and anti-Asian hate," Choi adds. Asian women contended not only with a long and brutal history of sexual fetishization; during the pandemic, they also faced the belief that they were vectors of disease. The murders—perpetrated by an evangelical Christian who blamed the workers for his "sexual addiction"—showed America's racial hierarchy at work once again.

As DJ mourns his mother, he blames that racial hierarchy for her death and dreams of better futures. "It's certainly heartbreaking and frustrating and you just ask yourself why that is and how it shouldn't be like that. The health-care system shouldn't be like that at all," DJ said. "That's not humane. That's not how we should be living. Everyone should be receiving the same and equal level of care across the board. That's definitely a problem. It was a problem during the pandemic, and still is." DJ knows that all too well. In 2023, I learned that his economic circumstances had further deteriorated. He'd launched a GoFundMe, and was facing eviction, again.

NINE

PROFIT OVER PEOPLE

Melissa Powers wants me to know that her mother, Deborah Smith, worked hard all her life. She was never without a job—sometimes two at once. But the jobs were never enough.

Melissa's father went to prison when she was ten, which left Deborah a single mother in Michigan. She'd grown up with a slight intellectual disability at a time when people with such diagnoses could expect little community support. Her daughter tells me she was sweet-natured, but she "could be naive in things," and had about the same maturity level as a teenager. If she had a teenager's naivety, she also had a teenager's energy and optimism, believing that everything would work out for her and her family as long as she tried for a better life.

After Melissa's father went to prison, Deborah started working at a grocery store as a stocker in the bulk foods section. She did temp work, factory work, whatever paid the bills. For a while, she worked at an envelope factory, and she'd return from her shifts with her hands cut up from the paper. She regularly drove forty-five minutes or an hour to work all night, then stayed up all day with her children. Somehow, she found time to take her children to the store or the occasional movie, though poverty often interfered: Deborah was unable to afford a reliable car, so she'd often walk forty-five minutes to the store to get some treat her children had requested. She applied for welfare programs to cover the rest, making sure her kids never went hungry. She mounded the family laundry onto a bicycle and biked it miles back and forth to the laundromat.

When Melissa was in middle and high school, the family moved twelve times in four years. They were frequently homeless, staying with whichever friend or relative could offer a bed or a couch. Once, they moved in with their mother's boyfriend: three generations in a small trailer. There was nowhere near enough room for all of them to sleep inside, though, so they made do at night with other structures on the property: a little outside camper, a barn, occasionally a tent.

When the latest junker car broke down or someone in the family got sick, Deborah wouldn't be able to get to work—and those absences generally meant the end of the job. Evictions were a fact of life. They had public housing for a time, but it was overrun with cockroaches, mice, and fleas. At night, on the other side of thin walls, Melissa could sometimes hear men beating women.

Such is the care America provides its disposable, who survive on the nation's scraps. From America's inception, wealth has flowed upward, whether from slave to master or from worker to boss. The disposable person stands in a chasm cut by centuries of movement. With great effort she can scale the walls: the victory of emancipation, and the gains won by the labor movement, have forced America to embody more of its self-professed democratic ideals. Yet those walls are still unacceptably high, and the disposable have far to reach before they know security. To get there, they must battle a political economy that sees them not as a people but as a site of extraction. When they are healthy, the system will siphon wealth from their labor. In sickness, their bodies are all that is left. Here at the end, the system sucks up its last profits until she is spent.

The hardworking Smith found happiness later in life, when she met Melissa's stepfather. Her daughter said the two were a good match. "They did so many fun things," she tells me.

At age sixty-four—though her living situation was finally stable, and her body was tired—Deborah was still working part-time at a local hotel, mostly just to have something to do, her daughter says. Even as the COVID drumbeat grew louder in the spring of 2020, she got out in the world to work.

On March 14, 2020, Deborah texted Melissa to tell her that she couldn't breathe. Powers sent her a link to information that could help her distinguish flu or allergy symptoms from COVID, and her mother told her that while she didn't have a fever, she was congested, and had trouble breathing. Though it was unclear if Smith's symptoms were due to COVID, they persisted, and gradually became worse. On March 23, she said she felt dizzy. She'd contacted a local outpatient clinic, but there were no appointments available until April, and on the phone, a clinic staff member had urged her to go to an emergency room instead. Smith balked, and with good reason. "They want me to go to emergency, I can't. It costs a lot more to go to the emergency," she told her daughter. Powers asked her how much the emergency room would cost. "And she said that they said it would cost $1,200, and they have to pay 80 percent of that because of their insurance," Powers remembers. "And that's if there's no tests or any procedures. That's strictly for the visit."

Smith couldn't afford it. So she grew weaker, until finally, on March 25, she decided an emergency room visit might be worth the expense. By then it was too late. "They admitted her immediately to the ICU," Powers says. "And I told her, 'I wish you had gone in sooner, money be damned, your life is more important.'" Smith apologized to her daughter. "And I said, 'I should have pushed you harder to go.' And she said it wasn't my fault. And I told her that she had to get better because too many people loved her," Powers tells me. A nurse called her, and told her that her mother had developed low blood pressure with bilateral pleural effusions and a heart arrhythmia. Soon the nurse would call again, with news that Powers did not expect. Smith had put out her hands, tried to stand up, and collapsed. She died of a heart attack, with suspected COVID on her death certificate. Powers is convinced that if her mother had felt like she could afford the emergency room, she might still be alive. "My stepdad thinks that he should have pushed her harder," she says. "And I mean, we all think that, but him, especially. He doesn't want it to come off like he was stingy or something."

Her stepdad wasn't stingy. Rather, her mother held back from seeking care. Years of struggle taught her that, in America, there are rules. Serious health care costs serious money, and even the middle class might someday need to choose between debt or death. A trip to the emergency room can cost thousands of dollars, and health insurance sometimes only covers so much. Smith wasn't the first American to die after deferring medical care, and without radical change, she also won't be the last. In March 2024, KFF reported that around a quarter of U.S. adults have delayed medical care in the last year because of the cost.[1] Their stories don't all end in death, but each is a study in justice denied. Vic, who asks to go by his first name to protect his identity, lost his grandfather to COVID. In life, the independent senior was reluctant to go to the doctor. "I could say it was because he was a much older Black man who grew up in the South. I could say it's because he didn't believe in going to the doctor unless you are dying," Vic says. "I could say it's because he didn't want to spend the money. He was notorious for buying things from the dollar store and walking to the ShopRite. And he had a car. He was very thrifty." For Vic's grandfather, medical care was just one expense among many, a thing to be avoided if possible. Vic would later find himself in a similar position for different reasons. The pandemic was difficult for him: not only did he lose his grandfather, he lost his job in customer service and his health insurance, too. "At the time, I was just so bitter. Just angry. It felt unfair," he says. "It was unfair that I was expected to put on a customer service face and act like you're going to get your package in three to five business days. Or, like, writing this bright, bubbly copy for this luxury product. It was unfair that I was expected to move over a weekend and still work while moving. They wouldn't give me the time off, and they're expecting me to not be burned out. And it's not fair that in the middle of a health crisis you can just let somebody go and there's no way for them to get access to any health care." Vic, who is trans, could no longer continue important transition care. Treatment for his eczema and joint pain was out of reach, and so was mental health care. "It was very depressing," Vic explains. At one low moment, Vic realized he needed to go to the hospital, but couldn't afford the cost. "In that moment, I was thinking both that I need to go to the hospital, I know I do, but I can't afford thousands of dollars in debt on top of what I'm already dealing with."

Kyle Paffhausen may be able to empathize. Though Paffhausen has health insurance and could afford surgery to repair a congenital heart defect, a trap awaited him. In addition to an internal defibrillator that would shock his heart back into a normal rhythm, he went home with a small box. The device had a button in the center and hooked up to Bluetooth, which in turn hooked up to the defibrillator located on the left side of his body. It came with a set of instructions. Every Monday, the box would blink blue. What happened next was simple enough: he had to press the button, and a far-away office would confirm the box was still working. If he experienced anything like an arrhythmia episode, he was to press the button again, and the same office would examine the signals they received to determine if anything was wrong with his heart.

But the box came with a catch. Paffhausen didn't know that, so he pushed the button every Monday. At first, there were no issues. Early on, after his heart fluttered, he pushed the button to send signals and called the twenty-four-hour on-call line. Then, about six months after his surgery, he received a statement in the mail for something called a device check. Only then did he learn that he'd generated the bill by pushing the button—the same button he'd been told to push as part of his regular care. "I said, okay, at that point, I still am obviously worried about my heart's health and I obviously want to be as safe as can be," he says. So he kept pushing it until he received a bill and realized he'd have to pay around $300 for so-called "quarterly check-ins." For a while, Paffhausen felt the expense was worth his peace of mind. "So this was done in November of 2020, and I think it was probably sometime this spring or early summer where financially it did not make sense," he explains in 2022. The button was too expensive, and so he disconnected the box. Now it sits in his basement, untouched. The defibrillator will still work, but Paffhauser has lost access to the on-call line. "My fear at this point is I don't have any way of telling the doctor himself, outside of me just calling 911," he tells me. He believes that the expense of a potential ambulance ride for a potential heart episode might be cheaper than the quarterly check-ins and payments associated with the device and its button. "It seems crazy for me to think this way," he says, but his expenses have become intolerable. Once he paid the bill for his surgery, and the anesthesia, and all the other costs associated with such a major operation, the recurring expenses caused by a single button had pushed him over the edge into financial insecurity. "We're not wealthy. We are very distinctly middle-class," he says. "A middle-class family was thrown into something that most people don't ever fathom having to deal with. And it was an unimaginable burden in terms of financial and emotional strife."

Medical expenses impose dual burdens on a household or individual. Not only can they exact a serious financial toll; they often inflict psychological stress. The combination sets a potentially disastrous process in motion. Because the American health-care system is driven by profit, it generates conditions that may cause a person to fall into insecurity or even outright poverty. The line that separates a middle-class life from that of the disposable can look especially thin with the arrival of a large medical bill or significant medical debt.

E.L., who asks to go by her initials only, can recall a "bodily relief" when she traveled to the UK on a student visa and could use the NHS, just as I once did. "We didn't have tons of money growing up. My dad was a special ed teacher and my mom worked in a warehouse," she explains. "This idea that you could get a bill out of nowhere that would put you in bankruptcy or make it impossible for you to live in a kind of normal way, meaning to not have to worry about going to a grocery store, that was so sharp in my mind," she adds. When she left the U.S. for England, the knowledge that she would never be surprised by a massive medical bill made life "viable." Nevertheless, old habits lingered. She says that at first she avoided the doctor, a legacy of her time in the U.S. "You just wait till things are bad and then you try to triage it," she continues. In the UK, she had to learn "a new way of thinking about health care because it wasn't something reserved for emergencies and rich people." In the U.S., she says, "poor people don't get to have dignity in health care. You just have to beg."

In addition to her time in the United Kingdom, E.L. spent a significant period of time elsewhere in Europe before returning to the U.S. to work for a campus of the University of Maine. Almost by luck, she chose a good health insurance plan that covered most of her needs, but her position ended during the first year of the pandemic and she lost her plan. She managed to get onto her partner's insurance, and says it wasn't as good. "I was having a chronic health issue, and I had to go to get ultrasounds. I would go because my fear of getting really sick was greater than my fear of paying the bill, or getting the bill and not being able to pay it," she tells me. "But every time I would go, I would just get sick to my stomach because I would be so anxious about what it was going to cost." One day she received a medical bill for $6,000 in a year when she'd made less than $14,000. She and her partner had moved from rural Maine to the more expensive city of Portland, where an apartment cost them $1,700 a month. Everything went to the landlord, and there was nothing left over to cover their health care. During the pandemic, she rationed her visits to the doctor because the bills cost too much money on top of insurance and rent.

Her partner had to ration health care, too, even though he suffered from terrible migraines that could derail his life once or twice per week. He was an adjunct professor, and he made just $6,000 a semester. A disposable person can be anywhere, even in the world of higher education; degrees are often no bulwark against the cold. "It just had to get to the point where he had ten migraines in a month, and an entire week with no sleep. And then we went to the ER," she says. At the same time, she watched her parents struggle with the costs of senior care. Her father had developed Lewy body dementia and Alzheimer's, and because of costs, her mother decided to care for him at home. Her parents lived in one level of the house; her brother, sister-in-law, and their child occupied another. "It was a decision about money, because there's just no way that my parents could pay for a nursing home. No way. And then there was also no way they could pay for a nursing home that would be staffed caringly enough," she adds. She and her partner have since relocated to Ireland for work. "As immigrants, we have to have private health insurance," she explains, but costs are more tightly regulated than they are in the U.S. Instead, they pay a certain amount per year, and their health-care costs are capped. The contrast with the U.S. remains jarring. "One of my mom's bills just for the anesthesiologist to check on her—not for the anesthetic, but just for the check from the guy beforehand—was $10,000. That was the part we were supposed to pay," she says. "My dad, I think he made $44,000 a year when he retired. How could you pay that?" Few can.

I, too, have put off health care I needed because of the cost, and so have members of my family. Though we were never quite destitute, our income fluctuated over the years and it was never very high. We survived because we lived in a low-cost area and because we cut expenses wherever we could. Health care became a luxury. Like Powers's stepfather, my parents weren't stingy, either; they merely faced a system that could break us without much effort. I recall watching my self-employed parents shop for health insurance, I recall learning what a "preexisting condition" was, and I recall knowing that my father had one, which was a problem. Later, I'd learn that I had one, too. My physical prognosis was good, but at the age of twenty-one my future still seemed dim, marked by symptoms I couldn't afford to treat and insurance plans that wouldn't cover my care.

Some light eventually broke through the gloom. With the passage of the Affordable Care Act, insurance companies could no longer refuse to insure people like me. The health-care exchanges made health insurance more accessible for many, and especially key to the cause of health justice is the law's expansion of Medicaid. When Virginia, our home state, finally voted to expand Medicaid, with the help of a few coalfield Republican legislators who crossed party lines, I felt relief at last. Medicaid expansion meant that my brother would have health care. At the time, I was the only person in my family to have health insurance through an employer. I watched from a slight distance as they balanced themselves on the edge of a knife. The wind could push them over into an abyss. My situation was more stable, but I knew that if I ever lost my job, I'd fall, too. Years later, that's still the case. I am entirely dependent on my employer for health insurance, so my ability to care for myself is bound up with my job. My future is not as dim as it once was, but I'm not at liberty, either. "The American health system, as it currently exists, functions as a form of social control, an engine of unfreedom," Hari Kunzru wrote in *Harper's* magazine.[2] "The truth is that Americans would be a great deal more free if they were liberated from the predations of a medical system that has become a parasite on the social body, extracting wealth and energy that could otherwise be directed toward human flourishing."

The Affordable Care Act reduced the ranks of the uninsured and kept people alive, but as my family learned, it's still possible to slip through the cracks in the law. As a market-based attempt at reform, the ACA was never that radical; it did not remove the profit motive from health care. Yet it, too, had enemies. The ACA provoked ludicrous hostility when first introduced: On her popular Facebook page, former Alaska governor and vice presidential candidate Sarah Palin accused President Obama of creating "death panels" to exterminate seniors and the sick. Palin's precise scenario never came to be, but the ex-governor hadn't quite invented the dynamic she allegedly feared. Death panels do exist. They predated the Affordable Care Act and survived its implementation. All countries ration health care to some extent, but the U.S. "is unique because of the complex, sometimes hidden, and frequently unintended ways it rations care," wrote Beatrix Hoffman in the introduction to her 2012 book, *Health Care for Some: Rights and Rationing in the United States Since 1930*.[3] The U.S. recognizes no universal right to health care, Hoffman observed; instead, it is only guaranteed for some groups, like veterans who are eligible to enroll in the VA system. Citing the scholar David Mechanic, Hoffman distinguished between explicit rationing, where official rules govern the distribution or denial of care, and implicit rationing, which is broader, and encompasses "different access to care" depending on a person's insurance status and ability to pay. Though Americans fear explicit rationing, the consequences of implicit rationing rarely make headlines, Hoffman wrote. That's beginning to change, due to public outcry and the rising popularity of proposals like Medicare for All. Though a mythology of personal liberty can obscure the extent to which the U.S. rations care, news outlets and some politicians are pulling back the veil. Reality is becoming difficult to ignore, although power lies, still, with the entities like private health insurance companies. Every day, insurance companies ration or deny care, and they don't yet fear the consequences of their actions. In 2023, the news website ProPublica obtained a damning recording: in it, a nurse employed by UnitedHealthcare told her colleague that a doctor under contract had decided that a patient's ulcerative colitis treatment was no longer necessary.[4] The colleague laughed. "I knew that was coming," he said.

Insurance officials can laugh. Patients cannot. They gather at kitchen tables around the country to weigh the terrible options some distant actuary allots them. Some, like Deborah Smith, deny themselves care with fatal consequences. Implicit rationing may not be as blunt as its more explicit counterpart, but it is just as brutal. The battle over health-care reform is thus a microcosm of a larger class war in the U.S.—and the disposable have few allies. Much of the Democratic Party appears unwilling to build on the ACA toward a more robust single-payer system. Republicans, meanwhile, once pledged to repeal and replace the ACA, with Donald Trump promising just such a fate for the law on the 2016 campaign trail. But public opinion was roughly divided on the ACA in 2016, and that was far from the popular revulsion the GOP counted on. With the American Health Care Act, proposed in 2017, Republicans intended to strike a major blow in the class war.[5] They planned to take $880 billion from Medicaid over the next decade by partially repealing the ACA and helping Trump fulfill a campaign promise, while also cutting taxes on the wealthy. Great news for the rich, but others, especially people with disabilities, would have gone without the services they needed to lead dignified lives. The bill also created a "back door" to permit discrimination against people with preexisting conditions, as Democratic advisers Gene B. Sperling and Michael Shapiro put it in a 2017 piece for the *Atlantic*, and it revived my old fears.[6] The law allowed insurers to offer so-called "skinny plans" that skimp on coverage to save on costs. For the able-bodied, these cheaper health-care plans can appear like a sound option (until something goes wrong), but people with preexisting conditions would have been forced into another, more expensive coverage pool. Insurance companies would profit at the expense of everyone else. Capitalism would have its due.

The AHCA was unpopular with the public at the time, and other versions of the bill failed in the Senate thanks in part to activists with disabilities, who put themselves at risk to oppose the bill. Members of ADAPT, a storied disability rights group, staged demonstrations across the nation and organized a die-in at then–Senate Majority Leader Mitch McConnell's office, only to face arrest.[7] Three Republican senators later crossed party lines to vote against the bill, killing it. Though the bill is dead, its legacy is instructive: Americans are caught between the Democratic Party, with its preference for incremental reform, and the Republican Party, which is even more deeply in thrall to capitalism. The window for change is narrow, and right now, it looks shut. Until it is forced open, through public pressure or shifting priorities in one of our major parties, people will continue to suffer. In 2021 a team of researchers found that Americans collectively hold over $140 billion in medical debt.[8] Debt loads were highest in states that did not expand Medicaid in 2014, as permitted by the Affordable Care Act, so debt is concentrated in the nation's poorest states, mostly in the South. The American health-care system, researchers observed, "leaves patients with high out-of-pocket costs" due to rising prices, increased cost-sharing, and a high number of individuals without health insurance.

• • •

The system isn't broken. Rather, it works precisely as designed, and profit, not care, is its priority. When Senator Bernie Sanders popularized Medicare for All during his first presidential run, he and his allies in Congress faced stiff resistance from hospital groups, pharmaceutical companies, and health insurance corporations. With progress blocked, when the pandemic struck the disposable had to contend with a hostile health-care system. As the pandemic welfare state withers, I fear any movement toward social democracy—let alone the democratic socialism of Senator Sanders—may falter. The future of health care looks uncertain, even as the events of the pandemic argue for substantial reform. The road to a single-payer system remains difficult, due largely to moneyed interests who profit from the health-care system as it is. UnitedHealthcare, for example, has no incentive to demand positive change as long as the law permits it to deny care at the expense of the collective good. Advocates for single-payer have to reckon, too, with public opinion, which can be divided on the subject of Medicare for All or reforms like it. Even so, there are clear signs of popular discontent with the system as it now works. In 2017, months after Clinton lost the presidential election to Donald Trump, the Pew Research Center reported that 60 percent of Americans believed the government "should be responsible for ensuring health care coverage for all Americans."[9] Two years later, as another presidential election dawned, a CNN poll found that 54 percent of Americans believe the government should institute a national health insurance program—even if it meant a tax hike.[10] Americans aren't quite ready to give up on private health insurance, the same poll showed. A national campaign for single-payer will have to change minds while it challenges powerful industries, which is a hard if necessary task. In doing so it will follow older civil rights movements that opposed rationing in health care as part of broader political projects.

Hoffman wrote that Black and Latino Americans, women's liberation activists, and members of the embattled middle class all helped formulate "a conception of the right to health care."[11] The fight to desegregate American hospitals and end discrimination in health care hinged partly on the notion that all human beings have a right to care; in a famous Chicago speech, Martin Luther King Jr. said, "Of all forms of discrimination and inequalities, injustice in health is the most shocking and inhuman. . . . It is more degrading than slums, because slums are a psychological death while inequality in health means a physical death."[12]

Leaders of the National Welfare Rights Organization—who were mostly women of color—"formed a Health Rights Committee early in 1970," Hoffman wrote.[13] The idea that the poor had a right to life-sustaining welfare was bound up with the conviction that the poor also had a right to health care, regardless of income status. Activists later sent the American Medical Association a list of demands, which they hoped the organization would incorporate into its Code of Ethics. The AMA should deem it unethical for any physician to refuse service to a Medicaid patient, they argued; furthermore, physicians should no longer "deny service on the basis of race, religion, ethnicity, or national origin" or "allow experimentation on poor patients that they would not allow on their own private patients," and they should not "deny poor patients the rights of privacy and dignity," Hoffman explained. They had one last request: that the AMA drop its long-held opposition to "National Compulsory Health Insurance."

The historian Premilla Nadasen has written that although women on welfare "didn't achieve everything they hoped to, their campaigns were a critical part of the push and pull of history: to reframe political debates, to think about what we value as a society, to demand more equitable and just social programs."[14] Nadasen added,

"The most powerful component of the welfare rights movement was the way in which poor women of color, battling social and economic exclusion, stood up and articulated their needs and desires." These activists belong to an organizing tradition that still carries deep meaning. Health care may be a right in the eyes of activists, or patients who need treatment, but the U.S. government has a long way to go before it fully agrees.

The Affordable Care Act softened the cruelty of the American health-care system, but it did not subvert the system itself. To the bill's defenders it is monumental legislation, and perhaps in some sense it is. As a patient with chronic illness I take its reforms seriously, but perhaps that says more about the low standards enforced by our political class than it does about the quality of the law. At its core the law further binds Americans to the market and to their employers, a form of mass labor discipline. To it we are not people first but rather consumers, and the distinction matters. The status of a person's bank account still determines the quantity and quality of care they receive, a fact that kept Deborah Smith out of an emergency room until an emergency room couldn't save her.

The nation's disposable know they can't count on the health-care system. That's to the clear detriment of the disposable person, but it also sets up a difficult situation for health-care providers, who must operate within an inhumane system. The emergency room has come to function as a social safety net in an era where few such safeguards exist. Within the hospital itself, providers confront not only the failures of the health-care system but the broader capitalist system of which it is a part. An occupational therapist, who asked to remain anonymous for professional reasons, struggled with proper protective gear at her rural hospital. "We had forty beds," she explains. "We ended up, because no one really knew how this virus was transmitted at that point, walking in full lead gowns and face shields and any kind of respirator we could find because we didn't have the equipment that bigger hospitals had." At the same time, she struggled with her own health-care costs. Advanced degrees have become an industry-wide expectation for people in her field, she tells me, which meant that many leave graduate school with high student loan debt. "You have these Medicare and Medicaid cuts, which are primarily providing funds for you as a therapist to be reimbursed," she adds. "So the money that you actually make coming out of school is very limited. In a lot of places, to save money, they are going to put you on an hourly schedule, and if you don't have a patient they send you home." She estimated that she made $1,300 per paycheck, as her health insurance siphoned $500 of her salary per month. Though that wasn't a poverty wage, she had little left over to cover whatever insurance did not. "I've had abscesses in my mouth and things that need to be taken care of medically that I've put off, and had infections," she says. An incident at work required stitches, which she couldn't afford. She had to ask family members for financial help. "The big emotion for me is hopelessness because I see this system from two different lenses, from a patient's perspective, as well as my own perspective," she continues. "I in some ways live some of those realities with them, and I sympathize with them. I think if it's bad for myself, how much worse is it for someone who maybe doesn't have the privilege of being able to go and get an education, or the privilege of being able to have some of the safety nets that I've had. And that is something that I struggle with."

The pandemic and its consequences argue for a transformation. The need to ration health care, or to avoid it altogether, was too common before the pandemic, and the consequences were just as potentially fatal. COVID merely raised the stakes. Melissa Powers will never know if her mother Deborah's death was preventable. What she does know is that her mother feared the cost of an emergency room visit more than she feared her own illness, and now she is gone. Smith's needless death is the product of a violent process in which capitalism triumphs over the human being. The U.S. spends more of its gross domestic product on health care than other similarly wealthy members of the Organisation for Economic Co-operation and Development, due partly to high prices for care.[15] Outcomes show little improvement compared to other countries, and by some metrics, like life expectancy, the picture is particularly grim: Americans die much sooner than residents of other wealthy nations. In 2021, the nonprofit Commonwealth Fund ranked the U.S. last of eleven nations in access to care. On affordability, the U.S. "has the poorest performance," the report noted.[16] "Compared to residents of the U.S., residents of the Netherlands, the U.K., Norway, and Germany are much less likely to report that their insurance denied payment of a claim or paid less than expected. Residents of these countries are also less likely to report difficulty in paying medical bills." In a different country where she didn't need to fear the cost of care when she most needed it, Deborah Smith might have lived. One 2022 research article published in *PNAS* estimated that a single-payer, universal health-care system like Medicare for All would have saved "about 212,000 lives" in 2020 alone.[17] Researchers also found that "$105.6 billion of medical expenses associated with COVID-19 hospitalization could have been averted by a single-payer universal healthcare system over the course of the pandemic." A single-payer system would not only be more humane, in crude economic terms it would be practical, too.

Capitalism is global, but some countries do more than others to rein it in. Though all countries had their health-care systems pushed to the brink by COVID, matters could have gone much differently in the U.S., argues Dr. Adam Gaffney, a pulmonary and critical care physician who is the past president of Physicians for a National Health Program. "In the United States, we have some of the most high-tech advanced health-care infrastructure of any country in the world. But at the same time, we have big disparities in that infrastructure," he says in a phone call. In disadvantaged areas, hospitals didn't have the resources to care for ill patients "even as other health systems that have far more resources and a generally more well-off clientele fared much better," he adds. "I think, in a better health-care system, we would have had more health care where it is needed and not necessarily where it is profitable." American health care is high-quality—if a person can afford it. If they don't, they can be denied care even when they need it the most. The access problem is widespread and it is the product of deep structural inequities: according to a 2020 study published in the journal *Health Affairs*, nearly half of the nation's lowest-income communities lacked ICU beds.[18] The same problem afflicts a mere 3 percent of our highest-income locales. Patients can suffer further from a lack of coordination, Gaffney explains. "So you saw doctors basically having to pick up the phone and call every single possible hospital, sometimes in the middle of a surge, to find a bed," he says. "I think other nations did do better in terms of setting up coordinated regional systems to know where the beds were available to move patients to where they were needed." Americans were also unhealthier than many other wealthy nations by the time the pandemic struck, he points out. "That is an indictment of our health-care system. It's also an indictment of our inequality and the injustice of a broader political economic system," he adds. "But in part, it relates to our health-care system not doing as good of a job as some other nations."

He believes our disjointed, for-profit system may have harmed vaccine outreach efforts. The U.S. got vaccines early and there were "extraordinary" efforts to get them to the public, he acknowledges. "But when you move beyond the initial vaccination campaign, and get into boosters and the bivalent updated boosters, a lot of this is falling on the traditional health-care infrastructure, and we're just not doing as good a job as other high-income nations," he explains. Though the vaccines were free, "having seen a physician regularly or having an ongoing relationship with a provider who can inform you of the need for a booster, or alleviate concerns, or even just provide it in the office, that can make a difference," he says, adding that many Americans don't have a relationship with a primary care provider. That's due partly to the fact that over 25 million people remain uninsured despite reforms like the Affordable Care Act. Because health insurance is so often linked to employment, job loss can also sever a person's relationship with a provider. "Those things are all connected with the way we finance health care, they're not accidental. That's what happens when you have the privatized and fragmented financing system that we have," he concludes.

Yet the system has its defenders, and they have deep pockets. The Partnership for America's Health Care Future, or PAHCF, is one example. An alliance of private hospitals, insurance companies, and other business interests, PAHCF exists to sabotage support of single-payer as well as any public option, which is a health insurance plan created by the government to compete with, and drive down the cost of, more expensive private offerings. A public option would exacerbate health-care worker shortages, they argue, and worsen existing disparities. There's little proof for such claims, and in its press releases PAHCF often cites research it paid for, so its evidence resembles an ouroboros. Despite the flaws in its efforts, PAHFC represents real money—and real power. Anyone who wants significant health-care reform in the U.S., whether it's Medicare for All or even a public option, will have to challenge these industries, and there's not much appetite to do so among the political class. Political cowardice is a common trait, and our COVID dead are the proof. For the first year of the pandemic, the ruling GOP served the very interests complicit in mass death. Their economic concerns defeated public health measures that could have saved lives. Trump's interventions were few, and temporary; he left the structure of the health-care system intact.

During COVID, America underperformed peer countries on major metrics, though "it was not an extreme outlier in terms of excess mortality," David Wallace-Wells observed in the *New York Times*.[19] A *JAMA* study published in 2022 found that the U.S. suffered "a higher infection-related and excess all-cause death toll" from COVID than did twenty other peer countries during the pandemic, according to CIDRAP News.[20] Our death toll may have been driven by low rates of vaccination in some states; meanwhile, states with higher rates of vaccination fared best. The overall picture is stark. "The US continued to experience significantly higher COVID-19 and excess all-cause mortality compared with peer countries during 2021 and early 2022, a difference accounting for 150,000 to 470,000 deaths," the researchers wrote. Many factors contribute to our high COVID death toll: we can attribute thousands of unnecessary deaths to state governments that did not maintain lockdown measures or prioritize vaccination. A right-wing media ecosystem spread fearful conspiracies to millions, which discouraged many from taking lifesaving precautions, but perhaps there's more than a conservative death cult at work. The profit motive in health care has no partisan affiliation, and its consequences are dire. When a health-care system prioritizes its bottom line over life, people suffer and some will not survive. The system was built on a lie: work hard enough, and that effort will pay off. The system and its defenders preach a fear of big government and wave toward personal liberty. Our choices dictate our fate, at least in this fantasy realm. Of course, fantasy has its attractions, and not even the disposable person is immune. The idea of America as a fundamentally fair and just place can be more seductive than the reality. Yet our health-care system is such that everyone who lacks true wealth can learn exactly how little America's promises can mean. In good health, Deborah Smith had a certain value to the free market. Her labor propped up a political economy that relied on her exploitation. When she fell ill, her life of hard work meant little to the health-care system, which was concerned not with her humanity but with her ability to pay. She was a dollar sign, and then she was dead.

The dead demand justice, but who will listen? Over a million gone and counting, but there is still little demand for change—at least on Capitol Hill. Americans themselves may be ready for a fairer system. In a 2022 Associated Press–NORC poll, 56 percent of Americans said that the U.S. handled health care poorly.[21] Seventy-four percent said that prescription drug costs were too high. Six out of ten Black and Hispanic adults said they were worried about access to health care, the AP reported, and women were more likely than men to worry about the same. People on the margins are restless. Though there's still no consensus on how the U.S. should fix the problems the public fears, the status quo is growing fragile. Cracks exist, and they are set to widen.

By December 2022, federal COVID funds had begun to run dry. The Biden administration had asked Congress for an additional

$9 billion, and as the *New York Times* reported, some funds would have covered COVID vaccinations and treatments for the uninsured. "We're back to the old ways," Michele Johnson, the executive director of the Tennessee Justice Center, informed the *Times*.[22] "People are going without vitally important services, and/or they're going into debt for the rest of their lives." Though millions may be ready to move on from the pandemic, the pandemic has not moved on from us. The risks it creates are still present, and so, too, are the holes it uncovered in the way we provide care. The federal government's interventions offered a brief sight of a different future. Even in America, with its disdain for the poor and its belief in the unfettered free market, lives can mean something. If we return to the old ways, we give way to death.

In America, excess death has become ordinary. Our health-care system is too often a slender lifeline in a time of crisis. Too fragmented and expensive to meet the needs of the many, the system reserves the best care only for those with the means to pay for it. For some others there's GoFundMe, but for most there's nothing. The safety net is too weak to catch us all. The dogma of personal responsibility poisons health care in America, and transforms even basic care into luxuries. Our broken health-care system is no impediment to national wealth, we can see that much clearly; America is a rich country. Equality is another matter. Not only does our health-care system contribute to inequality, industry opposition to health-care reform reflects a ruling class commitment to maintaining inequality at all costs. Before COVID, transformative health-care reform had few champions among the powerful. Politicians like Sanders and Representative Pramila Jayapal of Washington have helped keep Medicare for All alive as an idea, but although they have committed supporters, these voters haven't yet coalesced into a mass movement. There's still time, though, for COVID to change that. For unnecessary death to feel extraordinary, for outrage to generate real change. "There's too many people out there that are having these problems like I am," the occupational therapist says. "It's just a matter of time before something gives."

TEN

FALLING OFF THE FINAL RUNG

Milton Perez was living in a Brooklyn men's shelter when he first learned of the new viral threat. "Of course, because of the population, phones and Wi-Fi and things of that nature are not always available," explains Perez, who is an activist with VOCAL-NY, a grassroots membership organization for low-income New Yorkers. The men looked out for each other, though. They'd lend each other their hot spots. Sometimes they'd show the older men among them how to use a phone. And they had questions, lots of them, as COVID tightened its grip on the city. "There are older gentlemen who are grandfathers and such, and who are very close with their family," he says. "So the initial days of the pandemic before the shutdown, you have people who visit their families on a regular basis and we start hearing that somebody's daughter or so became positive, and people are concerned."

Men began to sleep completely covered up, "like mummies," he remembers, but says his claustrophobia prevented him from doing the same. The shelter offered them little information, so they kept their wary eyes open and they waited. For the virus, for more news, for a move out of the shelter. A supervisor went into quarantine, then staff members arrived in his dorm, dressed for a cleanup. A maintenance worker who often looked out for the residents later told Perez that someone had tested positive. "But they're not telling us anything directly," he tells me. To Perez, staff decisions seemed arbitrary and even callous. They decided to spray the dorm down a different day, but the men had already packed their belongings and couldn't get to things they needed. "They packed up whatever drugs, whether mental or physical, that they need. Somebody says, 'I need my heart medicine, I need diabetes medicine,' those type of things," he explains. Staff tossed their bags into a stairwell; Perez managed to remove his belongings and place them in a shower that wasn't working. "So people are grabbing other people's property. Some people might have an issue with this," he says. "Bags are being ripped open mistakenly." The next day, when they returned to their dorm, they could still see the residue from whatever staff had sprayed in the room. Perez eventually learned that staff had never removed the sick man's property or cleaned the area where he lived. At the time, he points out, nobody knew that the virus poses little threat on surfaces. "Everybody freaked out when we realized some of the bags that were ripped open, that we were handling, was the guy's property," he adds.

Eventually staff put up signs with information about the virus and how to social distance. "But when we brought that up in the dorm, one of the guys said the first sign was put up as something that he looked up and downloaded and insisted that they put up," he says. Residents exercised whatever agency they could inside a system they didn't control. "The whole initial part of the pandemic there was very little communication, most of it was initiated by us," he asserts. The flyers didn't accomplish much, he adds; the type was so small that older residents struggled to read them. Life in the shelter became stricter, and the few small pleasures they enjoyed disappeared. Staff banned residents from ordering pizza to the dorm. "I used to get a large iced tea and drink it throughout the day. All of a sudden we couldn't do that," he remembers. Outside, people stockpiled goods. "It just began to get to people that they entrust our safety into the hands of people that truly do not care about us," he explains. "Their main concern is their paycheck and to do as little as possible for that paycheck, and the pettiness and the overall attitude was in full display." Residents eventually moved into a hotel, which Perez described as an improvement over the shelter, and some men believed they might soon acquire more permanent housing. Yet the hotel presented its own indignities. At first residents could even bring food back to the hotel: canned items, or anything that could be cooked in microwaves, but the rules once again tightened over time. A security guard once blocked Perez from returning to the hotel with hot dogs and a bag of cooked shrimp, which both insulted him and cost him precious money. The specter of death was never very far removed from him, either. "One time I'm coming back from work and saw this huge black truck, and somebody told me, 'Oh, that's an emergency type of hearse thing that the city has that looks something out of G.I. Joe,'" he says. The deaths weren't all from COVID, but each reminded him of his own precarity.

Perez has since moved into an apartment, but he remains angry with the system and the city that oversees it. City officials and "their copartners in these so-called nonprofits" like to congratulate themselves for their charitable work, he argues. "But you never hear a kind word being said about the clients or a positive note about us. We're not even mentioned." The omission rankles him. "If that's their attitude, what chance does somebody like myself have who was in the shelter, saying any type of complaints?" he asks.

By becoming an activist with VOCA-NYL, Perez has increased the likelihood that he will be heard. A slim chance is better than no chance at all. But the odds don't favor him, and he knows it. To be unhoused in New York City—or anywhere else—is to be outcast, subject to formal erasure and even violence. Under the administration of Mayor Bill de Blasio, sweeps of homeless encampments increased during the pandemic. The sweeps destroyed property, displaced human beings, and contradicted guidelines from the Centers for Disease Control and Prevention, as Gothamist reported at the time, but de Blasio had promises to keep.[1] At a May 2020 press conference, the mayor—who'd run as a progressive—said it was "unacceptable to have [a] single encampment anywhere in New York City," and the city's most vulnerable shouldered the weight of his pledge.[2] The open-air encampments were arguably safer than the crowded shelter system endured by Perez, though this didn't deter de Blasio or the NYPD. The sweeps not only continued but increased under Mayor Eric Adams, a former cop who has repeatedly targeted the unhoused for official abuse. "You can't put a band-aid on a cancerous sore," he said in February 2022, referring to homelessness.[3] "You must remove the cancer and start the healing process."

During Adams' tenure as mayor, he has often blamed the unhoused for all the problems he hasn't solved. They are responsible, he argues, for crime in the subway system, and he has promised to remove them. To accomplish this, he has deployed cops and mental health professionals with the power to involuntarily hospitalize anyone they consider dangerous—incarceration by another name. "No more just doing whatever you want," Adams said at a press conference in 2022.[4] "Those days are over. Swipe your MetroCard, ride the system, get off at your destination. That's what this administration is saying." He's less concerned with what happens to people after they're removed from the subway. The encampment sweeps similarly fail to place most people in the shelter system—a fate many don't even want.

To Adams, and people who think like him, an unhoused person isn't truly a person, but a problem to be fixed by any means. When the means turn violent, as they did in the 2023 killing of Jordan Neely, the comfortable make excuses. Neely was unhoused and struggled with severe mental health problems, and on an F train in May, he began shouting at passengers. He was hungry, he said, and he was ready to go to jail, or die. When an ex-marine named Daniel Penny stood up, walked over, and then choked him to death, nobody intervened. Some filmed. The resulting video provoked outrage among many and equivocation from others. Adams, in his earliest remarks, almost seemed to side with the killer. "This is what highlights what I've been saying throughout my administration," he said on CNN. "People who are dealing with mental health illness should get the help they need and not live on the train. And I'm going to continue to push on that." Online, others implied that Penny got what was coming to him, or defended Penny outright. "Maybe have a little humility before you tell a working class person that it is the human right of a mentally ill drug addicted person wearing no pants to scream in their face and wildly gesticulate at them every other day while they try to get to work so they can feed their kids," tweeted Batya Ungar-Sargon, an opinion editor at *Newsweek*.[5] Senator J. D. Vance of Ohio, who is also a marine veteran, claimed falsely that Neely had threatened passengers and emphasized the dead man's arrest record on Twitter. "I find the response to this story completely disgusting. Let's all gang up on the guy whose protective instinct kicked in, not the people who allow the mentally ill to harass bystanders," he tweeted.[6] Congressman Wesley Hunt, a Republican from Texas, tweeted that "New York should put a medal" on Penny.[7]

In each remark Jordan Neely is nameless: an example, a warning, a threat. But he had a name, and he was a person. A talented Michael Jackson impersonator, his mental health had reportedly declined after the 2007 murder of his mother.[8] By the time of his death he had indeed been arrested dozens of times for offenses that ranged from assault to fare beating and disorderly conduct. To those who would defend his killing, Neely's record is evidence of his criminality. The truth is more complex: Neely had needed help for decades. The city knew it, too. "Jordan was reportedly on the 'top 50' list, a city roster of homeless people considered to be most urgently in need of help," wrote journalist Wilfred Chan for the *Guardian*.[9] As a child Neely floated through the city's foster care system and dropped out of school. Had he possessed an advocate, he might have thrived, Kerry Moles of the Court Appointed Special Advocates of New York City told Chan. Neely had no one, and at twenty-one, he was discharged from foster care with a MetroCard to his name. He turned to the streets, the subway system, and the shelters, Chan added. Conditions inside the city's shelters are often poor, as Perez knows too well, and it can be difficult to access mental health care. Neely interacted, too, with the city's homeless mobile teams. Mobile crisis teams, assertive community treatment teams, and intensive mobile treatment teams are intended to get help to people like Neely. But they suffer from limitations that staff often can't control. ACT and IMT teams have wait lists for care that can be "hundreds of people long," Chan explained. Workers are underpaid, and the nature of their work means they can lose track of their clients. From there, Chan wrote, Neely hit "the system's bottom layer," or outright criminalization. Less than three months after Neely left a court-ordered intensive inpatient treatment center, Penny killed him.

Neely had most needed housing, Matt Kudish of NAMI-NYC told Chan. "Give people a safe place to lay their head, and supportive housing with wraparound services," he said. "If you start to meet those basic needs, then maybe—and there's no one easy answer to this stuff—but maybe all the rest would have started to fall in place over time." Neely contended with an underfunded, patchwork system of services overseen by officials that may have considered him to be subhuman.

Stereotypes perpetuated in the media and by politicians like Adams assume that unhoused people are lazy or a persistent danger to the public. The truth is far more complicated. A person's lack of shelter implies nothing about their employment status: many unhoused people work, and simply don't earn enough money to have a stable address. A person's housing status implies more about the policy priorities of their state or local municipality than their work ethic or supposed criminal nature. Unhoused people are also much more likely to become the victims of violent crime than they are to commit it.[10] Yet vagrancy laws place the unhoused in proximity to the criminal justice system, and bans on camping, panhandling, and loitering are designed to make it impossible for people without housing to exist in public. The National Law Center on Homelessness & Poverty reported in 2019 that, nationwide, "a person experiencing homelessness is up to 11 times more likely to be arrested than a housed person."[11] The cycle continues after a person is released from incarceration. A person who has been incarcerated once is seven times more likely to be unhoused, the Prison Policy Initiative reported, and that rate almost doubles for a person who has been incarcerated more than once.[12]

People of color are not only disproportionately likely to be unhoused; they are also more likely than whites to be arrested and incarcerated. Death visits them frequently, and that was true before COVID. A person who is unhoused can expect to live forty-eight years, on average.[13] Chris Wildeman, a Duke University sociology professor, told NPR in 2023 that the average American life expectancy may be falling in part due to conditions in prisons. "It's a health strain on the population," he said.[14] "The worse the prison conditions, the more likely it is incarceration can be tied to excess mortality." Even proximity to incarceration can take years off a person's lifespan. One study published in 2021 by a team of researchers from the University of California–Los Angeles, University of Massachusetts–Amherst, Yale School of Medicine, University of Cincinnati College of Medicine, Duke University, and Washington University in St. Louis found that people with an incarcerated or formerly incarcerated family member have lives that are 2.6 years shorter on average.[15]

"If race has no essence, racism does," the scholar and prison abolitionist Ruth Wilson Gilmore wrote in her essay "Fatal Couplings of Power and Difference: Notes on Racism and Geography." "Racism is singular because, whatever its place-based particularities, its practitioners exploit and renew *fatal* power-difference couplings. Fatalities—premature deaths—are not simply an objective function of any kind of power differential. . . . Rather, the application of violence—the cause of premature deaths—produces political power in a vicious cycle."[16] Death is not an accidental by-product of racism, or of the laws that prop it up. Death is the manner through which power maintains itself.

In the lives of unhoused and incarcerated people, America's

hostility toward its surplus populations is undeniably clear. Members of both groups learn daily what it is to be outcast and disposable. Stripped of their dignity by administrators, staff, and public officials, they carve out lives on the edges of things. Nobody can truly wrest their humanity from them, but people try to do so all the time. When Eric Adams refers to homelessness—and by extension, people who experience it—as a "cancerous sore," he merely says what many already believe. When a person dies behind bars, the system is working as designed. The unhoused and the incarcerated both represent cheap labor and sources of profit. Perez was right to be skeptical of nonprofit officials: a 2021 *New York Times* investigation uncovered widespread self-dealing and financial abuses among the nonprofits that administer homeless services in New York City.[17] The disposable thus learn to rely on each other for aid. The encampments destroyed by Adams and de Blasio are small worlds of their own, where neighbors look out for each other. Both groups confront widespread cruelty. Their experiences before and during COVID are a testament to inhumane policy priorities that deprive people of the services they most need to survive. Rather than provide shelter or health care to people who need it, American public officials throw those same people out into the cold. On the streets, in a shelter, in a cage, he must scrape by on his own, or die.

The U.S. does not provide a universal basic income, or universal health care, or even guarantee a right to housing, but it does incarcerate. The U.S. is home to over 20 percent of the world's incarcerated population, the ACLU has reported, making it a dubious leader among developed nations.[18] Our incarcerated population has grown by 500 percent since 1970, and in 2023, federal, state, local, and tribal systems caged nearly 2 million people in the United States alone.[19] That number doesn't fully represent the number of Americans forced to interact with prisons or jails. People went to jail "almost 7 million times" in 2021 alone, the Prison Policy Initiative said in a report.[20] During the pandemic, the advocacy group said that American jails "were particularly ill-prepared to respond to the pandemic."[21] People pass in and out of them, which creates a "significant" risk to communities inside and outside the jail walls, and though reduced admissions meant that jails, like prisons, "saw an initial decline in their populations," that didn't last long. Populations returned to pre-pandemic levels as the virus continued to ravage the country. When the virus reached Rikers Island in New York City, in 2020, it quickly engulfed the jails. People incarcerated there told CNN in May 2020 that they used do-rags and T-shirts to cover their faces: the Department of Corrections only began to provide masks and cleaning supplies in April, weeks after New York City reported its first case of COVID.[22] Though officials insisted that no one in custody was forced to reuse masks, advocates said otherwise. "Communication with those inside the walls makes it obvious that these procedures are not the lived reality," Claudia Forrester, a jail services advocate with Brooklyn Defender Services, told CNN.

Nearly 88 percent of the people held on Rikers at the time were in pretrial detention, meaning they had not been convicted of a crime. They are nonetheless treated like human refuse—and some will die before they ever go to trial. Though the Department of Corrections had released more than 1,500 people from Rikers by September 2021, the population rebounded, in keeping with national trends, and rates of self-harm increased. Staff shortages due to COVID "slowed the basic functions of Rikers to a crawl," the New York Times reported, "starting with the intake process, where people normally spend less than 24 hours receiving clothes, undergoing medical checkups and being assigned to housing units."[23] The process stretched out over days, sometimes weeks, the *Times* added, which meant that people sometimes went without beds. People began to die, often by suicide. Fifteen people died at or shortly after leaving Rikers in 2021 alone, *New York* magazine reported.[24] Their deaths—most by suicide, overdose, or COVID—were preventable tragedies in a system that didn't view them as such. In conditions this dire, COVID would exact a devastating toll.

Wanda Bertram, a spokesperson for the Prison Policy Initiative, tells me that people incarcerated in American jails and prisons during the pandemic had to contend, also, with a troubled health-care system. People who are incarcerated tend to have higher rates of chronic illness, the result partly of conditions inside, but also of the poverty many experienced before they were incarcerated. One PPI report found that 50 percent of people in state prisons lacked health insurance before they entered custody. Although people in jails and prisons often suffer from poor health, they can't get care without the approval of a corrections staffer. "There's also the problem that prisons and jails are not the environment that anyone really wants to work in, so they tend to get the doctors and the nurses that, for lack of a better way of putting it, nobody else wants," Bertram says. People can receive poor treatment, if they receive treatment at all, and they must also shoulder the costs of their care. Co-pays are "really small, like three dollars, but for somebody who's making pennies every day for their work, if anything at all, they're actually a burden, and they're designed to be a burden," she adds.

COVID thrived in such circumstances. Within the walls of America's extensive prison system, people learn, early, that their lives mean little to the powers that keep them caged. COVID did not alter that fundamental reality, despite official protestations. "Please take care of yourself," urged a superintendent's memo, slipped through the bars of Arthur Longworth's cell. "It's the beneficent framing of that last line that gets me," Longworth wrote in a dispatch for the Prison Journalism Project.[25] "When you're pushed through the gate into one of these places, you either find a way to survive, or you don't. The one thing you can count on in here is that no one is going to do it for you." At the time of Longworth's report, his prison, the Washington State Penitentiary, was under formal investigation for ten prisoner deaths. When a medical staff member failed to replace her gloves before sliding a new plastic sleeve onto her thermometer, he wrote that a free person might complain. He doesn't. "I've come to expect to be treated this way," he wrote.

The carceral system takes human beings and reduces them to disposable people. To administrators and officers, and to public officials brandishing tough-on-crime credentials, a person's humanity vanishes when handcuffs hit their wrists. Whether a person is incarcerated in a public or private prison, they are useful chiefly as labor, and their exploitation is ceaseless. The pandemic exacerbated the worst characteristics of this carceral system, and heightened the stakes for people behind bars. Sentenced to time, many faced death instead.

When the virus struck Seattle in January 2020, the news eventually reached Michael Linear, who is incarcerated inside the Washington Corrections Center in Shelton, Washington. At first, he said, he "downplayed" the virus in his mind. He didn't know how it spread, or how severe the symptoms could be; it loomed as a distant threat. Cases multiplied in the outside world, but within the walls of the WCC, prison staff said little at first, he tells me. They only warned Linear and others that programming might soon shut down. Then, in mid-January, more news: visits were over, and volunteers could no longer enter the prison. "Then we were like, 'Whoa, this is a little bit serious,'" he says. "That was the first words that we heard from custody in the administration."

In the crowded prison setting, the virus would spread quickly and potentially take lives. Linear needed protective equipment: at minimum a good mask and hand sanitizer. Instead, prison officials told them to make do with coffee filters and handkerchiefs, an anecdote confirmed by a spokesperson for the Washington State Department of Corrections. "In April of 2020 mandatory face coverings were required for all DOC staff and Incarcerated Individuals prior to any statewide requirements from Washington State per recommendations from the Centers for Disease Control," the spokesperson said in a written statement. "However, there was a nationwide shortage of face coverings and masks, and the goal was to quickly provide as effective of a solution as possible. This included facilities using the pattern for homemade face coverings provided by the CDC and sewing them for distribution to the population. The guidance issued in April 2020 for required face coverings was consistent with that of the CDC." The incarcerated men did receive hand sanitizer, the spokesperson added, "in supervised locations where soap and water were unavailable."

"That was our first form of protection," Linear remembers. The virus hadn't entered the prison yet, as far as he knew, so he tried not to worry. Things would be fine, he thought, as long as staff didn't bring COVID into the prison. "That was actually the wrong state of mind to have," he adds. "Because as we started to see how careless they were and nonchalant, I personally was like, well, if this is their move here, there's no way that we can be protected." Later he realized that coffee filters and handkerchiefs wouldn't protect him from COVID, and he became anxious, and "felt powerless." His safety depended partly on the actions of staff. If they didn't take precautions, inside and outside the prison, men like Linear would suffer.

Soon he heard the news he'd dreaded. A member of the WCC's kitchen staff had tested positive for COVID. (A spokesperson for the DOC said that the WCC confirmed its first staff case on March 29, 2020, and its first case among the incarcerated population nearly a month later on April 27.) The prison shut down, and testing revealed multiple positive cases. Linear alleges that although the staff member had exposed several incarcerated kitchen workers, prison administrators allowed the men to return to their units. "We went on complete lockdown," he says, and then he began to feel ill. He had pains all over his body, and grew nauseous and faint. "There was actually nobody to come check on us and tell us what was transpiring," he asserts. "It wasn't until a couple days later that staff came and we was just like, for one, we wanted answers." According to Linear, men refused to return to their units until staff told them more about the danger they all faced. A team of officers arrived, and threatened to mace the men, and forced them into dry cells that lacked toilets. Linear says they were left without bathrooms for hours and that people urinated into bottles, if they had any at hand. "People felt really hopeless," he tells me. When officers returned with medical staff, Linear says they told the men they were being moved into a gymnasium for quarantine.

"The place was really unsanitary," he continues. "That really bothered us." He estimates there were around a hundred men packed into the gymnasium, and staff wouldn't tell them if they'd tested positive for the virus. He says that he learned, later, that not everyone who'd been sent to the gymnasium had COVID, and the error had exposed them to a deadly virus. When Linear returned to his living unit, he discovered that the prison had shut down all programming save the work program. Men could still labor in so-called correctional industries, but that was all. Profit, he claims, "was all they cared about." Linear worked on the prison's hazmat team, so he shouldered unique risks. When someone became infected with COVID, workers, including Linear, would be sent out to clean their cell. "They would just send us in there with no gown, no face shield, and say, 'Hey, go do your job and be good at it,'" he remembers. "If you was too intimidated to go on the call because you didn't feel comfortable, they was actually taking away from your livelihood, your means of income as a result."

The first outbreak faded, only to be replaced by another. Real protective gear was still scarce. Linear says the absence of programming, the threat of illness, and the indignities of prison life all contributed to a sense of despair. Inside the walls of the WCC, the men's mental health began to decline. In 2023, when we spoke, the effects were still palpable. "One guy, it's an older Muslim brother, he just took all his medication one day," adds Linear, who is Muslim himself. "About six months ago. He just was like, 'Man, I got to get out of here, I'm tired of sitting in here.'" The man's actions shocked Linear, who knew him; he had seemed strong, mentally, and Linear calls him an example to the younger men. He began to question his own sanity. "It actually made me think, 'Man, am I messed up or am I convincing myself that I'm mentally disturbed?'" he asks.

Linear has been vocal about his concerns, a risk for anyone behind bars. He is a member of the Industrial Workers of the World's Incarcerated Workers Organizing Committee, and in 2021, he joined *Rush v. DOC*, a lawsuit filed by the Seattle-based Columbia Legal Services against the Washington Department of Corrections, the Washington State Department of Health, and Dr. Umair Shah, the state's health secretary.[26] The suit's goals were threefold: The Washington DOC should immediately make the COVID vaccine available to people in custody, provide accurate information about the vaccine, and prohibit unvaccinated staff from contact with people who are incarcerated, argued attorneys for the plaintiffs.[27] At the time of the lawsuit, the incarcerated population of Washington State suffered a COVID infection rate 8.5 times greater than that of the general population.[28]

Vaccines offered people who are incarcerated a new way to protect themselves from the virus, but in the declaration Linear filed with Columbia Legal Services, he described a chaotic vaccine rollout, and said that the prison did not have enough vaccine for everyone who wanted to receive it. He still believes the DOC was prioritizing people who had jobs within the prison: people who were profitable. A spokesperson said the DOC followed the CDC's guidance in determining who was eligible to receive vaccinations when they first became available in December 2020. "This was not a matter of the amount of doses, but a matter of following CDC guidelines on who should receive the vaccine," the spokesperson said. "This specific guidance was given to medical providers on prioritizing vaccine doses everywhere, not just in [the] prison setting."

Linear is not the only person to depict a dangerous situation behind bars. Journalist Jeffrey McKee reported that men in his Washington State prison didn't receive N95 masks until March 2022. Prisoners were first "issued a handkerchief, hair ties and a coffee filter to make a mask," he wrote in a piece for the Prison Journalism Project.[29] When a 2022 outbreak shut the prison down, conditions quickly degraded. "Because prisoners cook and serve the meals, clean the units, take out the trash, and wash the clothing and linen, none of this was getting done," he wrote. Trash piled up, and some men started flushing it down their toilets, which caused his to overflow with feces and garbage. Though he had symptoms of COVID, he said he faked the test "because I would rather die" from the virus "than spend one day in the hole."

During the pandemic, conditions in Washington State prisons resembled those in other states. In May 2020, an attorney told *Mother Jones* magazine that when his client, a man in an upstate New York prison, asked to keep one of the surgical masks he'd been tasked to sew, a correctional officer refused, and told him to tie his state-issued handkerchief around his face instead.[30] Incarcerated people in the state of New York had sewed at least 371,000 cloth masks for correctional officers and first responders by May, "while often being denied access to these same masks themselves," *Mother Jones* continued, and added that Washington, Linear's home state, had provided "face coverings that consist of bandannas, rubber bands, and coffee filters, plus a tutorial to assemble them." Although the Centers for Disease Control and Prevention said early that handkerchiefs could make adequate masks, the state-issued pieces of cloth that people who are incarcerated receive were often too small to protect anyone.

The pandemic made life harsher not only for people who are incarcerated, but for the people who love them, too. "Dealing with the Department of Corrections is never going to be a wonderful experience, no matter what, whether you are incarcerated or a visitor," says Aqirah Stanley, the deputy director of the New York–based Alliance of Families for Justice. Founded in 2016, AFJ provides legal and emotional support to the families of people who are incarcerated in the state of New York.[31] Stanley tells me that the organization has a "healing aspect," and facilitates retreats and events for family members along with the provision of legal support to families and to people who are incarcerated. "Those issues are usually stemming from acts of mistreatment, if they're not getting the proper medication, if they're not being treated properly, if they're being abused," Stanley explains. As the virus closed in on New York, the staff of AFJ were in a unique position to hear exactly how the state DOC would respond.

The world of the New York DOC "fluctuates within the bad," she adds; it's not a nurturing place. She describes it as "an environment of punishment, built on a punitive system designed originally to destroy the Black community, moving from slavery into this current carceral system to maintain a system of free labor as well as punishment." Stanley, a formerly incarcerated person who has a loved one in prison, tells me that when COVID struck, the New York DOC did little at first. "Schools were shutting down, places were saying no movement, and meanwhile, nothing was happening inside. There was no talk about it," she remembers. When the DOC did decide to take action, it was to shut down visitation.

Visits offered people behind bars a tenuous but important link to the lives they'd once led. When COVID arrived, the DOC severed that link altogether. "When the pressure became too much, and this is a very small window of time, they decided the way they were going to deal with it was they're going to shut down visits," Stanley says. People inside still didn't have the appropriate protective gear, and she adds that department officials "issued ridiculous directives" ordering people who are incarcerated to make masks from handkerchiefs. When a person inevitably got sick, staff "would immediately remove them from their cell, throw them into an empty cell on a created quarantine block or quarantine area with nothing. None of their belongings, sometimes no mattress, very sick," she says. Prison porters didn't have the same protective gear worn by frontline workers on the outside.

In minimum- and medium-security prison settings, people lived in crowded dormitories, adds Soffiyah Elijah, the founder and executive director of AFJ. There the virus could—and did—spread rapidly. "The increase of people getting sick in the dorm settings was even higher than in the maximum-security facilities because there was no way to isolate yourself from other people who are sick," she says. When people couldn't get masks, they tried to cover their faces with T-shirts—only to receive disciplinary tickets for doing so. When the DOC did issue masks, they were cloth. Disposable masks arrived later, and people would only receive two for the week. As in Washington State, programming got suspended. Idle time was already common in prison, Elijah explains, but the pandemic increased it. "People suffered severe behavioral health challenges from the isolation and no stimulation for days and days, weeks and months on end," she tells me. The psychological toll that Linear described, and felt, spread throughout America's vast incarcerated population.

The virus inflicted pain and suffering on the unhoused, too. Though a popular right-wing meme claimed the virus could not be real because the unhoused still lived, they faced dangerous realities during the height of the pandemic. According to data analyzed by the Coalition for the Homeless, the age-adjusted COVID mortality rate for people in New York City's shelter system was almost 50 percent higher than the city's cumulative rate by the end of February 2021.[32] COVID also coincided with the wider prevalence of fentanyl in the nation's drug supply, which contributed to sharp increases in deaths due to overdose and created special challenges for people who were unhoused, and the professionals who cared for them, too. In the city of Boston, health-care workers affiliated with the Boston Health Care for the Homeless Program knew they had to act quickly if they were to protect their vulnerable patients from the devastations of COVID.

Barry Bock, who was the CEO of the Boston Health Care for the Homeless Program until 2022, says that the program's senior leadership knew they faced a serious challenge as soon as they heard reports of COVID spreading through parts of Asia and Europe. Most people who live in Massachusetts shelters sleep in bunk beds, he adds, which tend to be about three feet apart. That made social distancing difficult, if not completely impossible. For a population that is disproportionately immunocompromised, the pandemic therefore presented extreme risks. Bock and his senior leadership team were afraid their patients would die, and in large numbers. "I can still feel it," he tells me. "I mean, it was like a visceral panic that we were all experiencing. So we were stunned." To combat the virus and protect their patients, the staff of the BHCHP got to work. As staff explain on a podcast produced by the BHCHP, they first sought to place their patients in hotel rooms. "I personally had reached out to FEMA and the Massachusetts Emergency Management Agency, and then I probably went to twenty hotels because, to me, the most elegant solution was to operate the hotels," Bock says. The hotels would be reimbursed "at a reasonable rate," he continues, and patients would receive care with dignity. The hotels didn't work out for reasons that included stigma, and staff resorted to tents—sophisticated tents that could function like negative pressure rooms to minimize the spread of infectious air. There, in a parking lot, staff could screen patients, and patients themselves could isolate.

The tents were a temporary solution to a burgeoning problem. In early April, staff identified a cluster of positive COVID cases inside the Pine Street Inn, a nearby shelter. When they tested the shelter's entire population as a precaution, around 30 percent of the tests came back positive, and people needed to be transported to facilities where they could safely isolate. Late at night, Bock and another senior staff member had convinced people in the shelter to accompany them to isolation facilities. "Some folks were frustrated, but no one was aggressive, no one was impolite. It was just the kind of frustration that all of us would expect," Bock remembers. Because it was so late at night, there was no one to drive the resulting bus load of people to a place where they could isolate themselves. Bock said the president of the Boston Medical Center decided to drive the bus herself.

The BHCHP had transformed a portion of its respite ward, which was designed with input from people who were unhoused, into a COVID unit, and that was difficult for some. Patients struggled, sometimes, with being indoors; others were still using drugs, and required support and understanding from staff. Later the same month, BHCHP staff began managing five hundred beds, all for people who were unhoused, inside a field hospital set up at the Boston Convention & Exhibition Center. Called Boston Hope, the temporary hospital represented another challenge for staff—and for patients, too. "Each room was fairly private, but we heard from patients very quickly the need to increase our mental health services, to increase the kinds of activities that we were doing," says Bock, who adds, "I have to say, our patients were amazing. They were so invested in not only their own health but not in infecting others." Though he heard stories from other cities about patients leaving care, "we had almost no one just walking out the door."

Despite the risks that patients faced, Bock says that BHCHP staff noted a low mortality rate among the people in their care. COVID, he explains, "just did not take hold in the homeless community in the way that we thought it would and result in the level of illness." Several factors—including luck, perhaps—helped keep death from the door. Some credit, though, must go to the staff of BHCHP themselves. The care and dignity they afforded their patients recognized the innate humanity of everyone in their care. Their patients weren't manifestations of some cancerous sore, as Mayor Eric Adams of New York put it, but human beings who wanted to protect themselves and everyone else from the virus. That reality cuts sharply against the example provided by public officials like Adams. The pandemic created a kind of moral test, which officials and caregivers could pass or fail. A stay in a hotel room likely helped protect Milton Perez from the virus—but the guards and staff responsible for his well-being did not treat him with dignity or respect, an insult he carries with him even now. What chance does he have, making a complaint about his treatment, in a society that is determined not to hear him?

The same resistance afflicts people behind bars. There, the wrongs a person may have committed become the whole story of their life. A punitive system strips their humanity away; a person becomes a number, and no more. If they try to better their conditions inside, they can expect severe punishment for their efforts. "The carceral system has always used sensationalized cases and the specter of unthinkable harm to create new mechanisms of disposability," wrote Mariame Kaba, an abolitionist scholar, and activist Kelly Hayes in a 2018 essay. "Those mechanisms are what feed bodies to hungry dungeon economies while we are distracted by our own fears of 'bad people' and what they might do if they aren't contained."[33] In such an environment, an infectious disease can only become another way to punish, and control. Even social distancing "just meant more punitive rules," explains Aqirah Stanley of AFJ. Prison administrators created schedules that cost people recreation time. The state department of corrections enforced different standards for officers and visitors, creating a regime that effectively penalized the loved ones of people who were incarcerated. "Visitors have been held to standards of having to provide tests in order to enter the facility. Again, officers were not held to that standard. In terms of vaccinations, at one point our loved ones were not being offered the vaccine," says Stanley, who stresses that vaccination should remain optional for people behind bars. "If we are being given the option out here for vaccines, people who are incarcerated should also have access and if they so choose, the ability to be vaccinated." Pandemic restrictions have largely lifted now, but each prison was allowed to return to "normal" as its officials saw fit, she adds.

Stanley—and Bock—insist on a world in which people who are incarcerated or unhoused can expect to have their humanity honored. They can be trusted with the responsibility of making their own health-care decisions, and are treated, ultimately, as human beings, not as the disposable.

Now, people are too often discarded or abandoned to death behind bars. Advocates and disposable people alike pit themselves against behemoths: stigma, callous public officials, and a public safety net not fit for purpose. In the absence of change, the disposable person still struggles. Linear says the pandemic inflicted lingering damage. "Even in times where you think you're strong and you think you have everything figured out, it is very important to have people or a person or a group of people on the outside that you could turn to and talk to about some of your deepest things," he explains. "Just because the pandemic is over, so to speak, it still exists in the minds of those incarcerated." He adds, "Physically, we have recovered, but mentally we have not recovered. Every day it feels like we're suffering and we're fighting for something still."

ELEVEN

AFTER SOCIAL MURDER

In my grandfather's cabin, the world is silent. Outside, the natural world goes on; I hear wind chimes, birds, the occasional cat. Someone might break in, I tell myself. I fear other humans, some threat I can touch. Two weeks pass like this and by the time I go home to New York I am certain there is no afterlife. If my grandfather could be any-where, I think he would be in the cabin. There he spent the last few years of his life, a thousand miles from where he grew up—a choice he'd made to be close to us, his family. I think he'd make that choice a second time, if anyone could, but the cabin holds nothing. The silence is absolute. I am haunted, but not by him, and that is a source of grief. A ghost might frighten me, but it would also prove that something remains of the dead.

What is for some a certainty is for me an absence. I reach out, and I only feel the air. Because I am an atheist, I believe the dead are no longer present. They were, and now they are not, and our loss is harsher for it. The most important fact of life is that it ends. Without eternity we have only a brief time on the earth, which means that we have certain responsibilities to each other, and to the dead. Once departed, the dead remain part of our world not because there is an afterlife, but because they still matter to us. They have no voice and do not speak except through our own mouths; they do not live on except in our minds. Mass death is a crisis of memory. When we speak of the people we've lost, the dead appear not as ghosts but as extensions of ourselves. Memories of the dead hold up a mirror to the living. What we choose to recall, and what we choose to forget, are personal decisions with political import.

My grandfather is not a ghost, but as a memory he is a warning. Over four years after COVID first appeared in China, it still kills hundreds by the week in the U.S. alone. On a global level the losses are even more catastrophic. Yet America is perilously close to choosing amnesia. Let the dead bury the dead, Jesus once told a man, but you go and proclaim the Kingdom of God. Here there is no God but the free market: the COVID dead cannot be saved, and there's work to do.

In a society calloused by capitalism, the act of memory is not only political but radical. To remember the disposable is to lose confidence in the process that killed him. Our recent losses, though, present at such scale that they can be difficult to fix in the mind. "Great epidemics, like world wars and famines, massify death into species-level events beyond our emotional comprehension," wrote the late historian Mike Davis in his 2005 book on the avian flu, *The Monster at Our Door.* "The afflicted, as a result, die twice: their physical agonies are redoubled by the submergence of their personalities in the black water of megatragedy." He added, "No one mourns a multitude or keens at the graveside of an abstraction." Well over a million lie dead from COVID in the United States, and there is no outcry. The streets are quiet. It may be, as Davis argues, that we lack some "biological solidarity that is automatically aroused by the destruction of our fellow kind."[1] Yet our hearts are less settled than they first appear. The dead do not haunt us, but they do not have to; we are haunting each other instead. Lockdowns are over and the world has reopened, but we cannot outrun our losses. Pick America apart at the seams, and there is grief underneath. Because the dead in their multitudes have become an abstraction, grief belongs to the individual bereaved, while power is ready to forget.

By early 2023, American schools, businesses, and places of worship had reopened to the public. Masks had become a rare sight, but the virus was still with us—still killing us—and those who remembered found themselves on the losing side of a popular battle. A dominant perspective held that the pandemic was over and its risks were no more. Vaccines had saved us, and we had paused long enough. "Your health is in your hands," then–CDC director Rochelle Walensky said in 2021, adding, "If you are unvaccinated, please get vaccinated as soon as you can to decrease your risk to #COVID19. If you choose not to be vaccinated, continue to wear a mask and practice all mitigation strategies to protect yourself from the virus."[2] The onus for COVID prevention was thus on the individual. That view has its critics, as journalist Emma Green noted in a piece for the New Yorker. Members of the People's CDC, a progressive grassroots pressure group, still urged universal masking and outdoor gatherings, plus pre-event testing and proper ventilation in schools and event spaces. "We cannot accept mass infection, and we cannot leave anyone behind," read one tool kit published by the group.[3] One way to memorialize the dead is to fight for the living, but Green sometimes made the group's members sound as though they were part of some nefarious left-wing conspiracy. "All the talk about empire-building and capital accumulation—a key component of Marxist economic theory—made me wonder whether 'the people' in the People's CDC are *those* people," Green wondered.[4]

No group is above criticism, and I haven't arranged my life around the suggestions of the People's CDC. I still mask in doctors' offices, but after I got my vaccinations, I decided to eat in restaurants, and I've gone to gatherings indoors. Eventually, though, there were consequences. In December 2022 I attended a concert unmasked and I got COVID. I felt ill the better part of a month even though I was fully vaccinated—a consequence, perhaps, of my genetic disease. The pandemic isn't over, and in our haste to move on we can endanger ourselves—and people with disabilities. The prospect of long COVID is an additional threat. The COVID "holdouts," as one *New York Times* piece called them, have a point.[5] Risks persist, even if we wish they were history.

COVID minimization has risen in recent years, and not just in the conservative movement. At the *Washington Post*, Dr. Leana Wen argued in January 2023 that we're overcounting COVID deaths.[6] There was no truth to the idea that hospitals are exaggerating COVID deaths for some nefarious purpose, she wrote, but if patients with "concurrent infections" die, "COVID might get added to their death certificate along with the other diagnoses. But the coronavirus was not the primary contributor to their death and often played no role at all." As the watchdog group Fairness & Accuracy in Reporting pointed out in response to the piece, Wen had inaccurately described the manner in which medical examiners determine cause of death. "For those of us who certify deaths routinely (classifying COVID-19 deaths) is not necessarily much harder," Dr. Joyce deJong, the president of the National Association of Medical Examiners, told CNN and added that with COVID, "maybe you're missing some and maybe you're over counting some, but probably the bulk of them are accurate."[7] Dr. Jeremy Faust, an emergency room physician at Brigham and Women's Hospital who has studied excess mortality, argued that officials are likely undercounting COVID deaths in Massachusetts, a state Wen cited in her piece.[8] Using mortality data he and researcher Benjy Renton had collected, Faust wrote in his newsletter that "if we were truly overcounting COVID deaths, an important piece of evidence to support that would be if COVID deaths were . . . exceeding all-cause excess deaths." That has happened in Massachusetts at certain points in the pandemic, but it doesn't appear to be the case right now, he added.

Dr. Emily Oster, an influential Brown University economist, has been a vocal critic of school closures since at least mid-2020. In October of that year, she wrote in the *Atlantic* that schools "do not, in fact, appear to be major spreaders of COVID-19."[9] As proof, she cited her own school response dashboard, which she'd created with assistance from data scientists at Qualtrics. Oster became a popular voice, and as epidemiologists Justin Feldman and Abigail Cartus observed in a piece for *Protean* magazine, she "has been quoted in hundreds of articles about school pandemic precautions and interviewed as a guest on dozens of news shows," and officials from both major parties have cited her work.[10] Yet that work has largely been funded by opponents of teachers' unions and other right-wing entities and figures, including the Walton Family Foundation and the far-right billionaire Peter Thiel, whose grant "was administered by the Mercatus Center, the think tank founded and financed by the Koch family," Feldman and Cartus pointed out. They are critical of Oster's "economic style of reasoning," a term they borrow from Elizabeth Popp Berman of the University of Michigan, and which "emphasizes individualism, market-based choice, and efficiency," while de-emphasizing "collective well-being" they argued. Indeed, Oster's work shows relatively little concern for the welfare of teachers and school support staff, who had to risk COVID to educate the nation's children.

As Keeanga-Yamahtta Taylor pointed out in a 2021 piece for the *New Yorker*, Black and Latino parents were much likelier than white parents to prefer remote learning in the earlier years of the pandemic.[11] According to one survey produced by the University of Southern California Dornsife's Center for Economic and Social Research, "only eighteen percent of Black parents and twenty-two percent of Latinx parents would prefer to send their children back to in-person schooling full time, compared with forty-five percent of white parents. Over fifty percent of Black and Latinx parents prefer to keep their children in remote learning," Taylor wrote. Oster inhabited a different, and perhaps safer, America.

Over time, a more nuanced picture of COVID spread in schools emerged. In January 2021, reporter Rachel M. Cohen covered a trio of studies that complicated the straightforward narrative that Oster preferred. Two studies "suggest that when community transmission is low, reopening school buildings, at least when schools are not operating at full capacity, does not contribute much to the virus's spread," Cohen wrote.[12] "But the risks change, the researchers found, when community transmission is higher." A third study found "that reopening Florida schools led to increased infections among school-age children, particularly among high schoolers." Children aren't as likely to develop severe complications from COVID, but they can and have died from the virus, especially if they have underlying medical conditions. They—and their teachers, and their families—are at the mercy of public officials, who may or may not adopt evidence-based approaches to the virus. In a state like Mississippi, which never enforced many pandemic restrictions, the risks for students and teachers and their communities might have been greater than elsewhere.

School closures did cause academic setbacks, and they may not be an advisable measure when the next pandemic hits, depending on how the virus behaves. In *Poverty in the Pandemic*, researcher Zachary Parolin wrote that school closures "were probably necessary to protect children's health and slow the spread of COVID-19," but there were consequences, especially for low-income students. The closures also exacerbated performance gaps between high- and low-income students—a discrepancy that America's underfunded public school system may struggle to remedy.[13] As David Wallace-Wells wrote in a 2022 newsletter for the *New York Times*, a "last to close, first to open" model would have been best, but the data shows modest declines overall.[14] "Next time, we should try to do better," he concluded. "But all things considered, the best data we have at the moment suggest that school closures were probably a fog-of-war-style social and political stumble, not, as some have suggested, a 'disastrous, invasion-of-Iraq magnitude (or perhaps greater) policy decision.'" There was a need to balance the needs of people with disabilities with the needs of working parents and their students. The groups aren't as opposed to one another as popular coverage would suggest; they overlap, and they benefit from a society that places more emphasis on the common good. The collapse of public school infrastructure can be solved, if there's the political will to do so, but in the absence of better policy, any call for empathy can sound uncomfortably radical. Individualism is a language that Americans know well. The economic style of reasoning, with its preference for the free market and its emphasis on individual choice, thus offers nothing new. To care for the collective is to risk accusations of

Marxism or at least a certain foolishness. Yet this is the only way to care for the living and to honor the dead.

If the pandemic dead die twice, as Davis thought, the bereaved grieve twice. They are afflicted first by the virus, which has stolen a loved one away, and then by society, which will not mourn with them. In the rush to move on, the dead are not merely an abstraction but a hindrance. Their memories betray an uncomfortable truth: There is no return to normal. Something new beckons. The post-COVID future is in motion, which means it can be influenced, but the window for doing so will close.

When I speak to Kristin Urquiza of Marked by COVID, I can detect both determination and urgency in her voice. Members of the group, which was cofounded by Urquiza after she lost her father to COVID, are lobbying for a national COVID Memorial Day. To date they've worked with 225 cities and 11 states to pass local ordinances and resolutions marking the first Monday of March as COVID Memorial Day. There is bipartisan support in the House and Senate to establish a national COVID Memorial Day, and the group is ambitious. "The other big thing that we've been working on and that I'll share is kind of along similar lines, building public support to establish a truth and reconciliation commission or a 9/11-style commission to investigate the pandemic response," Urquiza tells me in 2022. She knows the group faces challenges. "There's two," she explains. The first is the environment, "going back to this urgency of normal, which is coming all the way from the top." The Biden administration has, she adds, "sort of hung their hat on a vaccine-alone-will-save-the-day approach and it's time to get back to business." She adds, "So that poses different challenges than two years ago, when I was like, 'My dad died and our government is failing us.' And everybody was like, 'Holy shit, you're right, the government is failing us. We all hate Trump. And oh yeah, your dad died, and that was bad.'" People are fatigued now, and long for a pre-COVID world that cannot be. The second challenge is "sustainable long-term funding," she explains. "Part of the work for me is centered around educating funders about the intersectionality of COVID and health justice and racial justice," she tells me. "It is incredibly frustrating at times for people like me. Not only did I lose my dad, it exposed, as you so intimately know as well, for everyone to see how the systems were working."

United across great distances, the COVID bereaved often gather online to grieve and memorialize the dead. On Facebook, Angelina Proia once organized regular Zoom meetings for people who lost someone to COVID. On Twitter, an account called Faces of COVID kept the dead in view of the living. Alex Goldstein, who ran the account, posted a photo, the date of death, and a short message from the loved ones of the deceased. "My kind of operating thesis has been that so long as people find meaning in sharing these types of stories about their family members, I am going to make sure the platform exists for them to do so," he tells me, adding, "There's, I think, a history-telling piece of this that becomes really important." In the template Goldstein created to post the tweets, he could input any date and read a list of past submissions. "There is a retelling that becomes meaningful as a reminder," he explains. "There's so many lessons it seems like we're destined to fail to learn from this pandemic. But perhaps, you know, a little bit of effort into trying to keep these stories in front of people, and remind them that these were real people who had beautiful and textured lives and families who missed them, who have not recovered, that this can try to help keep them in the forefront." Goldstein, a communications professional who commonly works on climate change issues, says that he sees a parallel between the national response to COVID, and its response to a warming world. "The IPCC report this morning said we have three years before it's too late," he tells me. There are no vaccines for climate change, he concedes, but adds, "I think that the biggest through line I see is the erosion of common cause and the erosion of common sacrifice." It is obvious to him "that we don't have the will right now to do what we need to do because folks aren't prepared to make those sacrifices, and because there's deeply entrenched and moneyed interests who are convincing them they shouldn't make those sacrifices."

The act of memorializing the dead must begin with a reckoning. There will be other pandemics, and without radical change, the disposable will suffer as much or more in the future as they have in the sorry present. The process of rendering the mass dead into an abstraction begins with social murder. As Beatrice Adler-Bolton and Artie Vierkant wrote in *Health Communism*, their 2022 manifesto, "Innumerable terms and theoretical formulations exist to define the endpoint of capital's immiseration, the one constant to human life that our political economy is particularly adept at expediting."[15] One such term is social murder, they added, quoting Engels.

"When one individual inflicts bodily injury upon another such that death results, we call the deed manslaughter; when the assailant knew in advance that the injury would be fatal, we call his deed murder," Engels wrote. Society, too, is responsible for murder when it deliberately puts its proletarians at risk of "a too early and an unnatural death," he added. It is "disguised, malicious murder, murder against which none can defend himself, which does not seem what it is, because no man sees the murderer, because the death of the victim seems a natural one, since the offence is more one of omission than of commission."[16]

The conditions of the working class have not remained static since Engels's time, whether in England, the land of his study, or in the United States. Defenders of the contemporary status quo will stress that standards of living are higher, labor laws are stronger, and there are more services available to people in poverty, but nothing is won for the working class without struggle, and the same is true of these reforms, which also fall far short of what an egalitarian society requires. The pandemic is evidence that Engels's basic charge is still relevant. Mass death revealed the human costs of the American political economy.

This process is social murder as surely as anything depicted by Engels in the nineteenth century, and it is a fact of life under capitalism; the price our ruling class is willing to pay for prosperity. It is easy to dismiss as natural the deaths that occurred due to COVID, or to invoke age, or comorbidity, as the most relevant factor in their demise. As the legal historian Nate Holdren has argued in an interview[17] for Adler-Bolton and Vierkant's *Death Panel* podcast and in a piece[18] for Harvard Law School's Petrie-Flom Center, "Capitalism produces both mass death and people in positions of institutional authority who are able to live with mass death." From a certain vantage, mass death not only looks acceptable but inevitable. There's nothing to mourn, and everything to forget.

Advocates for a COVID Memorial Day ask for more than twenty-four hours to remember and pause. Their request indicts a system that is determined to ignore the dead. Jennifer Ritz Sullivan, who is lobbying the state of Massachusetts for a COVID Memorial Day, says, "Grief isn't meant to be experienced alone, it requires validation from community." Instead, she bears her burdens without much help. "I'm sick of seeing it constantly be on the backs of us who are most impacted," she tells me. "Without a doubt we should be leading the way, but why am I also fighting for funding this? I didn't have funding for this memorial. Things came out of my pocket. We don't get paychecks. We're volunteers sharing our story and fighting for remembrance and for justice and accountability." Mass death did not change the world, she observes. "Why are we doing this? Where are all those people who were outraged back in 2020?" she asks. "I don't understand that. With Biden coming in, my loved one's not here. My mom's still dead and all those systems that harmed us are still in place."

The systems that oppressed Sullivan's mother in life, and contributed to her death, remain intact as the pandemic entered its fourth year. The dead are not ghosts. As memories they are still with us, and they are evidence of a crime in progress. An act of social murder demands justice—not only for the dead, who cannot be helped, but for the living, who can still be saved. Justice is not inevitable but a future to create, and it cannot exist without a reckoning. According to popular belief, in America a person's success or failure typically depends on the decisions they make. Once again, the disposable live a different reality: a person's future is influenced by factors in motion before birth, and true freedom can be scarce. It's real enough for those at the peak, but they hoard it for themselves. Both political parties deny this fundamental truth, though to different degrees and to varying levels of harm. Without public pressure, nothing will change.

Although the future could be grim, it's still in motion, and a more egalitarian world is still possible. We glimpsed it during the pandemic, even in the middle of mass death. Federal relief measures such as the stimulus payments, expansions to the federal Child Tax Credit, and food assistance reduced poverty and likely shortened the COVID-era recession in the U.S.[19] "Man, I'm just grinning ear to ear," H. Luke Shaefer, the coauthor of *$2.00 a Day*, told the *New York*

Times.[20] "Americans wonder if the government can shape successful policies that address poverty. This offers incontrovertible evidence that it can." Zachary Parolin finds evidence that 2021's policy changes significantly reduced child poverty in the U.S., which "temporarily" brought the country "in line" with other developed nations.[21] Food insufficiency also declined for lower-income respondents from December 2020 to March 2021, which, as Parolin noted, coincided with both stimulus payments and "the payout of many refundable tax credits." From here, policymakers can draw several conclusions, he argued. One is to reduce "barriers" to unemployment insurance and expand eligibility, as the government did during the pandemic; another is to provide "unconditional payments" to families with children, a policy common to America's peer nations.

Such policies have their opponents, however, and they aren't all Republicans. Senator Joe Manchin of West Virginia, a Senate kingmaker, killed the expanded Child Tax Credit. In 2024, the House passed a bipartisan extension of the CTC, but it faces a troubled path through the Senate.[22]

The American political class does not seem to think of mass death as social murder at all. Though certain pandemic-era policies reduced poverty and may have even saved lives, they were temporary, and they arguably didn't go far enough. Policymakers excluded thousands of workers, many undocumented, from expanded unemployment benefits and other economic measures during the pandemic. "For instance, my mom, being a housekeeper, certain times she had to stop working and their employers didn't pay what she missed out on work," explains Diana Sanchez, an organizer with the National Day Laborer Organizing Network, or NDLON. She adds, "We had people who work as domestic workers, who worked in restaurants, and all of these businesses got shut down. But because they were cash earners, they never had any aid. There was no funding from their employers and no funding from the government." People relied on food distributions from churches and charities and would line up for hours, Sanchez says. Others went into debt to pay their rent or buy medication. "We had community members that share that they had to buy insulin. And even insulin, they didn't even have money for that," she tells me. When her brother fell ill during the early weeks of the pandemic, he went to the doctor, and paid $200 to be told he likely had COVID but couldn't get a test to confirm. He had no health insurance, she says, and "ended up worse when he got back than when he got there."

A day laborer who belongs to NDLON tells me the pandemic had affected him in nearly every way it could. Through Sanchez as translator, he says "there's really no words to describe" how it impacted him. "It's hard to go back to that time," he adds, and explained that he lost friends and work partners to the pandemic. "The death, it was very hard," he remembers. Sanchez explains further. "He's saying it's such a huge thing. He even used the word extraordinary," she says. "It's out of this world to even imagine what they went through in the pandemic." Then he found out that he would be excluded from some pandemic aid by watching the news with his son, who thought the family might qualify for unemployment benefits. Though his son is a citizen, his father, the day laborer, is undocumented. He would receive no stimulus checks, no unemployment benefits. "No, unfortunately we don't have the same rights that everyone else does," he told his son.

He began to meet with groups that would later launch the Fund Excluded Workers campaign. Nearly two hundred organizations eventually formed a coalition, and the public pressure was effective. They secured $2.1 billion in funding for excluded workers. At first the day laborer's friends asked him why he wasn't celebrating the victory. "Not until we receive the checks, not until we see everyone have the checks in the hands, will I believe it," he told them. Through Sanchez, he says he could not believe the state government had done this for undocumented people.

The program operated in two tiers, Sanchez explains. Workers like the day laborer could submit their tax returns and other identifying documents to qualify for the maximum benefit. To receive a smaller benefit, workers could submit a letter from their employer that verified that they had lost employment during the pandemic. The program ran out of funding within nine weeks. Coalition members pushed for an extension called Excluded No More, but according to Sanchez, they were unsuccessful. They've pivoted, since, to calling for a permanent solution in what they call the Unemployment Bridge Program. "Not only were we advocating for undocumented workers, but we were advocating for freelancers, for cash earners, for recently incarcerated folks who had immigration and low immigration status," Sanchez says.

Should the Unemployment Bridge Program ever exist in New York, it would insulate thousands against the whims of their employers or even another pandemic. For now, though, it remains an unrealized demand. The pandemic altered political reality—for a while. Though the Biden administration has canceled billions in student loan debt, payments have resumed for millions of Americans. The expanded Child Tax Credit is no more, for now. States "unwound"[23] the COVID-era continuous coverage requirement for Medicaid, which means that millions face gaps in their coverage or may lose it altogether. In May 2023, then-President Biden brought the nation's formal COVID emergency to a close.[24] The White House disbanded its COVID response team the same month, and a senior administration official told the *Washington Post* that "transitioning out of the emergency phase is the natural evolution of the COVID response."[25] COVID does pose fewer dangers than it did in 2020, but as I write in 2024, we are not yet through with the years of grief, and an emergency persists even if the powerful do not acknowledge it as such. The virus has altered America, irrevocably. "Close to a half a million who would have been working . . . died from COVID," Federal Reserve chair Jerome Powell said in late 2022.[26]

The dead had years that are now lost to silence. After Lucy Esparza-Casarez lost her husband, nephew, mother-in-law, and sister-in-law to COVID in 2020, she spent her next Thanksgiving alone. "I made myself a little turkey breast and a mix of mashed potatoes and whatever else, opened a bottle of wine, and that was it," she tells me. "God, I spent so many days alone." When news outlets called the election for Joe Biden that year, she opened a bottle of champagne that she and her husband, David, had been waiting to drink. She finished it on her own, and spent Christmas by herself, too. "David didn't even get to make it to his seventieth birthday," says Lucy, who also belongs to Marked by COVID. David lost his life, and Lucy lost the time she thought she'd spend with him. There are over a million tragedies like Lucy's, and there is grief yet to come. Too often, though, that grief is absent from the headlines, from the debates, and from the statements of our political class. Silence is felt from below, and it is also enforced from above. My grandfather's empty cabin is an indictment.

If an act of social murder goes unrecognized and unchallenged, it might reoccur. We are already repeating the patterns that led to mass death during COVID. Our brief experiment with social democracy may be over, and our welfare state has fallen back into disrepair. After the expiration of a pandemic-era policy that prohibited states from removing people from Medicaid, Texas dropped half a million people from the program between April and July in 2023. Texas, like a handful of other conservative-run states, has not expanded Medicaid under the provisions of the Affordable Care Act. Health care, one new Texas mother told the *New York Times*, "is always about the cost."[27] Complicating matters, the party that controls Texas is actively COVID-denialist; the other barely mentions COVID at all.

In the early months of 2024, as inflation began to wind down and wage growth crept up, the economy made significant gains. Biden even struck a populist note in his State of the Union address that year, calling for higher taxes on corporations and the wealthy.[28] Though Biden's pledge was welcome, it remained subject to limitations; the president did not promise transformation. In its absence, a disposable class of person persists.

I fear I have lost more than my grandfather. When I am angry, and this is often, I am angry at a system that oppressed him in life and erased him in death. We who mourn the COVID dead are not haunted by their ghosts, but by a political economy that reduces many human beings to their labor or worse. In such a system there is hardly room for millions to live. For them, there is work, and then death. COVID merely accelerated the cycle, but we can break it if we try.

"Every benefit industrialism and capitalism have brought us, every wonderful advance in knowledge and health and communication and comfort, casts the same fatal shadow," the late science fiction writer Ursula K. Le Guin once warned.[29] She spoke of capitalism's environmental crimes, but as it attacks the earth it assaults the human spirit as well. The only answer is a radical one. Excise an inhuman political economy from the national body, and replace it with something else, something we haven't yet tried. That future need not be science fiction at all, as Le Guin suggested before her death. "We live under capitalism," she once said in a now-famous speech. "Its power seems inescapable. So did the divine right of kings. Any human power can be resisted and changed by human beings." We need nothing less than a new and more democratic order.

First, that reckoning. No one mourns a multitude, as the historian Mike Davis said. "In order to grieve over a cataclysm, we must personify it," he wrote.[30] The dead have names: Richard Proia. Anna Mae Morris. Florcie Yves Chavannes Versailles. We may draw political conclusions from their lives and their deaths. To the philosopher Martin Hägglund, our finite lives are worth more than the machinery of capitalism will ever allow. "To make our emancipation actual will require both our political mobilizations and our rational arguments; it will require our general strikes and our systematic reflections, our labor and our love, our anxiety and our passion," he wrote in *This Life*.[31] An egalitarian country will be the hard work of decades, but it is still possible. Our future did not end with the dead.

Pandemics reshape the world and remove a veil. We put our masks aside, and most of us have gone back to our parties, but we will not return to normal. Nor should we try. There's too much grief, and too many absent people. What is normal, anyway? In America, normal for millions can mean fear and hunger and, sometimes, death. When we put off an emergency room visit because of the cost, that is normal. When we risk illness at work because we cannot afford to rest, that is normal, too. Our normal state of affairs left America ill-prepared for an event like a pandemic. There were too few protections for workers, and seniors, and people with disabilities. There were too many disposable people. The pandemic, then, caught America between extremes. The country showed itself at its most humane, as medical professionals struggled to save lives on the frontline, and its cruelest, as its institutions failed vulnerable people in a dangerous time. We must recall both truths if we are to prevent future acts of social murder.

In May 2024, as summer loomed and the lockdowns of 2020 felt especially distant, the writer Jonathan V. Last asked if Trump was right about America. "Because as unpleasant as it is to acknowledge, Trump has been right about a great many things," he argued in a piece for the Bulwark.[32] To Last, COVID was an area where Trump's callous politics may have triumphed. "At the end of the day, people cared more about the economy than the deaths," he went on, adding that when he talked to people about what went wrong during the height of the pandemic, they'd talk about business closures, remote schooling, and the occasional inconvenience of masking in public parks. "They never talk about the 1 million Americans who died from COVID during the pandemic," he wrote. "Trump understood that the living do not care about the dead." Last was right in one sense: many seem to ignore about the dead, if they didn't lose a loved one to the virus. Nevertheless, I don't think that means Trump is right about America. We can't afford such defeatism. Trump has yet to win the popular vote in a presidential election, as I write this in the summer of 2024, and even if that changes, I'm still not sure that Last would be correct—not entirely, anyway. America is an unequal place, and brutality is common. I don't say that out of hatred. For me, to criticize America is to love what it could become. Right now, there is indeed little systemic incentive for the living to even remember the dead, though this hardly means Americans are incapable of empathy or even solidarity. The work goes on, no matter who is the president.

Policymakers could end disposability, if they choose; if they're forced to, by the people. America may function like an oligarchy all too often, but its transformation is not quite complete. For now we still live in a democracy, and we have power, which we can wield by organizing. "Self-blame demobilizes people, and it is a strategy," the late Jane McAlevey wrote toward the end of her 2016 book, *No Shortcuts: Organizing for Power in the New Gilded Age*. There is, McAlevey argued, "a mountain of evidence" that Americans "possess a deep sense of human solidarity." She added, "We see it with every disaster, in critical situations such as the aftermaths of September 11 and Hurricane Sandy."[33] We saw it during COVID, too. Now solidarity is the only path forward.

Memorials for the dead have always been for the living. In honoring them, we honor something deep in ourselves and in each other, too. We will all die someday, and our brevity confers deep meaning on our lives and urgency on our endeavors. The future will come. As we move forward, let us move together, leaving no one behind. Health care could be a universal right instead of a privilege. Our seniors could flourish, surrounded by support and loving care. Workers could have real power over what they produce and over the places where they labor. We could erase the racial wealth gap, and establish a measure of equality that America has never truly known. Society could adapt to people with disabilities rather than abandon them. COVID was a natural disaster, but injustice is a human creation. Unmake it now, before the next disaster strikes.

ACKNOWLEDGMENTS

Writing a book takes years of effort—and a community, too. The road to publication began with my family, to whom I owe just about everything. I'm grateful to my husband and partner of ten years, Ed, for endless rounds of feedback, steadfast emotional support, and the unwavering conviction that I could indeed pull this off. Parts of my family history appear in this book, and I'm thankful that my parents, Gene and Melody Jones, and my brother, Tim, allowed me to tell our story. My grandfather Charles still has a voice because they helped me bring him to life after death. Many thanks to Dennis and Terri Beck for being the best in-laws anyone could want and for supporting Ed and I as we navigate our life together.

I also thank Sally Weathers, who talked me off the proverbial ledge many times over the past several years. So has my wonderful agent, Anna Sproul-Latimer, who's spent years reassuring me that I could actually write a book. You would not be reading any of this if Ben Loehnen, my editor at Avid Reader Press, had not polished raw material into something worth reading, or if Alexandra Primiani, also of Avid Reader Press, had believed in this project a little bit less. I owe much to my fact-checkers, Julian Epp and Rosemarie Ho, who made sure that you're reading a truthful account.

After my grandfather died, editors Justin Miller and Eric Bates helped me transform a howl of outrage into a *New York* magazine essay that would eventually help form the basis of this book. (Eric also gave me my first job in journalism during his time at the *New Republic,* so in a way this all starts with him.) I'm grateful to my colleagues at *New York* magazine for their advice and guidance over the years, and to the *New York* magazine union, wonderful comrades all. I'm also grateful to editors Ryu Spaeth, now of *New York* magazine; Ezekiel Kweku, who is now at the *New York Times;* Ryan Kearney and Laura Marsh of the *New Republic;* and Natasha Lewis of *Dissent* magazine, who have all edited me extensively over the years and who helped teach me the craft.

Thank you to Matt Sitman, who reviewed an early version of chapter seven and told me that I was on the right track, and to Kim Kelly for taking a panicked phone call out of nowhere. Chris Stedman not only officiated my wedding but helped me with some of my earliest writing opportunities. I thank Rob Boston of Americans United for Separation of Church and State and Rev. Barry Lynn, who once led the same organization, for not only giving me a job but for helping me discover a purpose. I owe my high school English teacher Randy White a debt of gratitude for teaching me how to write a decent essay in the first place.

During a sabbatical from *New York* magazine (thanks for that, *New York!*), I spent time at the Virginia Center for the Creative Arts, where I completed most of chapter seven in a beautiful writing studio in the countryside. Thank you for the space to write and for the support you provide artists of all kinds.

My deep thanks to my sources, who shared their grief with me, and without whom there would no book at all. Your loved ones mattered. May we remember them, and honor them, by creating a better future.

NOTES

ONE: AN ACT OF SOCIAL MURDER

1. "Get the Facts on Economic Security for Seniors," National Council on Aging, February 22, 2024, https://www.ncoa.org/article/get-the-facts-on-economic -security-for-seniors.

2. Lydia DePillis and Jason DeParle, "Pandemic Aid Cut U.S. Poverty to New Low in 2021, Census Bureau Reports," *New York Times*, updated September 26, 2022, https://www.nytimes.com/2022/09/13/business/economy /income-poverty-census-bureau.html.

3. Lydia DePillis, "An Uptick in Elder Poverty: A Blip, or a Sign of Things to Come?" *New York Times*, October 17, 2022, https://www.nytimes.com/2022 /10/17/business/economy/elder-poverty-seniors.html.

4. Elder Index, Gerontology Institute, University of Massachusetts Boston, last updated December 15, 2023, https://elderindex.org/elderindex?state _county%5B%5D=8878&views_fields_combined_on_off_form=0&fields _on_off_hidden_submitted=1&views_fields_on_off_form%5Bfield_hous ing_renter%5D=field_housing_renter&views_fields_on_off_form_1=field _health_poor.

5. Peter S. Goodman, *Davos Man: How Billionaires Devoured the World* (New York: Custom House, 2022), 2.

6. Philip Bump, "Places That Backed Trump Skewed Poor; Voters Who Backed Trump Skewed Wealthier," *Washington Post*, December 29, 2017, https:// www.washingtonpost.com/news/politics/wp/2017/12/29/places-that -backed-trump-skewed-poor-voters-who-backed-trump-skewed-wealthier/.

7. Jane Mayer, "The Reclusive Hedge-Fund Tycoon behind the Trump Presidency," *New Yorker*, March 17, 2017, https://www.newyorker.com

/magazine/2017/03/27/the-reclusive-hedge-fund-tycoon-behind-the-trump
-presidency.

8. Justin Elliott and Robert Faturechi, "Secret IRS Files Reveal How Much
the Ultrawealthy Gained by Shaping Trump's 'Big, Beautiful Tax Cut,'"
ProPublica, August 11, 2021, https://www.propublica.org/article/secret
-irs-files-reveal-how-much-the-ultrawealthy-gained-by-shaping-trumps-big
-beautiful-tax-cut.

9. Terry Gross, "How the CARES Act Became a Tax-Break Bonanza for the
Rich, Explained," NPR, April 30, 2020, https://www.npr.org/2020/04/30
/848321204/how-the-cares-act-became-a-tax-break-bonanza-for-the-rich
-explained.

10. "Wealth of World's Top 10 Billionaires Doubled during COVID-19 Pandemic;
Here's How the Rich Got Richer," CNBC-TV18, January 17, 2022, https://
www.cnbctv18.com/world/wealth-of-worlds-top-10-billionaires-doubled
-during-COVID-19-pandemic-heres-how-the-rich-got-richer-12147522.htm.

11. Sarah Jones, "The Coronavirus Is Radicalizing Workers," *New York*, April 1,
2020, https://nymag.com/intelligencer/2020/04/the-coronavirus-may-be-a
-tipping-point-for-labor.html.

12. Paul Blest, "Leaked Amazon Memo Details Plan to Smear Fired Warehouse
Organizer: 'He's Not Smart or Articulate,'" *Vice*, April 2, 2020, https://www
.vice.com/en/article/5dm8bx/leaked-amazon-memo-details-plan-to-smear
-fired-warehouse-organizer-hes-not-smart-or-articulate.

13. Richard Hofstadter, *Social Darwinism in American Thought* (Boston: Beacon
Press, 1992), 40, Kindle.

14. Hofstadter, *Social Darwinism in American Thought*, 41, Kindle.

15. John Kelly, *The Graves Are Walking: The Great Famine and the Saga of the Irish
People* (New York: Picador, 2012), 51, Kindle.

16. Kelly, *The Graves are Walking*, 208, Kindle.

17. Niamh Gallagher, "'Their own wickedness': How the British Press Reported
the Famine," RTÉ, updated November 25, 2020, https://www.rte.ie/history
/famine-ireland/2020/0917/1165825-their-own-wickedness-how-the-brit
ish-press-reported-the-famine/.

18. Friedrich Engels, "Friedrich Engels on Why Capitalists Are Guilty of Social
Murder," *Jacobin*, November 28, 2022, https://jacobin.com/2022/11/fried
rich-engels-social-murder-condition-of-the-working-class-in-england.

19. Paul Blest, "Leaked Amazon Memo Details Plan to Smear Fired Warehouse
Organizer: 'He's Not Smart or Articulate,'" *Vice*, April 2, 2020, https://www
.vice.com/en/article/5dm8bx/leaked-amazon-memo-details-plan-to-smear
-fired-warehouse-organizer-hes-not-smart-or-articulate.

20. Years after Landmark Law," NPR, July 23, 2015, https://www.npr.org/sec
tions/health-shots/2015/07/23/424990474/why-disability-and-poverty-still
-go-hand-in-hand-25-years-after-landmark-law; Azza Altiraifi, "Advancing
Economic Security for People with Disabilities," Center for American Progress, July 26, 2019, https://www.americanprogress.org/article/advancing-eco
nomic-security-people-disabilities/.

21. "Policy Basics: Top Ten Facts about Social Security," Center on Budget and Policy Priorities, updated May 31, 2024, https://www.cbpp.org/research /social-security/top-ten-facts-about-social-security.

22. "Get the Facts on Economic Security for Seniors," National Council on Aging.

23. Nancy Ochieng et al., "How Many Older Adults Live in Poverty?," KFF, May 21, 2024, https://www.kff.org/report-section/how-many-seniors-live-in -poverty-issue-brief/.

24. "How Neighbors Affect the Health and Well-Being of Older Americans," Population Reference Bureau, accessed July 2, 2024, https://www.prb.org /resources/how-neighborhoods-affect-the-health-and-well-being-of-older -americans/.

25. Yascha Mounk, "Open Everything: The Time to End Pandemic Restrictions Is Now," *Atlantic*, February 9, 2022, https://www.theatlantic.com/ideas/archive /2022/02/end-coronavirus-restrictions/621627/.

26. Stephanie Soucheray, "US Records 60,000 COVID-19 Deaths in January," Center for Infectious Disease Research & Policy, University of Minnesota, February 7, 2022, https://www.cidrap.umn.edu/news-perspective/2022/02 /us-records-60000-COVID-19-deaths-january.

27. "The Morning at Night: A Virtual Event on Ukraine and COVID," *New York Times*, updated March 9, 2022, https://www.nytimes.com/2022/02/01/brief ing/omicron-david-leonhardt-event.html.

28. Martin Hägglund, *This Life: Secular Faith and Spiritual Freedom* (New York: Pantheon Books, 2019), 251, Kindle.

29. Veronica Stracqualursi, "Biden Reflects on 900,000 Americans Dead from COVID-19: 'Each Soul Is Irreplaceable,'" CNN Politics, February 4, 2022, https://www.cnn.com/2022/02/04/politics/biden-COVID-900000-deaths /index.html#:~:text=%22Today%2C%20our%20nation%20marks%20 another,Each%20soul%20is%20irreplaceable.%22.

TWO: AMERICAN SACRIFICE

1. Felicia Sonmez, "Texas Lt. Gov. Dan Patrick Comes under Fire for Saying Seniors Should 'Take a Chance' on Their Own Lives for Sake of Grandchil- dren during Coronavirus Crisis," *Washington Post*, March 24, 2020, https:// www.washingtonpost.com/politics/texas-lt-gov-dan-patrick-comes -under-fire-for-saying-seniors-should-take-a-chance-on-their-own -lives-for-sake-of-grandchildren-during-coronavirus-crisis/2020/03/24 /e6f64858-6de6-11ea-b148-e4ce3fbd85b5_story.html.

2. R. R. Reno, "Say 'No' to Death's Dominion," *First Things*, March 23, 2020, https://www.firstthings.com/web-exclusives/2020/03/say-no-to-deaths-do minion.

3. Craig Palosky, "Medicare Advantage Is Close to Becoming the Predominant Way That Medicare Beneficiaries Get Their Health Coverage and Care," KFF, August 5, 2022, https://www.kff.org/medicare/press-release/medicare -advantage-is-close-to-becoming-the-predominant-way-that-medicare-ben eficiaries-get-their-health-coverage-and-care/.

4. Ryan Cooper, "Medicare Advantage Is a Massive Scam," *American Prospect*, April 29, 2022, https://prospect.org/health/medicare-advantage-is-a-massive-scam/.

5. Reed Abelson and Margot Sanger-Katz, "'The Cash Monster Was Insatiable': How Insurers Exploited Medicare for Billions," *New York Times*, October 8, 2022, https://www.nytimes.com/2022/10/08/upshot/medicare-advantage -fraud-allegations.html.

THREE: BODIES ON THE LINE

1. "Study Shows Increased COVID-19 Mortality Risk for People with Lupus," Lupus Foundation of America, August 30, 2021, https://www.lupus.org /news/study-shows-increased-COVID19-mortality-risk-for-people-with -lupus.

2. Andrew Siddons, "The Never-Ending Crisis at the Indian Health Service," Roll Call, March 5, 2018, https://rollcall.com/2018/03/05/the-never-ending -crisis-at-the-indian-health-service/.

3. Azza Altiraifi, "A Deadly Poverty Trap: Asset Limits in the Time of the Coronavirus," Center for American Progress, April 7, 2020, https://www.american progress.org/article/deadly-poverty-trap-asset-limits-time-coronavirus/.

4. Rebecca Vallas, Kimberly Knackstedt, and Vilissa Thompson, "7 Facts about the Economic Crisis Facing People with Disabilities in the United States," Century Foundation, April 21, 2022, https://tcf.org/content/commentary /7-facts-about-the-economic-crisis-facing-people-with-disabilities-in-the -united-states/?agreed=1.

5. Sara Luterman, "Why Businesses Can Still Get Away with Paying Pennies to Employees with Disabilities," *Vox*, March 16, 2020, https://www.vox.com /identities/2020/3/16/21178197/people-with-disabilities-minimum-wage.

6. David J. Kim, "'He Just Loved Everybody': Longtime Salvation Army Bell Ringer Robert McCoskey Dies of COVID-19," Louisville *Courier-Journal*, updated May 15, 2020, https://www.courier-journal.com/story/news/local /2020/05/14/salvation-army-bell-ringer-robert-bobby-mccoskey-dies-coro navirus/3114587001/.

7. Priya Chidambaram, "Over 200,000 Residents and Staff in Long-Term Care Facilities Have Died from COVID-19," KFF, February 3, 2022, https://www .kff.org/policy-watch/over-200000-residents-and-staff-in-long-term-care-fa cilities-have-died-from-COVID-19/.

8. Libby Cathey, "Trump Now Calling Coronavirus Fight a 'War' with an 'Invisible Enemy,'" ABC News, March 17, 2020, https://abcnews.go.com /Politics/trump-coronavirus-task-force-economic-public-health-steps /story?id=69646672.

9. Sarah Jones, "Trump Has Turned the GOP into the Party of Eugenics," *New Republic*, February 15, 2017, https://newrepublic.com/article/140641 /trump-turned-gop-party-eugenics.

10. Jones, "Trump Has Turned the GOP into the Party of Eugenics."

11. Fred C. Trump III, "My Uncle Donald Trump Told Me Disabled Americans

Like My Son 'Should Just Die," *Time*, July 24, 2024, https://time.com /7002003/donald-trump-disabled-americans-all-in-the-family/.

12. Editorial Board, "A Jewish Revolt against Lockdowns," *Wall Street Journal*, October 8, 2020, https://www.wsj.com/articles/a-jewish-revolt-against-lock downs-11602198987.

13. Melanie Zanona, "'Abusive, Dictatorial, Tyrannical': Republicans Ramp Up Attacks on Lockdowns," *Politico*, May 11, 2020, https://www.politico.com /news/2020/05/11/conservative-protest-lockdown-243638.

14. Francis Galton, "Eugenics: Its Definition, Scope and Aims," *The American Journal of Sociology* X, no. 1 (July 1904).

15. Liat Ben-Moshe, *Decarcerating Disability: Deinstitutionalization and Prison Abolition* (Minneapolis: University of Minnesota Press, 2020), 41, Kindle.

16. "Virginia Sterilization Act (Footnote from Opinion of Circuit Court of Amherst County, Virginia)," DocsTeach, November 12, 1925, https://www.doc steach.org/documents/document/virginia-sterlization-act-1924-buck-v-bell.

17. *Buck v. Bell*, 274 U.S. 200 (1927), https://www.oyez.org/cases/1900-1940 /274us200.

18. Adam Cohen, *Imbeciles: The Supreme Court, American Eugenics, and the Sterilization of Carrie Buck* (New York: Penguin Books, 2016), 239–40, Kindle edition.

19. "Forced Sterilization of Disabled People in the United States," National Women's Law Center, January 24, 2022, https://nwlc.org/wp-content/uploads /2022/01/%C6%92.NWLC_SterilizationReport_2021.pdf.

20. Elizabeth Catte, *Pure America: Eugenics and the Making of Modern Virginia* (Cleveland: Belt Publishing, 2021), 23, Kindle.

21. Catte, *Pure America*, 60, Kindle.

22. Premilla Nadasen, *Welfare Warriors: The Welfare Rights Movement in the United States* (New York: Routledge, 2005), 216, Kindle.

23. Nadasen, *Welfare Warriors*, 216, Kindle.

24. Tim Evans, Emily Hopkins, and Tony Cook, "Poor Staffing, Missed Reforms, 3,100 COVID Deaths: How Indiana Failed Nursing Home Residents," *Indianapolis Star*, updated January 23, 2021, https://www.indystar.com/in-depth /news/investigations/2020/12/17/COVID-indiana-how-indiana-failed-nurs ing-home-residents/5673575002/.

25. "League of the Physically Handicapped," National Park Service, accessed August 13, 2024, https://www.nps.gov/articles/000/league-of-the-physically -handicapped.htm.

26. Kitty Cone, "Short History of the 504 Sit-in," Disability Rights Education & Defense Fund, accessed July 2, 2024, https://dredf.org/504-sit-in-20th-anni versary/short-history-of-the-504-sit-in/.

27. Sarah Jones, "How Trumpcare Turns Back the Clock on Disability Rights," *New Republic*, May 11, 2017, https://newrepublic.com/article/142647/trump care-turns-back-clock-disability-rights.

28. "Topic: Fitter Family Contests," Eugenics Archive, accessed July 2, 2024, http://www.eugenicsarchive.org/eugenics/topics_fs.pl?theme=8.

29. Jacob Bacharach, "Why Is David Leonhardt So Happy?," *New Republic*, March 15, 2022, https://newrepublic.com/article/165729/david-leonhardt -happy-review-new-york-times-morning-newsletter.

30. Ed Yong, "The Millions of People Stuck in Pandemic Limbo," *Atlantic*, February 16, 2022, https://www.theatlantic.com/health/archive/2022/02/covid -pandemic-immunocompromised-risk-vaccines/622094/.

31. Leana Wen (@DrLeanaWen), "For those who don't agree that the vaccinated can return to pre-pandemic normal . . . ," X, March 22, 2022, https://x.com /drleanawen/status/1506438947366449156?lang=enhttps://twitter.com /drleanawen/status/1506438947366449156?lang=en.

32. Alyssa Paolicelli, "How New Yorkers Are Reacting to Mayor Adams Calling for a Return to Offices," Spectrum News NY1, February 18, 2022, https:// www.ny1.com/nyc/all-boroughs/news/2022/02/19/adams-calls-for-new -yorkers-to-return-to-offices.

33. Emma G. Fitzsimmons, "Can Eric Adams Cheerlead New Yorkers Past the Pandemic?," *New York Times*, March 20, 2022, https://www.nytimes.com /2022/03/20/nyregion/pandemic-recovery-masks-nyc.html.

34. Lena H. Sun and Fenit Nirappil, "CDC Officially Drops Five-Day COVID Isolation Guidelines," *Washington Post*, March 1, 2024, https://www.washing tonpost.com/health/2024/03/01/new-cdc-covid-isolation-guidelines/.

35. Sarah Jones, "How Trumpcare's Failure Sets the Stage for Single-Payer," *New Republic*, March 28, 2017.

36. Aimee Picchi, "The Rising Cost of Insulin: 'Horror Stories Every Day,'" CBS News, May 9, 2018, https://www.cbsnews.com/news/the-rising-cost-of-insu lin-horror-stories-every-day/.

FOUR: THE WORTHY AND THE UNWORTHY

1. Aimee Picchi, "50 Years of Tax Cuts for the Rich Failed to Trickle Down, Economics Study Says," CBS News, December 17, 2020, https://www.cbsnews .com/news/tax-cuts-rich-50-years-no-trickle-down/.

2. Spencer Rich, "Reagan Welfare Cuts Found to Worsen Families' Poverty," *Washington Post*, July 28, 1984, https://www.washingtonpost.com/archive /politics/1984/07/29/reagan-welfare-cuts-found-to-worsen-families-poverty /077278f9-a875-4791-9c34-d1cf3cd148b5/.

3. John Burn-Murdoch, "Britain and the US Are Poor Societies with Some Very Rich People," *Financial Times*, September 15, 2022, https://www.ft.com/con tent/ef265420-45e8-497b-b308-c951baa68945.

4. "Statement on Visit to the USA, by Professor Philip Alston, United Nations Special Rapporteur on Extreme Poverty and Human Rights," Office of the High Commissioner, Human Rights, United Nations, December 15, 2017, https://www.ohchr.org/en/statements/2017/12/statement-visit-usa-profes sor-philip-alston-united-nations-special-rapporteur?LangID=E&NewsID=22 533e.

5. *Report of the Special Rapporteur on Extreme Poverty and Human Rights on His Mission to the United States of America* (New York: United Nationa General

Assembly, 2018), https://documents.un.org/doc/undoc/gen/g18/125/30/pdf /g1812530.pdf.

6. Judith Solomon, "The Healthy Indiana Plan's Uncertain Impact," *Off the Charts* blog, Center on Budget and Policy Priorities, February 7, 2017, https:// www.cbpp.org/blog/the-healthy-indiana-plans-uncertain-impact.

7. Maureen Groppe, "Indiana's Medicaid Alternative Life-Saving and Frustrating," *Indianapolis Star*, updated April 3, 2017, https://www.indystar .com/story/news/politics/2017/04/03/indianas-medicaid-alternative-life -saving-and-frustrating/99828916/.

8. Ian Hill and Emily Burroughs, "Lessons from Launching Medicaid Work Requirements in Arkansas," Urban Institute, October 3, 2019, https://www .urban.org/research/publication/lessons-launching-medicaid-work-require ments-arkansas.

9. Centers for Medicare & Medicaid Services, "Verma Outlines Vision for Medicaid, Announces Historic Steps Taken to Improve the Program," press release, November 7, 2017, https://www.cms.gov/newsroom/press-releases/verma -outlines-vision-medicaid-announces-historic-steps-taken-improve-program.

10. Michael Harrington, *The Other America: Poverty in the United States* (New York: Scribner, 2012), 6, Kindle.

11. Barbara Ehrenreich, *Fear of Falling: The Inner Life of the Middle Class* (New York: Twelve, 2020), 47, Kindle.

12. Zachary Parolin, *Parolin, Poverty in the Pandemic: Policy Lessons from COVID-19* (New York: Russell Sage Foundation, 2023), 1, Kindle edition.

13. Harrington, *The Other America*, 13.

14. John F. Harris and John E. Yang, "Clinton to Sign Bill Overhauling Welfare," *Washington Post*, August 1, 1996, https://www.washingtonpost.com/wp-srv /politics/special/welfare/stories/wf080196.htm.

15. Martin Gilens, *Why Americans Hate Welfare: Race, Media, and the Politics of Antipoverty Policy* (Chicago: University of Chicago Press, 1999), 233.

16. Michael B. Katz, *In the Shadow of the Poorhouse: A Social History of Welfare in America* (New York: Basic Books, 1996), 327.

17. Katz, *In the Shadow of the Poorhouse*, 9.

18. Katz, *In the Shadow of the Poorhouse*, 11.

19. Katz, *In the Shadow of the Poorhouse*, 34.

20. Ramesh Ponnuru, "Some Republicans Go Back to Fighting the 'Takers,'" *Washington Post*, January 31, 2024, https://www.washingtonpost.com/opin ions/2024/01/31/child-tax-credit-republican-conservative-arguments/.

21. Alicia Adamczyk, "Joe Manchin Reiterates That He Won't Support Enhanced Child Tax Credit without a Work Requirement," CNBC, January 4, 2022, https://www.cnbc.com/2022/01/04/manchin-wont-support-enhanced -child-tax-credit-without-work-requirement.html.

22. Katz, *In the Shadow of the Poorhouse*, 287.

23. Alain Sherter, "Nearly 40% of Americans Can't Cover a Surprise $400 Expense," CBS News, May 23, 2019, https://www.cbsnews.com/news/nearly -40-of-americans-cant-cover-a-surprise-400-expense/.

24. William Darity Jr., Fenaba R. Addo, and Imari Z. Smith, "A Subaltern Middle Class: The Case of the Missing 'Black Bourgeoisie' in America," *Contemporary Economic Policy* 39, no. 3 (July 2021): 494–502, https://onlinelibrary.wiley.com/doi/full/10.1111/coep.12476.
25. Darity, Addo, and Smith, "A Subaltern Middle Class."
26. William A. Darity Jr. and A. Kirsten Mullen, *From Here to Equality: Reparations for Black Americans in the Twenty-First Century*, 2nd ed. (Chapel Hill: University of North Carolina Press, 2022), 409, Kindle.
27. Eugene T. Richardson et al., "Reparations for Black American Descendants of Persons Enslaved in the U.S. and Their Potential Impact on SARS-CoV-2 Transmission," *Social Science & Medicine* 276 (May 2021): 113741, https://www.sciencedirect.com/science/article/pii/S0277953621000733?via%3Dihub.
28. Olúfémi O. Táíwò, *Reconsidering Reparations* (New York: Oxford University Press, 2022), 147, Kindle edition.
29. Matthew Desmond, *Poverty, by America* (New York: Crown, 2023).
30. Jason DeParle, "Pandemic Aid Programs Spur a Record Drop in Poverty," *New York Times*, updated September 14, 2021, https://www.nytimes.com/2021/07/28/us/politics/covid-poverty-aid-programs.html.

FIVE: THE CHERRY ON THE FUCK-YOU SUNDAE

1. "Trump: 'We Have Met the Moment and We Have Prevailed,'" video, Politico, May 11, 2020, https://www.politico.com/video/2020/05/11/trump-we-have-met-the-moment-and-we-have-prevailed-075095.
2. Jeremy W. Peters and Michael M. Grynbaum, "How Right-Wing Pundits Are Covering Coronavirus," *New York Times*, March 11, 2020, https://www.nytimes.com/2020/03/11/us/politics/coronavirus-conservative-media.html.
3. Colleen Shalby, "As Coronavirus Cases Surge, L.A. County Death Toll Tops 3,500," *Los Angeles Times*, July 6, 2020, https://www.latimes.com/california/story/2020-07-06/coronavirus-cases-surge-la-county-death-toll-tops-3500.
4. Sam Levin, "'I Can't Grieve': LA Families Wait Months to Bury Loved Ones as COVID Deaths Rise," *Guardian*, January 23, 2021, https://www.theguardian.com/us-news/2021/jan/23/los-angeles-funeral-homes-covid-19-deaths.
5. Studs Terkel, *Working: People Talk about What They Do All Day and How They Feel about What They Do* (New York: New Press, 2004), xi.
6. Elizabeth Anderson, *Private Government: How Employers Rule Our Lives (and Why We Don't Talk about It)* (Princeton, NJ: Princeton University Press, 2017), 53, Kindle.
7. Samantha Christmann, "NLRB Tells Starbucks to Reinstate 10 Fired Buffalo Workers with Back Pay," *Buffalo News*, February 7, 2024, https://buffalonews.com/news/local/business/nlrb-tells-starbucks-to-reinstate-10-fired-buffalo-workers-with-back-pay/article_87fa5d28-c5bf-11ee-a4fe-ab6745eca3ec.html.
8. "Over 60% of Low-Wage Workers Still Don't Have Access to Paid Sick Days on the Job," Economic Policy Institute, September 23, 2022, https://www.epi.org/blog/over-60-of-low-wage-workers-still-dont-have-access-to-paid

-sick-days-on-the-job/#:~:text=by%20Elise%20Gould-,Over%2060%25%20
of%20low%2Dwage%20workers%20still%20don't,in%20the%20U.S.%20
labor%20market.

9. Cory Stieg, "Line Cooks Have the Highest Risk of Dying during Pandemic, Plus Other Riskiest Jobs: Study," CNBC, updated February 3, 2021, https://www.cnbc.com/2021/02/02/jobs-where-workers-have-the-highest-risk-of-dying-from-covid-study.html.

10. "Amazon Ends COVID Paid Leave for U.S. Workers," Reuters, April 30, 2022, https://www.reuters.com/world/us/amazon-ends--paid-leave-us-workers-2022-05-01/.

11. "Over 60% of Low-Wage Workers," Economic Policy Institute.

12. Rachel Lerman et al., "What You Need to Know about the Threat of a Rail Strike and Congress," *Washington Post*, November 30, 2022, https://www.washingtonpost.com/business/2022/11/30/rail-strike-union-demands-congress/.

13. Tony Romm and Lauren Kaori Gurley, "Senate Adopts Deal to Block Rail Strike, Sending It to Biden," *Washington Post*, December 1, 2022, https://www.washingtonpost.com/business/2022/12/01/rail-deal-strike-senate-vote-congress/.

14. Aaron Gordon, "The Freight Rail Labor Dispute Was Never about 'Sick Days,'" *Vice*, December 5, 2022, https://www.vice.com/en/article/g5v9xy/the-freight-rail-labor-dispute-was-never-about-sick-days.

15. Aaron Nelsen, "The Disposable US Workforce: Life as an 'Essential' Meatpacking Plant Worker," *Guardian*, November 19, 2021, https://www.theguardian.com/environment/2021/nov/19/the-disposable-us-workforce-life-as-an-essential-meatpacking-plant-worker.

16. "Blood, Sweat, and Fear: Workers' Rights in U.S. Meat and Poultry Plants," Human Rights Watch, January 24, 2005, https://www.hrw.org/report/2005/01/25/blood-sweat-and-fear/workers-rights-us-meat-and-poultry-plants.

17. Nebraska Appleseed, *"The Speed Kills You": The Voice of Nebraska's Meatpacking Workers*, 2009, https://neappleseed.org/wp-content/uploads/downloads/2013/01/the_speed_kills_you_100410.pdf.

18. "Poultry Companies Are Denying Their Workers Bathroom Breaks. Tell Tyson to #GiveThemABreak," Oxfam America, May 10, 2016, https://www.oxfamamerica.org/explore/stories/no-relief-for-poultry-workers/.

19. Brian Stauffer, "'When We're Dead and Buried, Our Bones Will Keep Hurting': Workers' Rights Under Threat in US Meat and Poultry Plants," Human Rights Watch, September 4, 2019, https://www.hrw.org/report/2019/09/04/when-were-dead-and-buried-our-bones-will-keep-hurting/workers-rights-under-threat.

20. Daniel Flaming et al., "Hungry at the Table: White Paper on Grocery Workers at the Kroger Company," Economic Roundtable, January 11, 2022, https://economicrt.org/publication/hungry-at-the-table/#:~:text=Food%20Insecurity,-Kroger%20says%20that&text=Kroger%20provides%20its%20employees%20a,eat%20healthy%20and%20balanced%20meals.

21. Jason Lalljee, "Kroger Workers Experienced Hunger, Homelessness, and Couldn't Pay Their Rent in 2021. Its CEO Made $22 Million the Previous Year," *Business Insider*, January 14, 2022, https://www.businessinsider.com /1-in-7-kroger-workers-homeless-many-food-insecure-rent-2022-1.

22. Jason Lalljee, "Kroger Workers Experienced Hunger, Homelessness, and Couldn't Pay Their Rent in 2021. Its CEO Made $22 Million the Previous Year," *Business Insider*, January 14, 2022, https://www.businessinsider.com /1-in-7-kroger-workers-homeless-many-food-insecure-rent-2022-1.

23. Kate Gibson, "Kroger Ending $2 an Hour 'Hero Pay' Bonus for Workers," CBS News, May 12, 2020, https://www.cbsnews.com/news/kroger-ending -hero-pay-workers-2-dollars-hour/.

24. Jennifer Aldrich, "Order a Medicine Ball at Starbucks to Cure What Ails You," *Better Homes & Gardens*, updated January 11, 2024, https://www.bhg.com /news/starbucks-medicine-ball/.

25. Janet I. Tu, "Starbucks CEO Howard Schultz Reportedly Was Hillary Clinton's Pick for Labor Secretary," *Seattle Times*, January 10, 2017, https://www .seattletimes.com/business/retail/starbucks-ceo-howard-schultz-reportedly -was-hillary-clintons-pick-for-labor-secretary/.

26. Daniel Wiessner, "Starbucks Case at US Supreme Court Could Limit Labor Board's Key Legal Tool," Reuters, January 18, 2024, https://www.reuters .com/legal/government/starbucks-case-us-supreme-court-could-limit-labor -boards-key-legal-tool-2024-01-18/.

27. Christmann, "NLRB Tells Starbucks to Reinstate 10 Fired Buffalo Workers with Back Pay."

28. Josh Eidelson, "Starbucks Threatens Trans Benefits in Anti-Union Push, Staff Say," Bloomberg, June 14, 2022, https://www.bloomberg.com/news /articles/2022-06-14/starbucks-threatens-trans-benefits-in-anti-union -push-staff-say.

SIX: THE TWO PANDEMICS

1. Mary Farrow, "Memento Mori—How Religious Orders Remember Death," Catholic News Agency, October 30, 2017, https://www.catholicnewsagency .com/news/37093/memento-mori-how-religious-orders-remember-death.

2. Jeffrey M. Jones, "More in U.S. Retiring, or Planning to Retire, Later," Gallup, July 22, 2022, https://news.gallup.com/poll/394943/retiring-planning-retire -later.aspx.

3. Trina Paul, "Americans Are Retiring Later and Expecting to Work Longer than in Past Decades," CNBC, July 30, 2023, https://www.cnbc.com/select /americans-are-retiring-later-than-they-did-in-the-1990s/.

4. Teresa Ghilarducci, *Work, Retire, Repeat: The Uncertainty of Retirement in the New Economy* (Chicago: University of Chicago Press, 2024), 4.

5. Peter Reuell, "For Life Expectancy, Money Matters," *Harvard Gazette*, April 11, 2016, https://news.harvard.edu/gazette/story/2016/04/for-life-ex pectancy-money-matters/.

6. Yasmin Rafiei, "When Private Equity Takes Over a Nursing Home," *New*

Yorker, August 25, 2022, https://www.newyorker.com/news/dispatch/when
-private-equity-takes-over-a-nursing-home.

7. Jordan Rau, "Why Glaring Quality Gaps among Nursing Homes Are Likely
    to Grow If Medicaid Is Cut," KFF Health News, September 28, 2017, https://
    khn.org/news/why-glaring-quality-gaps-among-nursing-homes-are-likely-to
    -grow-if-medicaid-is-cut/.

8. Michelle Andrews, "Is Cuomo Directive to Blame for Nursing Home COVID
    Deaths, as US Official Claims?," KFF Health News, August 24, 2020, https://
    kffhealthnews.org/news/is-cuomo-directive-to-blame-for-nursing-home
    -COVID-deaths-as-us-official-claims/.

9. Jesse McKinley and Luis Ferré-Sadurní, "N.Y. Severely Undercounted
    Virus Deaths in Nursing Homes, Report Says," *New York Times*, updated
    September 23, 2021, https://www.nytimes.com/2021/01/28/nyregion/nurs
    ing-home-deaths-cuomo.html.

10. Veronica Stracqualursi, "*New York Times* and *Wall Street Journal*: Top Cuomo
    Aides Rewrote Nursing Home Report from State Health Officials to Hide
    Higher Death Toll," CNN Politics, March 5, 2021, https://www.cnn.com
    /2021/03/05/politics/andrew-cuomo-nursing-homes-report.

11. Maysoon Khan, "Report: Cuomo Wrongly Used State Resources to Promote
    Book," Associated Press, July 8, 2022, https://apnews.com/article/COVID
    -health-new-york-andrew-cuomo-47db38685c00e280325875d118e7cf6f.

12. Alexia Fernández Campbell, "Home Health Aides Care for the Elderly. Who
    Will Care for Them?," *Vox*, August 21, 2019, https://www.vox.com/the-high
    light/2019/8/21/20694768/home-health-aides-elder-care.

13. "Cost of Care Trends & Insights," Genworth Financial, accessed July 2, 2024,
    https://www.genworth.com/aging-and-you/finances/cost-of-care/cost-of
    -care-trends-and-insights.html.

14. Serah Louis, "Caregiver Crisis: Nearly 1 in 3 Have Left Their Jobs to Help
    Ailing Family, and the Cost of Lost Wages Could Hit $147 Billion by
    2050," Yahoo, April 16, 2023, https://www.yahoo.com/video/caregivers
    -crisis-nearly-1-3-120000441.html#:~:text=America%20is%20dealing%20
    with%20a%20'caregiving%20crisis'&text=The%20number%20of%20em
    ployees%20in,according%20to%20Federal%20Reserve%20data.

15. Silvia Federici, "10. On Elder Care," Libcom.org, 2009, https://files.libcom
    .org/files/silvia-federici-on-elder-care.pdf.

16. Matthew Goldstein, Jessica Silver-Greenberg, and Robert Gebeloff, "Push for
    Profits Left Nursing Homes Struggling to Provide Care," *New York Times*,
    May 7, 2020, https://www.nytimes.com/2020/05/07/business/coronavirus
    -nursing-homes.html.

17. "US: Concerns of Neglect in Nursing Homes," Human Rights Watch, March 25,
    2021, https://www.hrw.org/news/2021/03/25/us-concerns-neglect-nursing
    -homes.

18. U.S. Government Accountability Office, *Infection Control Definiciences Were
    Widespread and Persistent in Nursing Homes Prior to COVID-19 Pandemic*,
    May 20, 2020, https://www.gao.gov/assets/gao-20-576r.pdf.

19. Mark S. Lachs, "COVID-19 and Aging, a Tale of Two Pandemics," *Nature Aging* 1, no. 1 (January 2021): 8–9, https://www.nature.com/articles/s43587 -020-00005-3.

20. Terry Carter, "With Their Picket, Nursing Home Workers in Chatsworth Again Sound Alarm on Unsafe Staffing Levels and Other Problems in Their Facility," SEIU 2015, May 19, 2022, https://www.seiu2015.org/stoney-point -picket/.

21. Mark S. Lachs, "COVID-19 and Aging, a Tale of Two Pandemics," *Nature Aging* 1, no. 8–9 (2021), https://www.nature.com/articles/s43587-020-00 005-3.

22. Paula Span, "For Older Americans, the Pandemic Is Not Over," *New York Times*, updated February 13, 2023, https://www.nytimes.com/2023/02/11 /health/covid-pandemic-seniors.html?smid=tw-share.

23. Marion Renault, "A French Village's Radical Vision of a Good Life with Alzheimer's," *New Yorker*, November 23, 2022, https://www.newyorker.com /culture/annals-of-inquiry/a-french-villages-radical-vision-of-a-good-life -with-alzheimers.

SEVEN: HOW THE FRINGE CAPTURED THE CENTER

1. Sam Adler-Bell, "Conservative Incoherence," *Dissent*, Summer 2020, https:// www.dissentmagazine.org/article/conservative-incoherence/.

2. Barbara Golder, "Why Masks Are Important during COVID-19 Pandemic," Fédération Internationale des Associations de Médecins Catholiques, May 14, 2020, https://www.fiamc.org/medical-specialties/infectology/why-masks-are -important-during-covid-19-pandemic/.

3. Matthew Sitman, "Anti-Social Conservatives," Gawker.com, July 25, 2022.

4. Daniel Victor, Lew Serviss, and Azi Paybarah, "In His Own Words, Trump on the Coronavirus and Masks," *New York Times*, October 2, 2020, https://www .nytimes.com/2020/10/02/us/politics/donald-trump-masks.html.

5. Eugene Scott, "A Down Economy Could Affect Mental Health, But Staying Connected Can Help, Expert Says," *Washington Post*, March 30, 2020, https:// www.washingtonpost.com/politics/2020/03/30/what-do-we-know-about -how-down-economy-will-affect-suicides/.

6. Beth LeBlanc and Craig Mauger, "Whitmer to Protesters: Rally Will 'Come at Cost to People's Health,'" *Detroit News*, updated April 15, 2020, https:// www.detroitnews.com/story/news/politics/2020/04/15/stay-home-protest -michigan-capitol-opposition-whitmer-order-coronavirus/2989230001/.

7. Igor Volsky, "Flashback: Republicans Opposed Medicare in 1960s by Warning of Rationing, 'Socialized Medicine,'" Physicians for a National Health Program, July 29, 2009, https://pnhp.org/news/flashback-republicans-opposed -medicare-in-1960s-by-warning-of-rationing-socialized-medicine/.

8. Anthony Zurcher, "Why Trump's Slamming Medicare for All as 'Socialist' Healthcare," BBC, October 10, 2018, https://www.bbc.com/news/world-us -canada-45817327.

9. Spencer Rich, "Reagan's Workforce Program Failed in California, Report

Reveals," *Washington Post*, March, 30, 1981, https://www.washingtonpost.com
/archive/politics/1981/03/30/reagans-workfare-program-failed-in-california
-report-reveals/c18ec063-e9e0-4f85-a1cf-30260b89a9be/.

10. Rich, "Reagan Welfare Cuts Found to Worsen Families' Poverty."
11. Kathleen Belew, "The Crunchy-to-Alt-Right Pipeline," *Atlantic*, December 14, 2022, https://www.theatlantic.com/ideas/archive/2022/12/fringe
-left-alt-right-share-beliefs-white-power-movement/672454/.
12. Phyllis Schlafly, "Experimenting on Teen Girls," Eagle Forum, March 7, 2007, https://eagleforum.org/column/2007/mar07/07-03-07.html.
13. Jay Root, "Under Scrutiny, Perry Walks Back HPV Decision," *Texas Tribune*, August 15, 2011, https://www.texastribune.org/2011/08/15/facing-new-scrut
iny-perry-walks-back-hpv-decision/.
14. Wade Goodwyn, "In Texas, Perry's Vaccine Mandate Provoked Anger," NPR, September 16, 2011, https://www.npr.org/2011/09/16/140530716/in-texas
-perrys-vaccine-mandate-provoked-anger.
15. Melissa Attias, "Hearing Gives Burton a Last Shot at Autism Issue," Roll Call, November 27, 2012, https://rollcall.com/2012/11/27/hearing-gives-burton
-a-last-shot-at-autism-issue/.
16. Maggie Fox, "California Governor Signs Tough New Vaccine Law," NBC News, June 30, 2015, https://www.nbcnews.com/health/health-news/cali
fornia-governor-signs-tough-new-vaccine-law-n384556.
17. Derek Beres, Matthew Remski, and Julian Walker, *Conspirituality: How New Age Conspiracy Theories Became a Health Threat* (New York: PublicAffairs, 2023), 40, Kindle.
18. "The Great Barrington Declaration," accessed August 13, 2024, https://gb
declaration.org/.
19. Sheryl Gay Stolberg, "White House Embraces a Declaration from Scientists That Opposes Lockdowns and Relies on 'Herd Immunity,'" *New York Times*, October 13, 2020, https://www.nytimes.com/2020/10/13/world/white-house
-embraces-a-declaration-from-scientists-that-opposes-lockdowns-and-relies
-on-herd-immunity.html.
20. Stephanie M. Lee, "These Scientists Have a Controversial Plan for 'Herd Immunity'—and the White House Is Listening," BuzzFeed News, October 9, 2020, https://www.buzzfeednews.com/article/stephaniemlee/herd-immu
nity-bhattacharya-atlas-barrington.
21. Paige Winfield Cunningham, "The Health 202: Health Officials Call an Anti-Lockdown Paper 'Dangerous.' Its Authors Say They Just Want the Idea Debated," *Washington Post*, October 16, 2020, https://www.washingtonpost
.com/politics/2020/10/16/health-202-health-officials-call-an-anti-lock
down-paper-dangerous-its-authors-say-they-just-want-idea-debated/.
22. Stephanie M. Lee, "These Scientists Have a Controversial Plan for 'Herd Immunity'—and the White House Is Listening," Buzzfeed News, updated October 9, 2020, https://www.buzzfeednews.com/article/stephaniemlee
/herd-immunity-bhattacharya-atlas-barrington.
23. Lee, "These Scientists Have a Controversial Plan for 'Herd Immunity.'"

24. Amanda D'Ambrosio, "New Institute Has Ties to the Great Barrington Declaration," MedPage Today, updated November 12, 2021, https://www.medpagetoday.com/special-reports/exclusives/95601.

25. Kiera Butler, "Meet Ron DeSantis' New 'Public Health Integrity Committee,'" *Mother Jones*, December 16, 2022, https://www.motherjones.com/politics/2022/12/meet-ron-desantis-new-public-health-integrity-committee/.

26. D'Ambrosio, "New Institute Has Ties to the Great Barrington Declaration."

27. Robert Costa (@costareports), "Per several people familiar, Steve Bannon had been encouraging this for months and believes RFK Jr. could be both a useful chaos agent in 2024 race and a big name who could help stoke anti-vax sentiment around the country . . . ," X, April 5, 2023, 6:39 p.m., https://x.com/costareports/status/1643745138978721792?lang=en.

28. Vinay Prasad, "It's the Compulsion That Needs to Be Restricted," Brownstone Institute, February 26, 2022, https://brownstone.org/articles/its-the-compulsion-that-needs-to-be-restricted/.

29. *Nikolao v Lyon, et al.*, No. 4:2016cv12545—Document 16 (E.D. Mich. 2017), Justia US Law, accessed July 2, 2024, https://law.justia.com/cases/federal/district-courts/michigan/miedce/4:2016cv12545/312502/16/.

30. "PAC Profile: National Federation of Independent Business," Open Secrets, accessed July 2, 2024, https://www.opensecrets.org/political-action-committees-pacs/national-federation-of-independent-business/C00101105/summary/2022.

31. Sean Feucht (@seanfeucht), "A police officer escorting me out tonight said he estimated 9,000–10,000 worshippers filled the courthouse steps in downtown Nashville! . . . ," Twitter, October 11, 2020, https://twitter.com/seanfeucht/status/1315455479037014016?lang=en.

32. Elaina Plott Calabro, "The Return of the John Birch Society," *Atlantic*, February 23, 2024, https://www.theatlantic.com/politics/archive/2024/02/john-birch-society-cpac-conservatism/677542/?taid=65d902a55dc11e00150627d&utm_campaign=the-atlantic&utm_content=true-anthem&utm_medium=social&utm_source=twitter.

33. Ben Goggin, "Calls to 'Fight' and Echoes of Jan. 6 Embraced by CPAC Attendees," NBC News, February 23, 2024, https://www.nbcnews.com/politics/2024-election/jack-posobiec-jan-6-2024-cpac-rcna140225.

34. Russell Gold, "The Billionaire Bully Who Wants to Turn Texas into a Christian Theocracy," *Texas Monthly*, March 2024, https://www.texasmonthly.com/news-politics/billionaire-tim-dunn-runs-texas/.

35. Jamelle Bouie, "Our Society Is Not a Bee Hive," *New York Times*, February 17, 2024, https://www.nytimes.com/2024/02/17/opinion/texas-tim-dunn-trump.html.

36. Darrell Scott, Kareem Lanier, and Tim Dunn, "Let's Get America Back on Her Feet—Together," Townhall, April 13, 2020, https://townhall.com/columnists/darrellscottkareemlanierandtimdunn/2020/04/13/lets-get-america-back-on-her-feettogether-n2566804.

37. Chaya Raichik (@ChayaRaichik10), "If I was vaccinated I'd be terrified right

now," Twitter, January 13, 2023, https://twitter.com/ChayaRaichik10/status
/1613966259636568065?lang=en.

38. Aria Bendix, "COVID Death Rates Are Higher among Republicans than
    Democrats, Mounting Evidence Shows," NBC News, October 6, 2022,
    https://www.nbcnews.com/health/health-news/COVID-death-rates-higher
    -republicans-democrats-why-rcna50883.

39. Thomas Massie (@RepThomasMassie), "CDC admits mRNA shots can cause
    myocarditis and blot clots . . . ," Twitter, January 19, 2023, https://twitter.com
    /RepThomasMassie/status/1616249150248452099?s=20&t=tkSF4QXUM6
    fiJ32v4Y1Rjg.

40. Lunna Lopes et al., "KFF COVID-19 Vaccine Monitor: December 2022,"
    KFF, December 16, 2022, https://www.kff.org/coronavirus-COVID-19/poll
    -finding/kff-COVID-19-vaccine-monitor-december-2022/.

41. Davey Alba, "Twitter Permanently Suspends Marjorie Taylor Greene's Ac-
    count," *New York Times*, January 2, 2022, https://www.nytimes.com/2022/01
    /02/technology/marjorie-taylor-greene-twitter.html.

42. Daniel Engber, "The Return of Measles," *Atlantic*, March 12, 2024, https://
    www.theatlantic.com/health/archive/2024/03/measles-outbreak-america
    -politics/677735/?utm_source=feed.

43. Clayton Henkel, "Declaring 'Medical Freedom' This North Carolina County
    Just Banned Fluoride in Its Water," NC Newsline, February 20, 2024, https://
    ncnewsline.com/2024/02/20/declaring-medical-freedom-this-north-caro
    lina-county-just-banned-fluoride-in-its-water/.

44. Lev Facher, "GOP Opposition to Vaccine Mandates Extends Far Beyond
    COVID-19," STAT, November 17, 2021, https://www.statnews.com/2021/11
    /17/gop-opposition-to-vaccine-mandates-extends-far-beyond-COVID-19/.

45. Chris Lehmann, "How the Prosperity Gospel Explains Donald Trump's Popu-
    larity with Christian Voters," *Washington Post*, July 15, 2016, https://www
    .washingtonpost.com/posteverything/wp/2016/07/15/how-the-prosperity
    -gospel-explains-donald-trumps-popularity-with-christian-voters/.

EIGHT: EXPOSING BEDROCK

1. Ashley Parker and Liz Goodwin, "Republicans Use 'Wokeism' to Attack
   Left—but Struggle to Define It," *Washington Post*, February 21, 2023, https://
   www.washingtonpost.com/politics/2023/02/21/wokeism-republicans-liber
   als/.

2. "Black History Boston: Mel King," City of Boston, last updated November 1,
   2022, https://www.boston.gov/news/black-history-boston-mel-king.

3. Sarah Betancourt, "COVID-19 Remembrance Day Effort Picking Up Steam
   on Beacon Hill," WGBH, updated December 9, 2021, https://www.wgbh.org
   /news/local-news/2021/12/01/COVID-19-remembrance-day-effort-picking
   -up-steam-on-beacon-hill.

4. Terry Gross, "A 'Forgotten History' of How the U.S. Government Segregated
   America," NPR, May 3, 2017, https://www.npr.org/2017/05/03/526655831
   /a-forgotten-history-of-how-the-u-s-government-segregated-america.

5. Catherine Elton, "How Has Boston Gotten Away with Being Segregated for So Long?," *Boston*, December 8, 2020, https://www.bostonmagazine.com /news/2020/12/08/boston-segregation/.

6. Candace Jackson, "What Is Redlining?," *New York Times*, August 17, 2021, https://www.nytimes.com/2021/08/17/realestate/what-is-redlining.html.

7. Jerusalem Demsas, "Black and Hispanic Renters Experience Discrimination in Almost Every Major American City," *Vox*, December 7, 2021, https:// www.vox.com/22815563/rental-housing-market-racism-discrimination.

8. Khristopher J. Brooks, "People of Color Face Higher Rental Costs than White Americans, Zillow Finds," CBS News, updated April 13, 2022, https://www .cbsnews.com/news/zillow-black-renters-hispanic-security-deposit/.

9. Teresa Wiltz, "'A Pileup of Inequities': Why People of Color Are Hit Hardest by Homelessness," Stateline, March 29, 2019, https://www.pewtrusts.org /en/research-and-analysis/blogs/stateline/2019/03/29/a-pileup-of-inequi ties-why-people-of-color-are-hit-hardest-by-homelessness.

10. Priya Chidambaram, Tricia Neuman, and Rachel Garfield, "Racial and Ethnic Disparities in COVID-19 Cases and Deaths in Nursing Homes," KFF, October 27, 2020, https://www.kff.org/coronavirus-COVID-19/issue-brief/racial -and-ethnic-disparities-in-COVID-19-cases-and-deaths-in-nursing-homes/.

11. Eric Carlson and Gelila Selassie, *Racial Disparities in Nursing Facilities—and How to Address Them* (Washington, DC: Justice in Aging, 2022), https://jus ticeinaging.org/wp-content/uploads/2022/09/Racial-Disparities-in-Nursing -Facilities.pdf.

12. Patrice Peck, "The Virus Is Showing Black People What They Knew All Along," *Atlantic*, December 22, 2020, https://www.theatlantic.com/health /archive/2020/12/pandemic-black-death-toll-racism/617460/.

13. "COVID-19 Is Affecting Black, Indigenous, Latinx, and Other People of Color the Most," COVID Racial Data Tracker, COVID Tracking Project, accessed July 2, 2024, https://COVIDtracking.com/race.

14. Nambi Ndugga, Latoya Hill, and Samantha Artiga, "COVID-19 Cases and Deaths, Vaccinations, and Treatments by Race/Ethnicity as of Fall 2022," KFF, November 17, 2022, https://www.kff.org/coronavirus-COVID-19 /issue-brief/COVID-19-cases-and-deaths-by-race-ethnicity-current-data -and-changes-over-time/.

15. Tiana N. Rogers, "Racial Disparities in COVID-19 Mortality among Essential Workers in the United States," *World Medical & Health Policy* 12, no. 3 (September 2020): 311–27, https://www.ncbi.nlm.nih.gov/pmc/articles/PMC 7436547/pdf/WMH3-12-311.pdf.

16. Zak Podmore, "Remote Navajo Mountain Clinic Now Ranks among Utah's Most Vaccinated Places," *Salt Lake Tribune*, February 12, 2021, https://www .sltrib.com/news/2021/02/12/remote-navajo-mountain/.

17. Jennifer W. Tsai, Rohan Khazanchi, and Emily Laflamme, "Death by Missing Data: Uncollected Racial and Ethnic Pandemic Data Will Drive Inequities for Decades to Come," *Stat*, January 30, 2023, https://www.statnews.com/2023/01 /30/covid-19-missing-data-race-ethnicity-drive-inequities-decades-to-come/.

18. LaShyra Nolen and Nicte I. Mejia, "Inequities in Neurology Amplified by the COVID-19 Pandemic," *Nature Reviews Neurology* 17, no. 2 (January/February 2021): 67–68, https://www.nature.com/articles/s41582-020-00452-x?fbclid=IwAR004b6GeER2CTKWGcpSV6K-CF33ZxxFo8nI6HZ3QIDz6mn215RFAnCBlOE.

19. LaShyra T. Nolen, Shibani S. Mukerji, and Nicte I. Mejia, "Post-Acute Neurological Consequences of COVID-19: An Unequal Burden," *Nature Medicine* 28, no. 1 (January 2022): 20–23, https://www.nature.com/articles/s41591-021-01647-5.

20. Tobi Haslett, "Magic Actions: Looking Back on the George Floyd Rebellion," *n+1*, no. 40 (Summer 2021): https://www.nplusonemag.com/issue-40/politics/magic-actions-2/.

NINE: PROFIT OVER PEOPLE

1. Lunna Lopes et al., "Americans' Challenges with Health Care Costs," KFF, March 1, 2024, https://www.kff.org/health-costs/issue-brief/americans-challenges-with-health-care-costs/#:~:text=Main%20takeaways%20include%3A,putting%20off%20due%20to%20cost.

2. Hari Kunzru, "The Social Body," *Harper's*, n.d., https://harpers.org/archive/2023/03/the-social-body-health-care-national-health-service/#:~:text=The%20American%20health%20system%2C%20as,them%20beholden%20to%20their%20bosses.

3. Beatrix Hoffman, *Health Care for Some: Rights and Rationing in the United States since 1930*, reprint ed. (Chicago: University of Chicago Press, 2012).

4. David Armstrong, Patrick Rucker, and Maya Miller, "UnitedHealthcare Tried to Deny Coverage to a Chronically Ill Patient. He Fought Back, Exposing the Insurer's Inner Workings," ProPublica, February 2, 2023, https://www.propublica.org/article/unitedhealth-healthcare-insurance-denial-ulcerative-colitis.

5. Robert Pear, "What's in the AHCA: The Major Provisions of the Republican Health Bill," *New York Times*, May 4, 2017, https://www.nytimes.com/2017/05/04/us/politics/major-provisions-republican-health-care-bill.html.

6. Gene B. Sperling and Michael Shapiro, "How the Senate's Health-Care Bill Would Cause Financial Ruin for People with Preexisting Conditions," *Atlantic*, June 23, 2017, https://www.theatlantic.com/business/archive/2017/06/ahca-senate-bill-preexisting-conditions/531375/.

7. Daniella Diaz and Pete Grieve, "Dozens Arrested after Disability Advocates Protest at McConnell's Office," CNN Politics, updated June 22, 2017, https://www.cnn.com/2017/06/22/politics/protests-mitch-mcconnell-office-health-care-bill/index.html.

8. Sarah Kliff and Margot Sanger-Katz, "Americans' Medical Debts Are Bigger than Was Known, Totaling $140 Billion," *New York Times*, July 20, 2021, https://www.nytimes.com/2021/07/20/upshot/medical-debt-americans-medicaid.html.

9. Kristen Bialik, "More Americans Say Government Should Ensure Health Care Coverage," Pew Research Center, January 13, 2017, https://www.pew

research.org/short-reads/2017/01/13/more-americans-say-government-should
-ensure-health-care-coverage/.

10. Grace Sparks, "CNN Poll: Most Think the Government Should Provide a National Health Insurance Program," CNN Politics, February 6, 2019, https://www.cnn.com/2019/02/06/politics/cnn-poll-healthcare-taxes/index.html.

11. Hoffman, *Health Care for Some*, 143, Kindle.

12. Hoffman, *Health Care for Some*, 144, Kindle.

13. Hoffman, *Health Care for Some*, 147, Kindle.

14. Premilla Nadasen, *Welfare Warriors: The Welfare Rights Movement in the United States* (New York: Routledge, 2005), 140.

15. Munira Z. Gunja, Evan D. Gumas, and Reginald D. Williams II, "U.S. Health Care from a Global Perspective, 2022: Accelerating Spending, Worsening Outcomes," Commonwealth Fund, January 31, 2023, https://www.com monwealthfund.org/publications/issue-briefs/2023/jan/us-health-care -global-perspective-2022#:~:text=In%202021%2C%20the%20U.S.%20 spent,higher%20than%20in%20South%20Korea.

16. Eric C. Schneider et. al., "Mirror, Mirror 2021: Reflecting Poorly," Commonwealth Fund, August 4, 2021, https://www.commonwealthfund.org/publica tions/fund-reports/2021/aug/mirror-mirror-2021-reflecting-poorly.

17. Alison P. Galvani et al., "Universal Healthcare as Pandemic Preparedness: The Lives and Costs That Could Have Been Saved during the COVID-19 Pandemic," *PNAS* 119, no. 25 (June 2022): e2200536119, https://www.pnas.org /doi/10.1073/pnas.2200536119.

18. Penn Medicine News, "Half of Low-Income Communities Have No ICU Beds," news release, August 3, 2020, https://www.pennmedicine.org/news/news-re leases/2020/august/half-of-low-income-communities-have-no-icu-beds.

19. David Wallace-Wells, "Who's to Blame for a Million Deaths?," *New York Times*, April 26, 2023, https://www.nytimes.com/2023/04/26/opinion/whos -to-blame-for-a-million-deaths.html.

20. Mary Van Beusekom, "US Pandemic Death Toll Higher than in 20 Peer Countries," Center for Infectious Disease Research & Policy, University of Minnesota, November 21, 2022, https://www.cidrap.umn.edu/covid-19/us -pandemic-death-toll-higher-20-peer-countries.

21. Amanda Seitz, "Americans Give Health Care System Failing Mark: AP-NORC Poll," Associated Press, September 12, 2022, https://apnews.com/article/CO VID-health-medication-prescription-drug-costs-drugs-63b342945f9b6ab 3ce0ed3920deb935a.

22. Noah Weiland and Sarah Kliff, "For the Uninsured, COVID Care Has Entered a New Stage of Crisis," *New York Times*, December 6, 2022, https://www.ny times.com/2022/12/06/us/politics/covid-testing-treatment-uninsured.html.

TEN: FALLING OFF THE FINAL RUNG

1. Akash Mehta, "Destruction of Homeless Encampments," Gothamist, May 29, 2020, https://gothamist.com/news/despite-cdc-guidance-de-blasio-ramps-de struction-homeless-encampments.

2. "Transcript: Mayor de Blasio Holds Media Availability," Official Website of the City of New York, May 6, 2020, https://www.nyc.gov/office-of-the-mayor/news/324-20/transcript-mayor-de-blasio-holds-media-availability.

3. Associated Press, "NYC Mayor Pushes to Remove Homeless People in Subway System," *Independent*, February 18, 2022, https://www.independent.co.uk/news/eric-adams-people-kathy-hochul-nyc-mayor-b2018553.html.

4. Andy Newman, Dana Rubinstein, and Michael Gold, "New York City Plans to Stop Homeless People from Sheltering in Subway," *New York Times*, February 18, 2022, https://www.nytimes.com/2022/02/18/nyregion/homeless-people-subway-trains-mta.html.

5. Batya Ungar-Sargon (@bungarsargon), "Maybe have a little humility before you tell a working class person ... ," Twitter, May 4, 2023, https://twitter.com/bungarsargon/status/1654135330411368448?s=20.

6. J. D. Vance (@JDVance1), "He was threatening innocent people on the train and had been arrested multiple times ... ," Twitter, May 5, 2023, https://twitter.com/JDVance1/status/1654476863828373506?s=20.

7. Sarah Jones, "The Sheepdog Defense," *New York*, May 16, 2023, https://nymag.com/intelligencer/2023/05/daniel-penny-and-the-sheepdog-defense.html.

8. Minyvonne Burke, "Jordan Neely Struggled with Not Being Able to Help His Mother before Her Murder, Attorney Says," NBC News, May 6, 2023, https://www.nbcnews.com/news/us-news/jordan-neely-struggled-not-able-help-mother-murder-attorney-says-rcna83218.

9. Wilfred Chan, "'It's a Failure of the System': Before Jordan Neely Was Killed, He Was Discarded," *Guardian*, May 12, 2023, https://www.theguardian.com/us-news/2023/may/12/jordan-neely-new-york-social-services-support-mental-health.

10. Steve Berg, "The Disturbing Realities of Homelessness and Violence," National Alliance to End Homelessness, January 24, 2022, https://endhomelessness.org/blog/the-disturbing-realities-of-homelessness-and-violence/.

11. *Housing Not Handcuffs, 2019: Ending the Criminalization of Homelessness in U.S. Cities*, National Law Center on Homelessness & Poverty, December 2019, https://homelesslaw.org/wp-content/uploads/2019/12/HOUSING-NOT-HANDCUFFS-2019-FINAL.pdf.

12. Lucius Couloute, "Nowhere to Go: Homelessness among Formerly Incarcerated People," Prison Policy Initiative, August 2018, https://www.prisonpolicy.org/reports/housing.html.

13. "Homelessness Makes You Sick," Health Care for the Homeless, accessed July 2, 2024, https://www.hchmd.org/homelessness-makes-you-sick.

14. Fred Clasen-Kelly, "When a Prison Sentence Becomes a Death Sentence," NPR, April 27, 2023, https://www.npr.org/sections/health-shots/2023/04/27/1172320844/when-a-prison-sentence-becomes-a-death-sentence.

15. Emily Widra, "New Data: People with Incarcerated Loved Ones Have Shorter Life Expectancies and Poorer Health," Prison Policy Initiative, July 12, 2021, https://www.prisonpolicy.org/blog/2021/07/12/family-incarceration/.

16. Ruth Wilson Gilmore, *Abolition Geography: Essays Towards Liberation* (New York: Verso, 2022), 136.

17. Amy Julia Harris, "Housing Boss Earns $1 Million to Run Shelters Despite a Troubled Past," *New York Times*, updated October 15, 2021, https://www.nytimes.com/2021/10/03/nyregion/jack-brown-homeless-nyc-core-services.html.

18. "Mass Incarceration," ACLU, accessed July 2, 2024, https://www.aclu.org/issues/smart-justice/mass-incarceration.

19. Wendy Sawyer and Peter Wagner, "Mass Incarceration: The Whole Pie 2023," Prison Policy Initiative, March 14, 2023, https://www.prisonpolicy.org/reports/pie2023.html.

20. Sawyer and Wagner, "Mass Incarceration."

21. "COVID-19 in Prisons and Jails," Prison Policy Initiative, July 2024, https://www.prisonpolicy.org/virus/.

22. Sonia Moghe, "Inside New York's Notorious Rikers Island Jails, 'the Epicenter of the Epicenter' of the Coronavirus Pandemic," CNN, May 18, 2020, https://www.cnn.com/2020/05/16/us/rikers-coronavirus/index.html.

23. Jonah E. Bromwich and Jan Ransom, "10 Deaths, Exhausted Guards, Rampant Violence: Why Rikers Is in Crisis," *New York Times*, updated November 8, 2021, https://www.nytimes.com/2021/09/15/nyregion/rikers-island-jail.html.

24. Bliss Broyard and Lisa Riordan Seville, "Fifteen People at the Jail Died in 2021. These Are Their Lives—and How They Came to an End," *New York*, December 27, 2021, https://nymag.com/intelligencer/article/rikers-inmates-died2021.html#:~:text=In%20all%2C%2015%20people%20died,be%20sent%20to%20the%20island.

25. Arthur Longworth, "Diary of an Incarcerated Man during a Pandemic," Prison Journalism Project, April 20, 2020, https://prisonjournalismproject.org/2020/04/20/diary-of-an-incarcerated-man-during-a-pandemic/.

26. "Declaration of Michael Linear," *Candis Rush et al. v. Washington State Department of Corrections et al.*, April 23, 2021, https://columbialegal.org/wp-content/uploads/2021/03/Rush-v-DOC-Declaration-of-Linear.pdf.

27. Adriana, "Litigation FAQ: *Rush v. DOC*," Columbia Legal Services, April 2, 2021, https://columbialegal.org/litigation-faq-rush-v-doc/.

28. Adriana, "Lawsuit Demands Immediate Access to COVID-19 Vaccine for All Individuals Living in DOC Custody," Columbia Legal Services, March 30, 2021, https://columbialegal.org/lawsuit-demands-immediate-access-to-COVID-19-vaccine-for-all-individuals-living-in-doc-custody/.

29. Jeffrey McKee, "Coffee Filters to N95: The Evolution of Masks in a Washington Prison," Prison Journalism Project, March 14, 2022, https://prisonjournalismproject.org/2022/03/14/coffee-filters-to-n95-the-evolution-of-masks-in-a-washington-prison/.

30. Samantha Michaels, "New York Prisoners Are Sewing Masks for Hospitals—but Most Don't Have Their Own," *Mother Jones*, May 6, 2020, https://www.motherjones.com/crime-justice/2020/05/new-york-prisoners-are-sewing-masks-for-hospitals-but-most-dont-have-their-own/.

31. "Our Team," Alliance of Families for Justice, accessed July 2, 2024, https://afj-ny.org/our-team.

32. "Age-Adjusted Mortality Rate for Sheltered Homeless New Yorkers," Coalition for the Homeless, accessed July 2, 2024, https://www.coalitionforthehomeless.org/age-adjusted-mortality-rate-for-sheltered-homeless-new-yorkers/.

33. Mariame Kaba, with Kelly Hayes, "A Jailbreak of the Imagination: Seeing Prisons for What They Are and Demanding Transformation," in *We Do This 'Til We Free Us: Abolitionist Organizing and Transforming Justice* (Chicago: Haymarket Books, 2021), 24, Kindle.

ELEVEN: AFTER SOCIAL MURDER

1. Mike Davis, *The Monster at Our Door: The Global Threat of Avian Flu* (New York: New Press, 2005), 3.

2. Mandy K. Cohen, MD, MPH (@CDCDirector), "Your health is in your hands. If you are unvaccinated, please get vaccinated as soon as you can to decrease your risk to #COVID19. If you choose not to be vaccinated, continue to wear a mask and practice all mitigation strategies to protect yourself from the virus," Twitter, May 14, 2021, 5:09 p.m., https://x.com/cdcdirector/status/1393312416373645317?lang=en. Please note that Walensky is no longer the director of the CDC, hence the different name on the account.

3. "Safer In-Person Gatherings," People's CDC, n.d., https://docs.google.com/presentation/d/e/2PACX-1vQSr1XqvRXt7Km1q6gn4jzZ6FyZqfe4ul_YPOnAC7j7kMVbFGSiIay5VAER0xM6B0QxNOpUmSZ_VH65/pub?start=true&loop=false&delayms=60000&slide=id.g1488323f9b4_0_81.

4. Emma Green, "The Case for Wearing Masks Forever," *New Yorker*, December 28, 2022, https://www.newyorker.com/news/annals-of-activism/the-case-for-wearing-masks-forever.

5. Amy Harmon, "The Last Holdouts," *New York Times*, December 26, 2022, https://www.nytimes.com/2022/12/26/us/covid-masks-risk.html.

6. Leana S. Wen, "We Are Overcounting COVID Deaths and Hospitalizations. That's a Problem," *Washington Post*, January 13, 2023, https://www.washingtonpost.com/opinions/2023/01/13/covid-pandemic-deaths-hospitalizations-overcounting/.

7. Deidre McPhillips, "COVID-19 Killed Fewer People in the US in 2022, but Early Data Suggests It Was Still a Leading Cause of Death," CNN Health, January 17, 2023, https://www.cnn.com/2023/01/17/health/covid-death-reporting-2022/index.html.

8. Jeremy Faust, "Data Snapshot: Are We Overcounting COVID-19 Deaths? No," Inside Medicine, January 16, 2023, https://insidemedicine.substack.com/p/data-snapshot-are-we-overcounting.

9. Emily Oster, "Schools Aren't Super-Spreaders," *Atlantic*, October 9, 2020, https://www.theatlantic.com/ideas/archive/2020/10/schools-arent-super spreaders/616669/.

10. Abigail Cartus and Justin Feldman, "Motivated Reasoning: Emily Oster's COVID Narratives and the Attack on Public Education," *Protean*, March 22,

2022, https://proteanmag.com/2022/03/22/motivated-reasoning-emily-osters-COVID-narratives-and-the-attack-on-public-education/.

11. Keeanga-Yamahtta Taylor, "What's at Stake in the Fight over Reopening Schools," *New Yorker*, February 9, 2021, https://www.newyorker.com/news/our-columnists/whats-at-stake-in-the-fight-over-reopening-schools.

12. Rachel M. Cohen, "As Virus Surges, New Studies Suggest Warning for School Reopening," January 6, 2021, Intercept, https://theintercept.com/2021/01/06/school-reopening-studies-COVID/.

13. Parolin, *Poverty in the Pandemic*, 16.

14. David Wallace-Wells, "How Big Were Pandemic Learning Losses, Really?," *New York Times*, September 21, 2022, https://www.nytimes.com/2022/09/21/opinion/pandemic-learning-loss.html.

15. Beatrice Adler-Bolton and Artie Vierkant, *Health Communism* (New York: Verso, 2022), 19, Kindle.

16. Friedrich Engels, *Condition of the Working Class in England* (1845), https://www.marxists.org/archive/marx/works/1845/condition-working-class/ch07.htm.

17. "Social Murder w/ Nate Holdren (Unlocked)," *Death Panel* podcast, SoundCloud, accessed July 2, 2024, https://soundcloud.com/deathpanel/social-murder-w-nate-holdren-unlocked?ref=clipboard&p=i&c=1&si=7783585D76FF485894247CAD591243CD&utm_source=clipboard&utm_medium=text&utm_campaign=social_sharing.

18. Nate Holdren, "Depoliticizing Social Murder in the COVID-19 Pandemic," *Bill of Health* blog, Petrie-Flom Center, Harvard Law School, March 21, 2022, https://blog.petrieflom.law.harvard.edu/2022/03/21/depoliticizing-social-murder-COVID-pandemic/.

19. "Robust COVID Relief Achieved Historic Gains against Poverty and Hardship, Bolstered Economy," Center on Budget and Policy Priorities, June 14, 2022, https://www.cbpp.org/research/poverty-and-inequality/robust-COVID-relief-achieved-historic-gains-against-poverty-and-0.

20. Lydia DePillis and Jason DeParle, "Pandemic Aid Cut U.S. Poverty to New Low in 2021, Census Bureau Reports," *New York Times*, updated September 26, 2022, https://www.nytimes.com/2022/09/13/business/economy/income-poverty-census-bureau.html.

21. Parolin, *Poverty in the Pandemic*, 122.

22. Aimee Picchi, "House Approves Expansion for the Child Tax Credit. Here's Who Could Benefit," CBS News, February 3, 2024, https://www.cbsnews.com/news/child-tax-credit-2024-who-qualifies/.

23. Suzanne Wikle and Jennifer Wagner, "Unwinding the Medicaid Continuous Coverage Requirement," Center on Budget and Policy Priorities, April 28, 2023, https://www.cbpp.org/research/health/unwinding-the-medicaid-continuous-coverage-requirement.

24. Lena H. Sun and Amy Goldstein, "What the End of the COVID Public Health Emergency Means for You," *Washington Post*, updated May 9, 2023,

https://www.washingtonpost.com/health/2023/05/04/covid-public-health
-emergency-end/.

25. Dan Diamond and Tyler Pager, "White House Disbanding Its COVID-19 Team in May," *Washington Post*, March 22, 2023, https://www.washington post.com/politics/2023/03/22/biden-disband-covid-team/.

26. Emily Peck, "The Missing Workers Who Are Never Coming Back," Axios, December 16, 2022, https://www.axios.com/2022/12/16/the-missing-workers -who-are-never-coming-back.

27. Noah Weiland, "After End of Pandemic Coverage Guarantee, Texas Is Epicenter of Medicaid Losses," *New York Times*, August 13, 2023, https://www .nytimes.com/2023/08/13/us/politics/texas-medicaid-coverage-loss.html.

28. David Lawder, "State of the Union: Biden Vows to Raise Taxes on Wealthy, Corporations," Reuters, March 8, 2024, https://www.reuters.com/world/us /state-union-biden-push-wealth-company-tax-ideas-2024-03-07/.

29. Ursula K. Le Guin, "Ursula K. Le Guin on the Future of the Left," *Vice*, February 4, 2015, https://www.vice.com/en/article/vvbxqd/ursula-le-guin-future -of-the-left.

30. Davis, *The Monster at Our Door*, 3.

31. Martin Hägglund, *This Life: Secular Faith and Spiritual Freedom* (New York: Pantheon Books, 2019), 390, Kindle.

32. Jonathan V. Last, "What If Trump Is Right about America?," Bulwark, May 24, 2024, https://www.thebulwark.com/p/what-if-trump-is-right-about -america.

33. Jane F. McAlevey, *No Shortcuts: Organizing for Power in the New Gilded Age* (New York: Oxford University Press, 2016), 201.

ABOUT THE AUTHOR

SARAH JONES is a senior writer for *New York* magazine, where she covers politics and religion. She was previously a staff writer for the *New Republic* and her work has been published by the *Nation*, the *Columbia Journalism Review*, and *Dissent* magazine. Jones won the 2019 Mirror Award for commentary. She is active on social media @OneSarahJones. Originally from rural Washington County, Virginia, she now lives in Brooklyn with her husband.